JOURNEY INTO MYSTERY

FEAR ITSELF FALLOUT

Writers
KIERON GILLEN (#627-631) & ROB RODI (#626.1)

#626.1
Artist: PASQUAL FERRY
Colorist: FRANK D'ARMATA

#627 & #630
Artist: RICHARD ELSON
Colorists: RACHELLE ROSENBERG (#627)
& JESSICA KHOLINE OF IFS (#630)

#628 & #631
Penciler: WHILCE PORTACIO
Inkers: ALLEN MARTINEZ
with JEFF HUET (#631)
Colorists: ARIF PRIANTO OF IFS
with JESSICA KHOLINE OF IFS (#628)
& JOHN RAUCH (#631)

#629
Pencilers: WHILCE PORTACIO
with DOUG BRAITHWAITE (pp. 6-8)
Inkers: ALLEN MARTINEZ
with DOUG BRAITHWAITE (pp. 6-8)
Colorists: ARIF PRIANTO OF IFS
& JOHN RAUCH
with ULISES ARREOLA (pp. 6-8)

Cover Art: STEPHANIE HANS (#627-631) & PASQUAL FERRY (#626.1)
Letterer: VC'S CLAYTON COWLES
Assistant Editor: JOHN DENNING • Editor: LAUREN SANKOVITCH
Executive Editor: TOM BREVOORT

Collection Editor: Jennifer Grünwald • Assistant Editors: Alex Starbuck & Nelson Ribeiro • Editor, Special Projects: Mark D. Beazley
Senior Editor, Special Projects: Jeff Youngquist • Senior Vice President of Sales: David Gabriel
SVP of Brand Planning & Communications: Michael Pasciullo • Book Design: Jeff Powell

Editor in Chief: Axel Alonso • Chief Creative Officer: Joe Quesada • Publisher: Dan Buckley • Executive Producer: Alan Fine

JOURNEY INTO MYSTERY: FEAR ITSELF FALLOUT. Contains material originally published in magazine form as JOURNEY INTO MYSTERY #626.1 and #627-631. First printing 2012. Hardcover ISBN# 978-0-7851-5261-3. Softcover ISBN# 978-0-7851-5262-0. Published by MARVEL WORLDWIDE, INC., a subsidiary of MARVEL ENTERTAINMENT, LLC. OFFICE OF PUBLICATION: 135 West 50th Street, New York, NY 10020. Hardcover: $19.99 per copy in the U.S. and $21.99 in Canada (GST #R127032852). Softcover: $15.99 per copy in the U.S. and $17.99 in Canada (GST #R127032852). Canadian Agreement #40668537. **Printed in the U.S.A.** ALAN FINE, EVP - Office of the President, Marvel Worldwide, Inc. and EVP & CMO Marvel Characters B.V.; DAN BUCKLEY, Publisher & President - Print, Animation & Digital Divisions; JOE QUESADA, Chief Creative Officer; DAVID BOGART, SVP of Business Affairs & Talent Management; TOM BREVOORT, SVP of Publishing; C.B. CEBULSKI, SVP of Creator & Content Development; DAVID GABRIEL, SVP of Publishing Sales & Circulation; MICHAEL PASCIULLO, SVP of Brand Planning & Communications; JIM O'KEEFE, VP of Operations & Logistics; DAN CARR, Executive Director of Publishing Technology; SUSAN CRESPI, Editorial Operations Manager; ALEX MORALES, Publishing Operations Manager; STAN LEE, Chairman Emeritus. For information regarding advertising in Marvel Comics or on Marvel.com, please contact John Dokes, SVP Integrated Sales and Marketing, at jdokes@marvel.com. For Marvel subscription inquiries, please call 800-217-9158. **Manufactured between 1/30/2012 and 2/27/2012 (hardcover), and 1/30/2012 and 9/3/2012 (softcover), by R.R. DONNELLEY, INC., SALEM, VA, USA.**

10 9 8 7 6 5 4 3 2 1

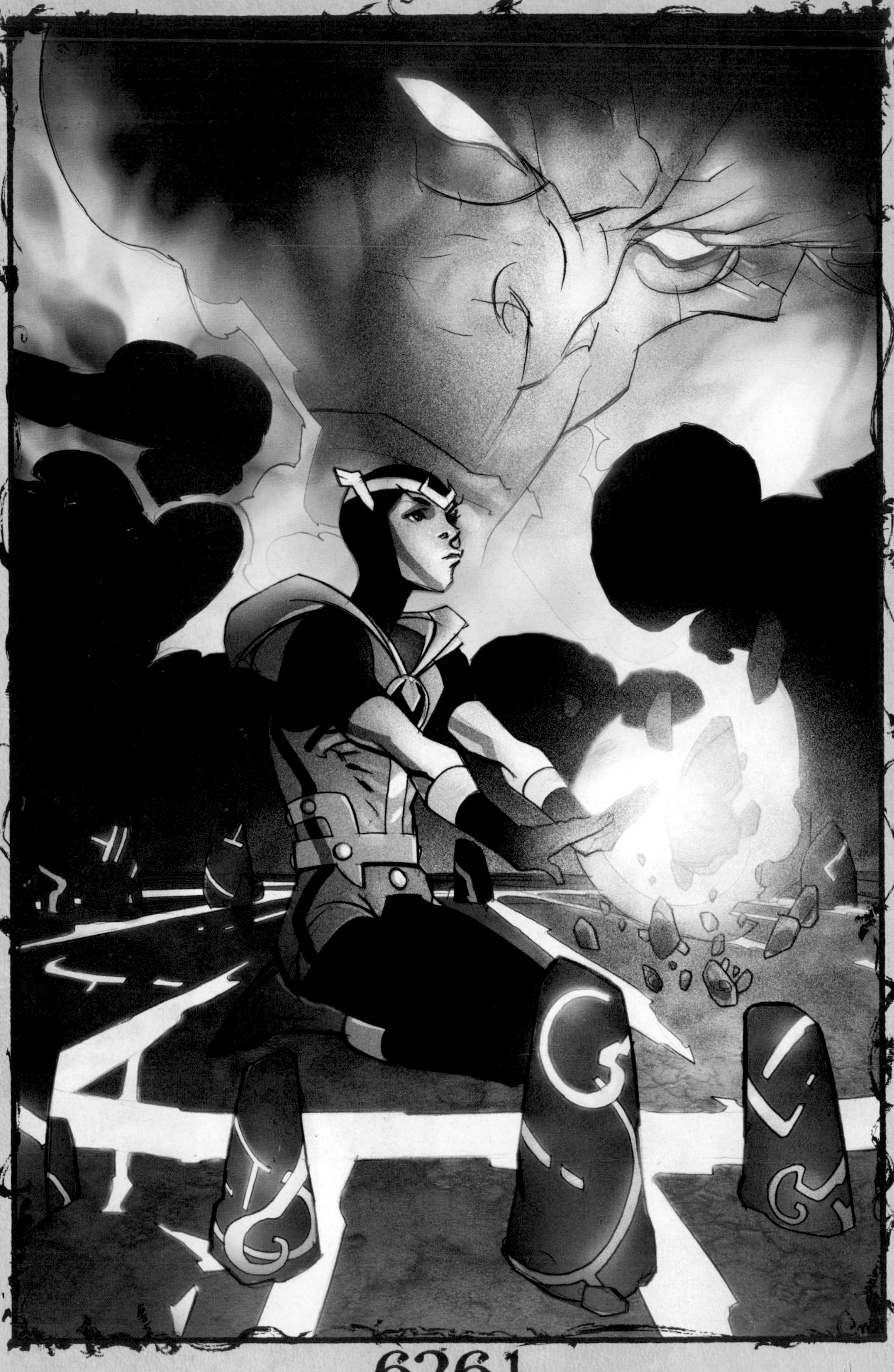

626.1

AS THE CULMINATION OF HIS GREATEST SCHEME, LOKI, GOD OF TRICKERY, GOT HIMSELF KILLED.

LOKI DIED DEFENDING ASGARD FROM A THREAT THAT HE HIMSELF HAD ARRANGED. NOT LONG BEFORE, HOWEVER, HE MADE AN AGREEMENT WITH HELA, GODDESS OF HEL, TO WRITE HIM OUT OF THE BOOK OF THE DEAD. HIS SOUL HAD ESCAPED THE CYCLE OF DEATH AND REBIRTH THAT DICTATES THE FATES OF ALL ASGARDIANS. WHEN THOR FOUND HIS SPIRIT AND RETURNED HIM TO THE LAND OF THE LIVING, LOKI WAS A NEW MAN. WELL, A NEW BOY.

AND HE DID IT ALL TO MAKE HIMSELF A BETTER PERSON. REALLY. HONEST TO ODIN. WE PROMISE.

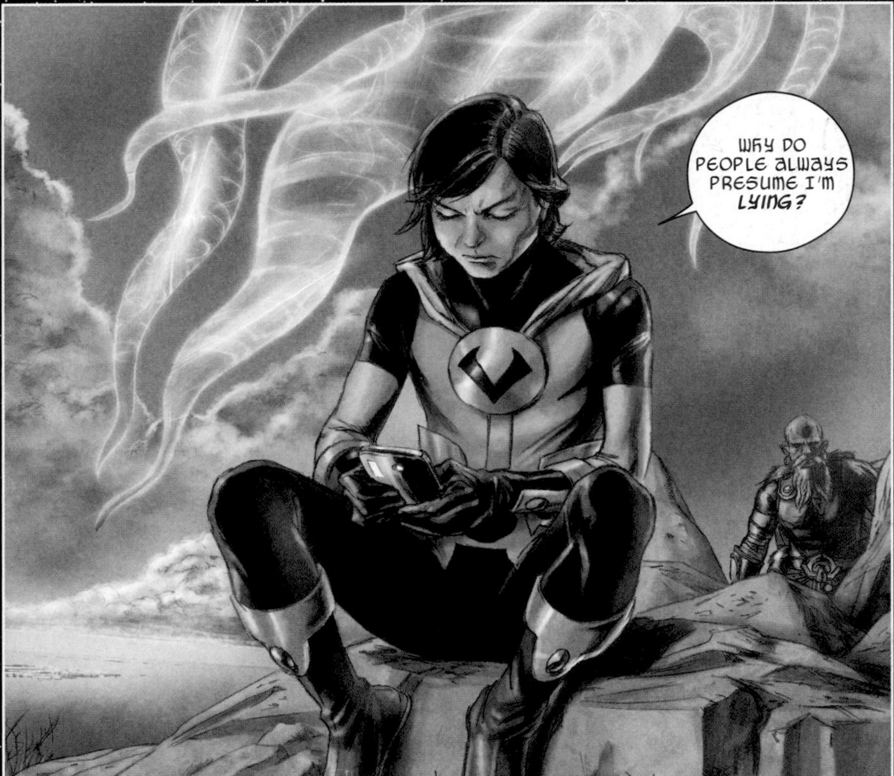
WHY DO PEOPLE ALWAYS PRESUME I'M *LYING?*

EDITOR'S NOTE: THIS ISSUE TAKES PLACE BETWEEN PANELS 4 & 5 ON PAGE 21 OF JOURNEY INTO MYSTERY #622. IN CASE YOU WERE WONDERING.

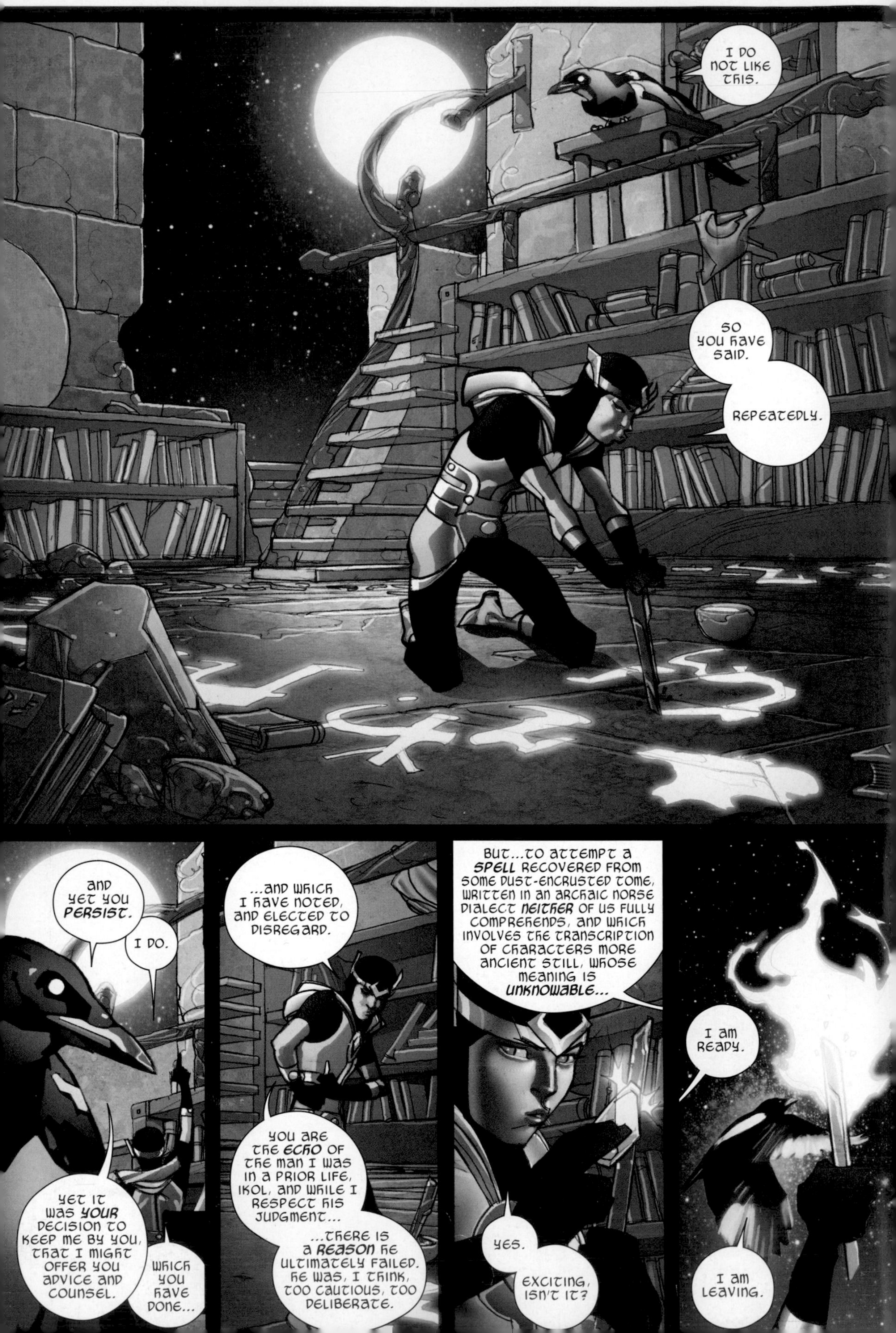
I DO NOT LIKE THIS.
SO YOU HAVE SAID.
REPEATEDLY.
AND YET YOU PERSIST.
I DO.
YET IT WAS YOUR DECISION TO KEEP ME BY YOU, THAT I MIGHT OFFER YOU ADVICE AND COUNSEL.
WHICH YOU HAVE DONE...
...AND WHICH I HAVE NOTED, AND ELECTED TO DISREGARD.
YOU ARE THE ECHO OF THE MAN I WAS IN A PRIOR LIFE, IKOL, AND WHILE I RESPECT HIS JUDGMENT...
...THERE IS A REASON HE ULTIMATELY FAILED. HE WAS, I THINK, TOO CAUTIOUS, TOO DELIBERATE.
BUT...TO ATTEMPT A SPELL RECOVERED FROM SOME DUST-ENCRUSTED TOME, WRITTEN IN AN ARCHAIC NORSE DIALECT NEITHER OF US FULLY COMPREHENDS, AND WHICH INVOLVES THE TRANSCRIPTION OF CHARACTERS MORE ANCIENT STILL, WHOSE MEANING IS UNKNOWABLE...
YES.
EXCITING, ISN'T IT?
I AM READY.
I AM LEAVING.

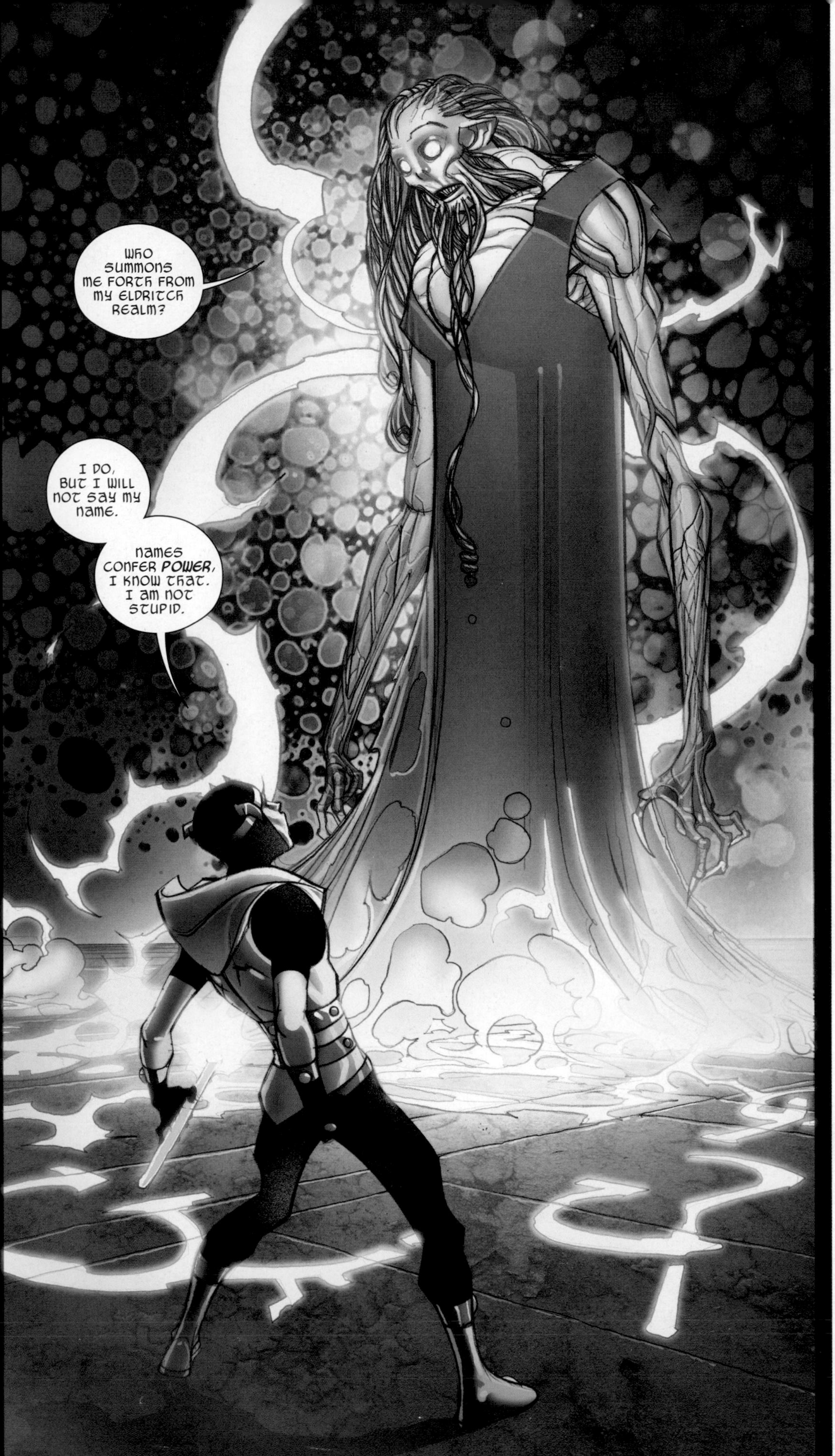
WHO SUMMONS ME FORTH FROM MY ELDRITCH REALM?
I DO, BUT I WILL NOT SAY MY NAME.
NAMES CONFER POWER, I KNOW THAT. I AM NOT STUPID.

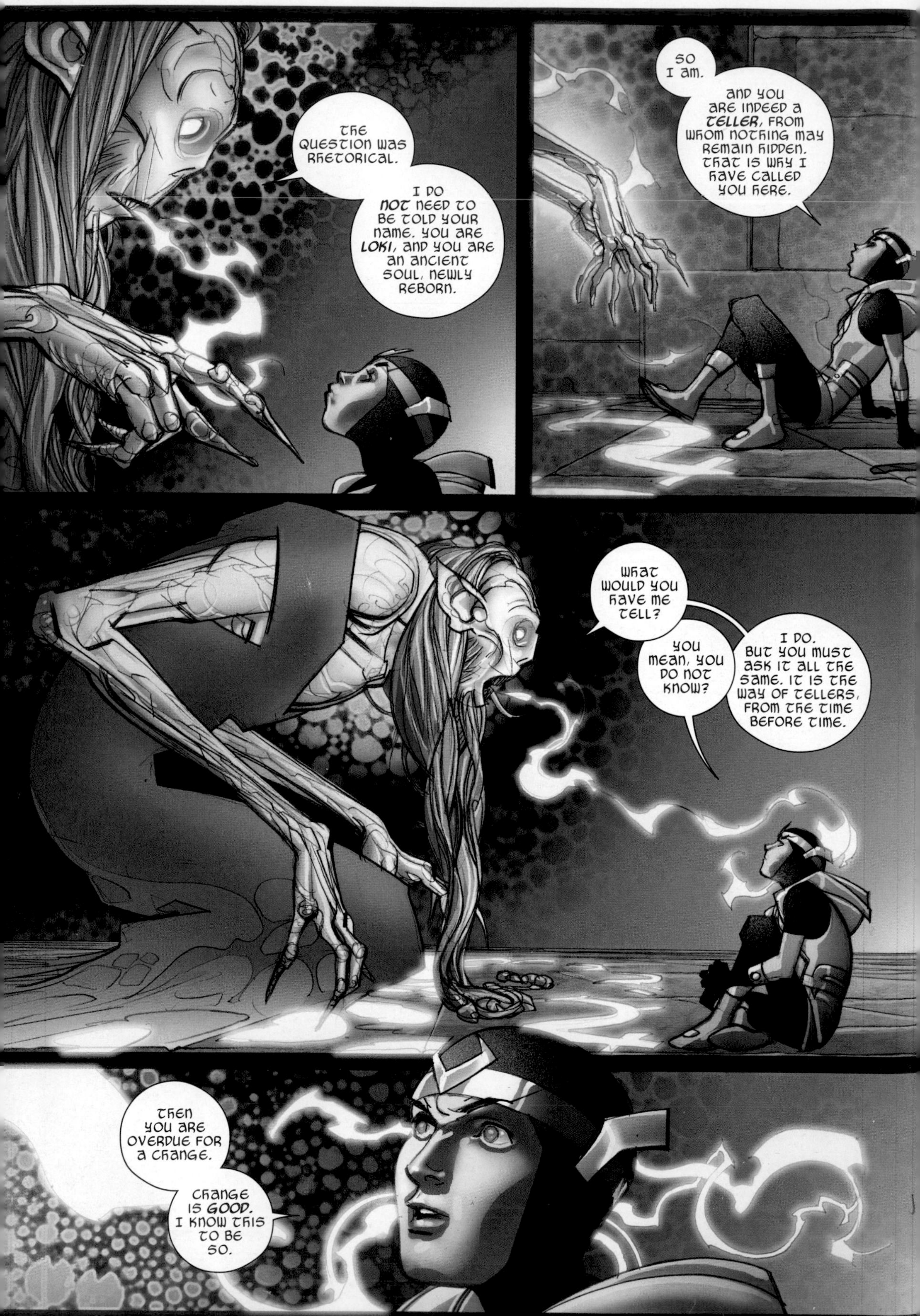
THE QUESTION WAS RHETORICAL.
I DO NOT NEED TO BE TOLD YOUR NAME. YOU ARE LOKI, AND YOU ARE AN ANCIENT SOUL, NEWLY REBORN.
SO I AM.
AND YOU ARE INDEED A TELLER, FROM WHOM NOTHING MAY REMAIN HIDDEN. THAT IS WHY I HAVE CALLED YOU HERE.
WHAT WOULD YOU HAVE ME TELL?
YOU MEAN, YOU DO NOT KNOW?
I DO. BUT YOU MUST ASK IT ALL THE SAME. IT IS THE WAY OF TELLERS, FROM THE TIME BEFORE TIME.
THEN YOU ARE OVERDUE FOR A CHANGE.
CHANGE IS GOOD. I KNOW THIS TO BE SO.

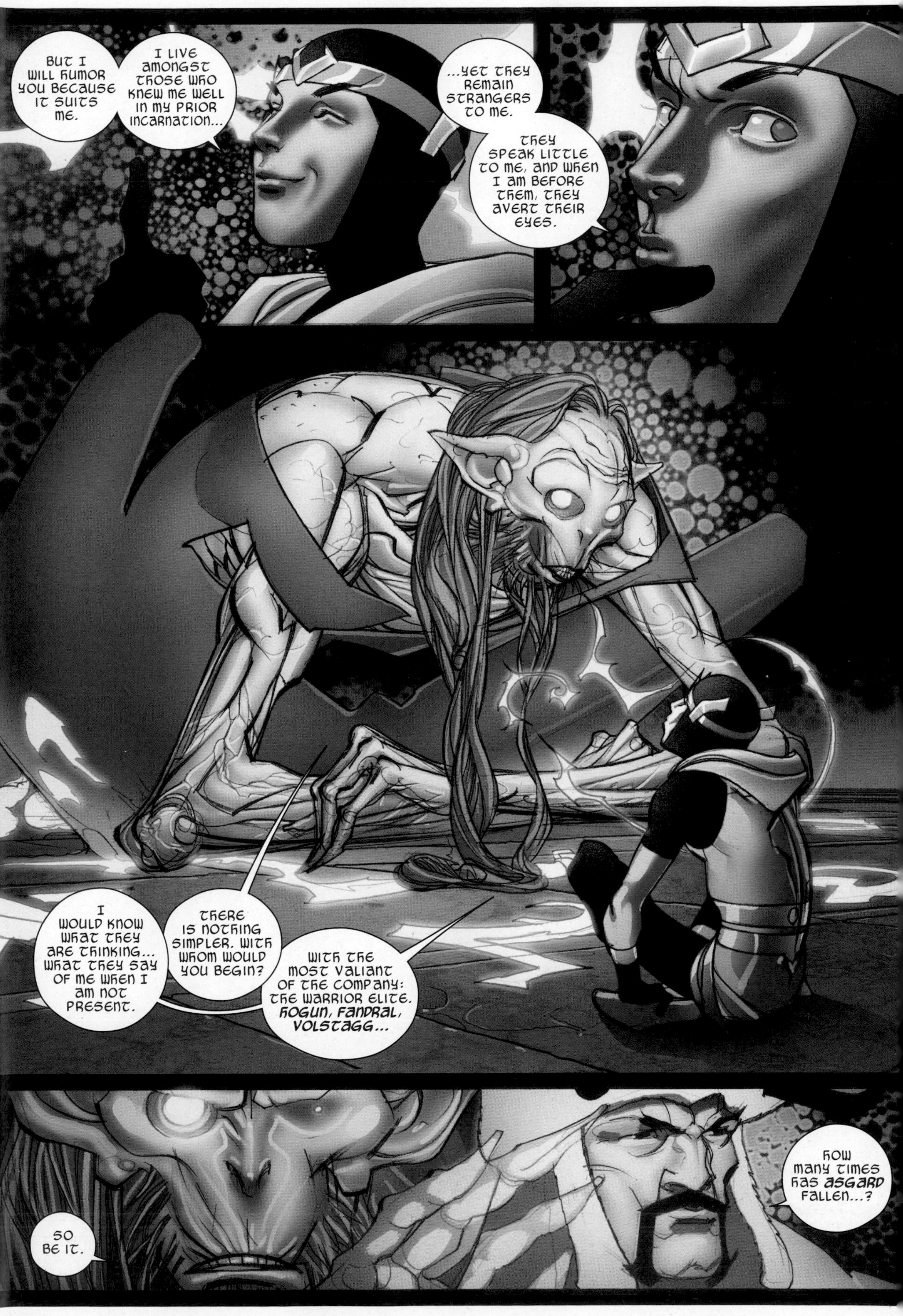
BUT I WILL HUMOR YOU BECAUSE IT SUITS ME.
I LIVE AMONGST THOSE WHO KNEW ME WELL IN MY PRIOR INCARNATION...
...YET THEY REMAIN STRANGERS TO ME.
THEY SPEAK LITTLE TO ME, AND WHEN I AM BEFORE THEM, THEY AVERT THEIR EYES.
I WOULD KNOW WHAT THEY ARE THINKING... WHAT THEY SAY OF ME WHEN I AM NOT PRESENT.
THERE IS NOTHING SIMPLER. WITH WHOM WOULD YOU BEGIN?
WITH THE MOST VALIANT OF THE COMPANY: THE WARRIOR ELITE. HOGUN, FANDRAL, VOLSTAGG...
SO BE IT.
HOW MANY TIMES HAS ASGARD FALLEN...?

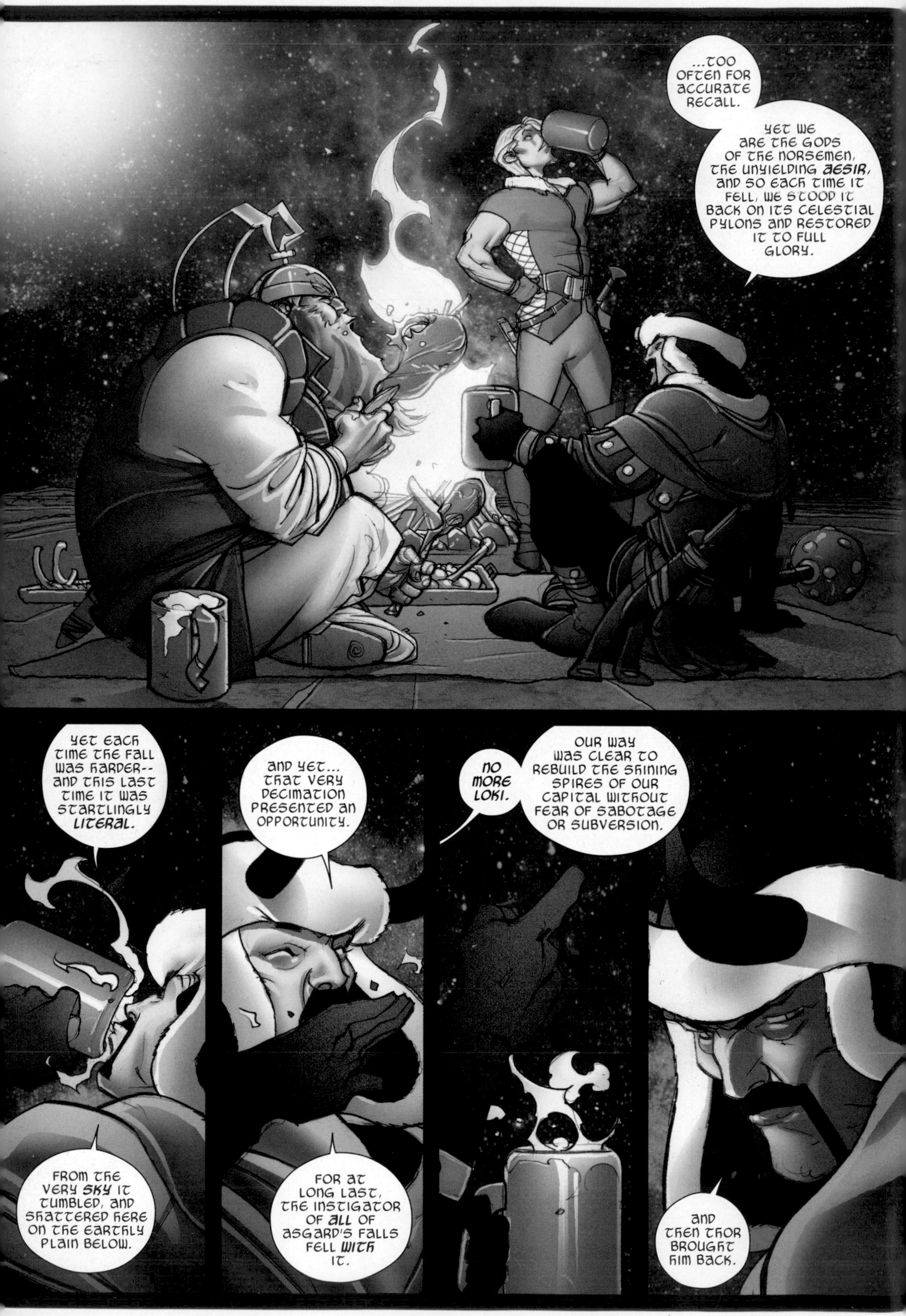
...TOO OFTEN FOR ACCURATE RECALL.
YET WE ARE THE GODS OF THE NORSEMEN, THE UNYIELDING AESIR, AND SO EACH TIME IT FELL, WE STOOD IT BACK ON ITS CELESTIAL PYLONS AND RESTORED IT TO FULL GLORY.
YET EACH TIME THE FALL WAS HARDER-- AND THIS LAST TIME IT WAS STARTLINGLY LITERAL.
FROM THE VERY SKY IT TUMBLED, AND SHATTERED HERE ON THE EARTHLY PLAIN BELOW.
AND YET... THAT VERY DECIMATION PRESENTED AN OPPORTUNITY.
FOR AT LONG LAST, THE INSTIGATOR OF ALL OF ASGARD'S FALLS FELL WITH IT.
NO MORE LOKI.
OUR WAY WAS CLEAR TO REBUILD THE SHINING SPIRES OF OUR CAPITAL WITHOUT FEAR OF SABOTAGE OR SUBVERSION.
AND THEN THOR BROUGHT HIM BACK.

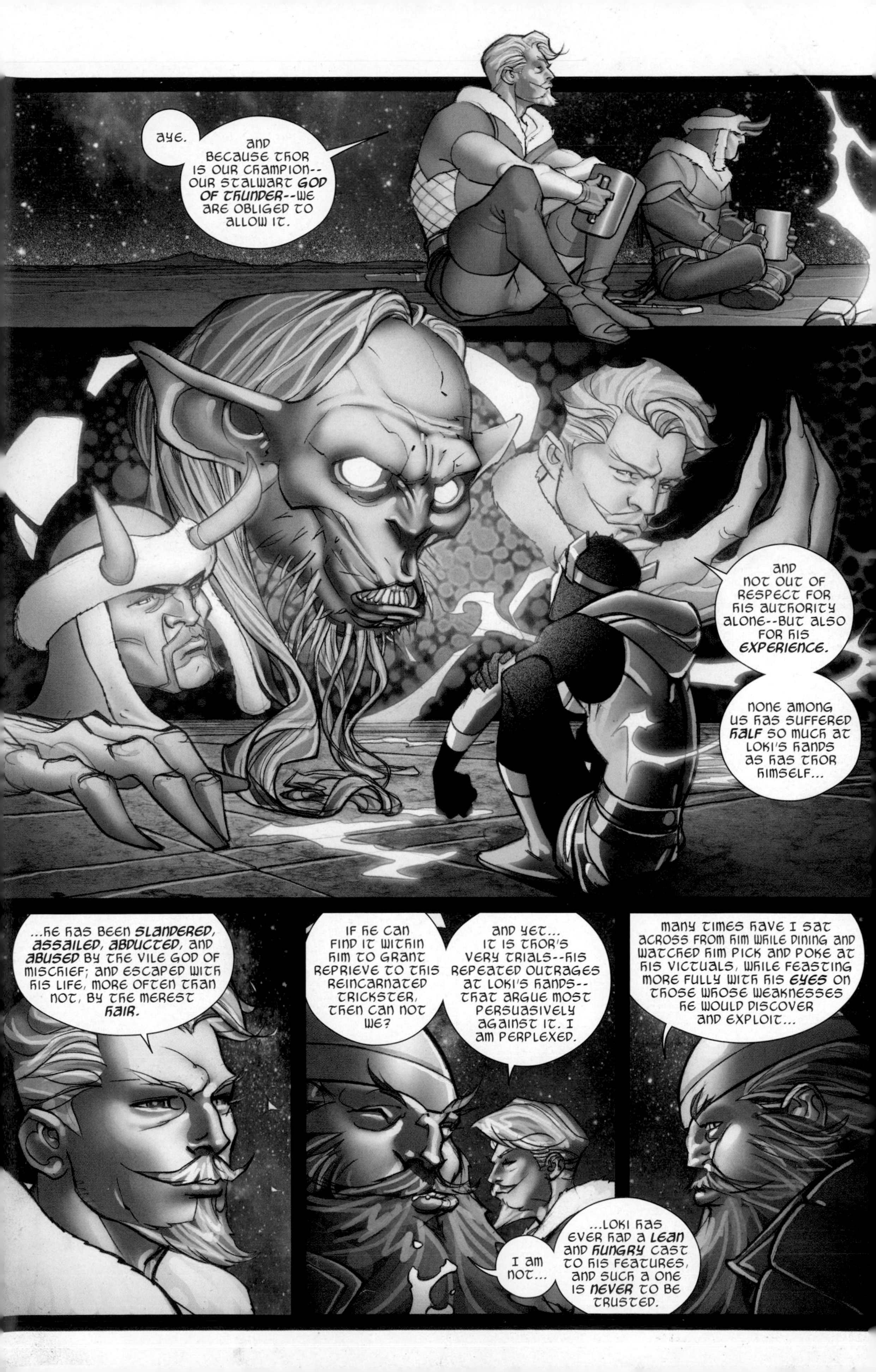
AYE.
AND BECAUSE THOR IS OUR CHAMPION--OUR STALWART GOD OF THUNDER--WE ARE OBLIGED TO ALLOW IT.
AND NOT OUT OF RESPECT FOR HIS AUTHORITY ALONE--BUT ALSO FOR HIS EXPERIENCE.
NONE AMONG US HAS SUFFERED HALF SO MUCH AT LOKI'S HANDS AS HAS THOR HIMSELF...
...HE HAS BEEN SLANDERED, ASSAILED, ABDUCTED, AND ABUSED BY THE VILE GOD OF MISCHIEF; AND ESCAPED WITH HIS LIFE, MORE OFTEN THAN NOT, BY THE MEREST HAIR.
IF HE CAN FIND IT WITHIN HIM TO GRANT REPRIEVE TO THIS REINCARNATED TRICKSTER, THEN CAN NOT WE?
AND YET... IT IS THOR'S VERY TRIALS--HIS REPEATED OUTRAGES AT LOKI'S HANDS--THAT ARGUE MOST PERSUASIVELY AGAINST IT. I AM PERPLEXED.
I AM NOT...
MANY TIMES HAVE I SAT ACROSS FROM HIM WHILE DINING AND WATCHED HIM PICK AND POKE AT HIS VICTUALS, WHILE FEASTING MORE FULLY WITH HIS EYES ON THOSE WHOSE WEAKNESSES HE WOULD DISCOVER AND EXPLOIT...
...LOKI HAS EVER HAD A LEAN AND HUNGRY CAST TO HIS FEATURES, AND SUCH A ONE IS NEVER TO BE TRUSTED.

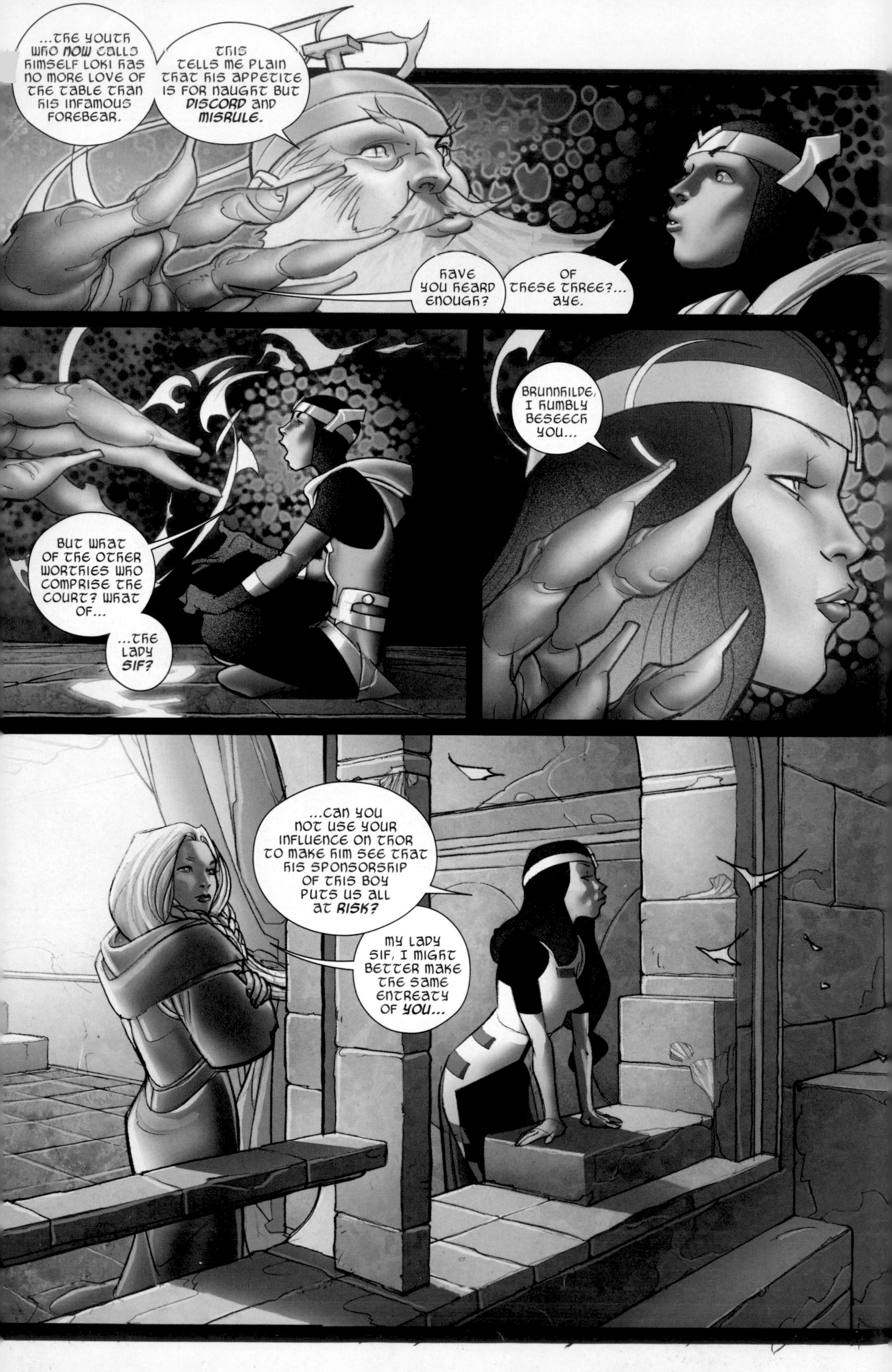

...THE YOUTH WHO NOW CALLS HIMSELF LOKI HAS NO MORE LOVE OF THE TABLE THAN HIS INFAMOUS FOREBEAR.
THIS TELLS ME PLAIN THAT HIS APPETITE IS FOR NAUGHT BUT DISCORD AND MISRULE.
HAVE YOU HEARD ENOUGH?
OF THESE THREE?... AYE.
BUT WHAT OF THE OTHER WORTHIES WHO COMPRISE THE COURT? WHAT OF...
...THE LADY SIF?
BRUNNHILDE, I HUMBLY BESEECH YOU...
...CAN YOU NOT USE YOUR INFLUENCE ON THOR TO MAKE HIM SEE THAT HIS SPONSORSHIP OF THIS BOY PUTS US ALL AT RISK?
MY LADY SIF, I MIGHT BETTER MAKE THE SAME ENTREATY OF YOU...

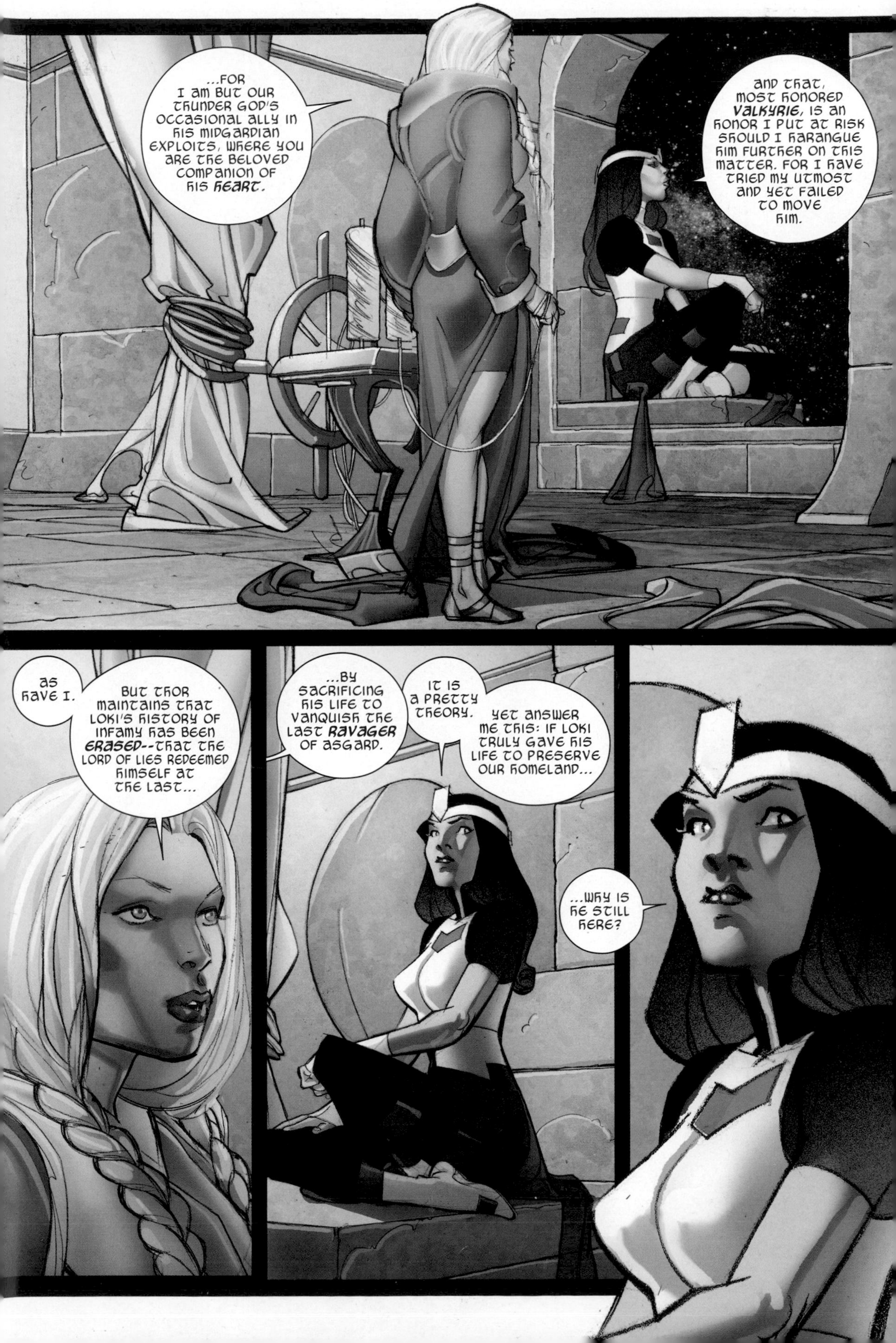
...FOR I AM BUT OUR THUNDER GOD'S OCCASIONAL ALLY IN HIS MIDGARDIAN EXPLOITS, WHERE YOU ARE THE BELOVED COMPANION OF HIS HEART.
AND THAT, MOST HONORED VALKYRIE, IS AN HONOR I PUT AT RISK SHOULD I HARANGUE HIM FURTHER ON THIS MATTER. FOR I HAVE TRIED MY UTMOST AND YET FAILED TO MOVE HIM.
AS HAVE I.
BUT THOR MAINTAINS THAT LOKI'S HISTORY OF INFAMY HAS BEEN ERASED--THAT THE LORD OF LIES REDEEMED HIMSELF AT THE LAST...
...BY SACRIFICING HIS LIFE TO VANQUISH THE LAST RAVAGER OF ASGARD.
IT IS A PRETTY THEORY.
YET ANSWER ME THIS: IF LOKI TRULY GAVE HIS LIFE TO PRESERVE OUR HOMELAND...
...WHY IS HE STILL HERE?

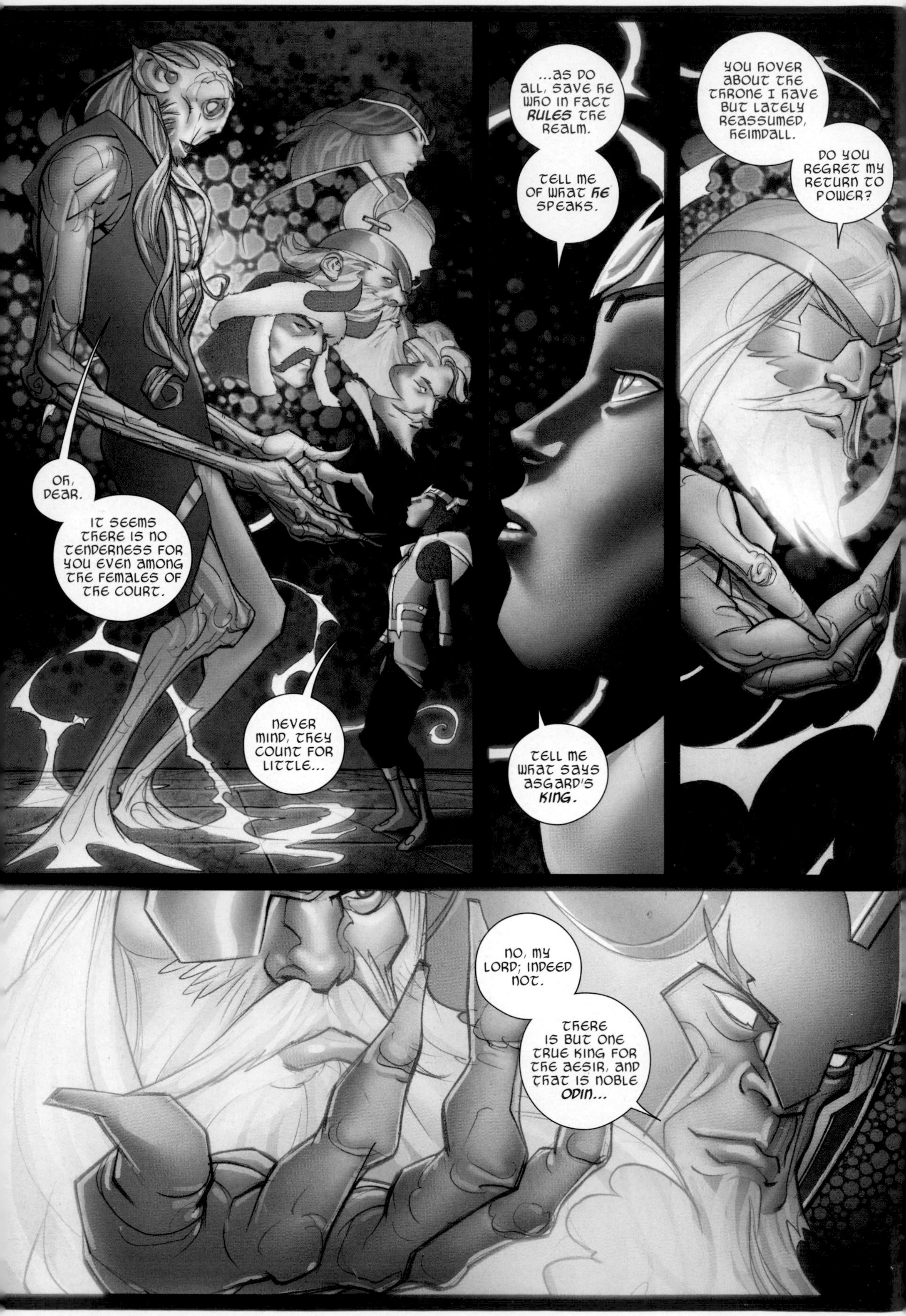

OH, DEAR.
IT SEEMS THERE IS NO TENDERNESS FOR YOU EVEN AMONG THE FEMALES OF THE COURT.
NEVER MIND, THEY COUNT FOR LITTLE...
...AS DO ALL, SAVE HE WHO IN FACT RULES THE REALM.
TELL ME OF WHAT HE SPEAKS.
TELL ME WHAT SAYS ASGARD'S KING.
YOU HOVER ABOUT THE THRONE I HAVE BUT LATELY REASSUMED, HEIMDALL.
DO YOU REGRET MY RETURN TO POWER?
NO, MY LORD; INDEED NOT.
THERE IS BUT ONE TRUE KING FOR THE AESIR, AND THAT IS NOBLE ODIN...

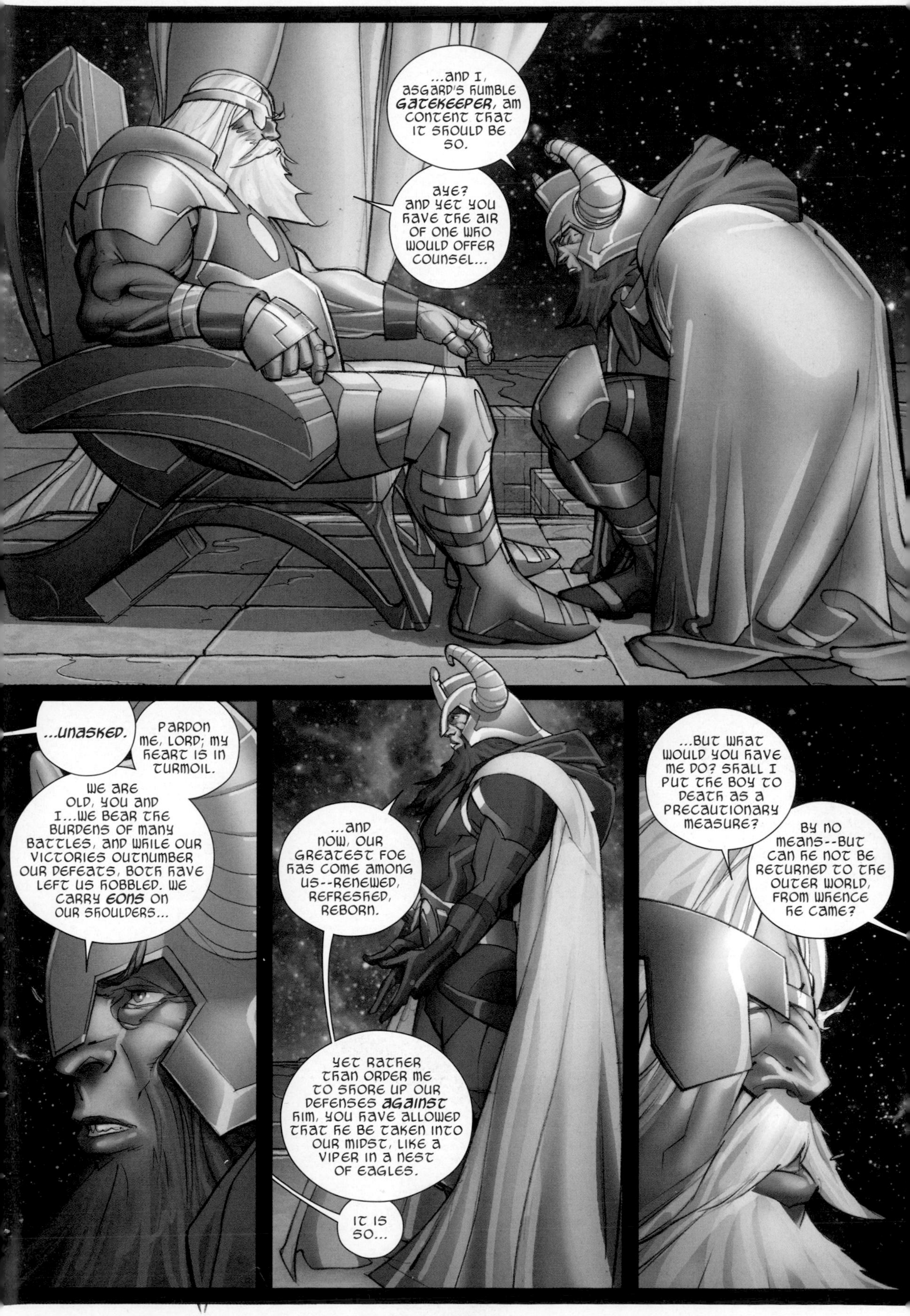
...AND I, ASGARD'S HUMBLE GATEKEEPER, AM CONTENT THAT IT SHOULD BE SO.
AYE? AND YET YOU HAVE THE AIR OF ONE WHO WOULD OFFER COUNSEL...
...UNASKED.
PARDON ME, LORD; MY HEART IS IN TURMOIL.
WE ARE OLD, YOU AND I...WE BEAR THE BURDENS OF MANY BATTLES, AND WHILE OUR VICTORIES OUTNUMBER OUR DEFEATS, BOTH HAVE LEFT US HOBBLED. WE CARRY EONS ON OUR SHOULDERS...
...AND NOW, OUR GREATEST FOE HAS COME AMONG US--RENEWED, REFRESHED, REBORN.
YET RATHER THAN ORDER ME TO SHORE UP OUR DEFENSES AGAINST HIM, YOU HAVE ALLOWED THAT HE BE TAKEN INTO OUR MIDST, LIKE A VIPER IN A NEST OF EAGLES.
IT IS SO...
...BUT WHAT WOULD YOU HAVE ME DO? SHALL I PUT THE BOY TO DEATH AS A PRECAUTIONARY MEASURE?
BY NO MEANS--BUT CAN HE NOT BE RETURNED TO THE OUTER WORLD, FROM WHENCE HE CAME?

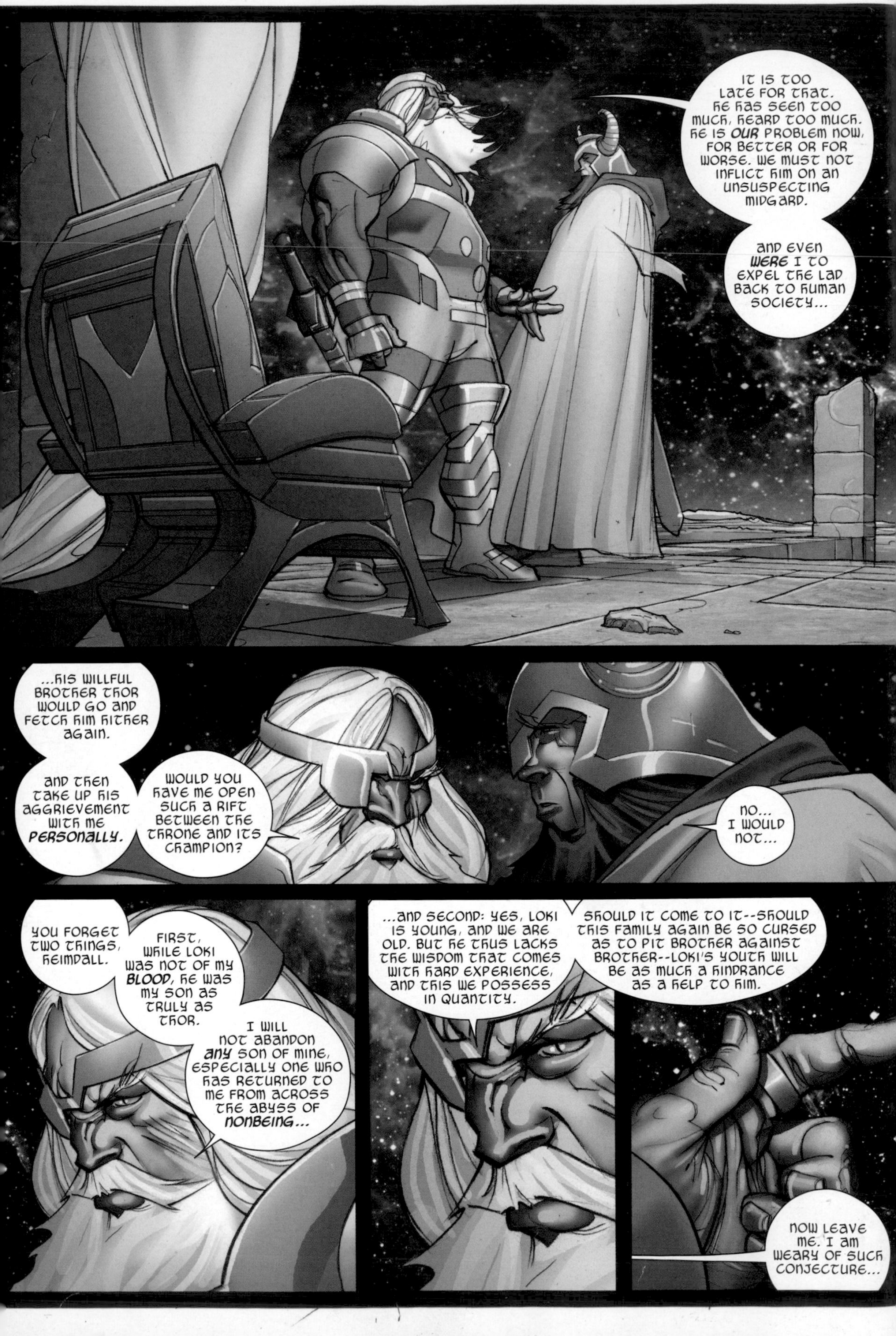

IT IS TOO LATE FOR THAT. HE HAS SEEN TOO MUCH, HEARD TOO MUCH. HE IS OUR PROBLEM NOW, FOR BETTER OR FOR WORSE. WE MUST NOT INFLICT HIM ON AN UNSUSPECTING MIDGARD.
AND EVEN WERE I TO EXPEL THE LAD BACK TO HUMAN SOCIETY...
...HIS WILLFUL BROTHER THOR WOULD GO AND FETCH HIM HITHER AGAIN.
AND THEN TAKE UP HIS AGGRIEVEMENT WITH ME PERSONALLY.
WOULD YOU HAVE ME OPEN SUCH A RIFT BETWEEN THE THRONE AND ITS CHAMPION?
NO... I WOULD NOT...
YOU FORGET TWO THINGS, HEIMDALL.
FIRST, WHILE LOKI WAS NOT OF MY BLOOD, HE WAS MY SON AS TRULY AS THOR.
I WILL NOT ABANDON ANY SON OF MINE, ESPECIALLY ONE WHO HAS RETURNED TO ME FROM ACROSS THE ABYSS OF NONBEING...
...AND SECOND: YES, LOKI IS YOUNG, AND WE ARE OLD. BUT HE THUS LACKS THE WISDOM THAT COMES WITH HARD EXPERIENCE, AND THIS WE POSSESS IN QUANTITY.
SHOULD IT COME TO IT--SHOULD THIS FAMILY AGAIN BE SO CURSED AS TO PIT BROTHER AGAINST BROTHER--LOKI'S YOUTH WILL BE AS MUCH A HINDRANCE AS A HELP TO HIM.
NOW LEAVE ME. I AM WEARY OF SUCH CONJECTURE...

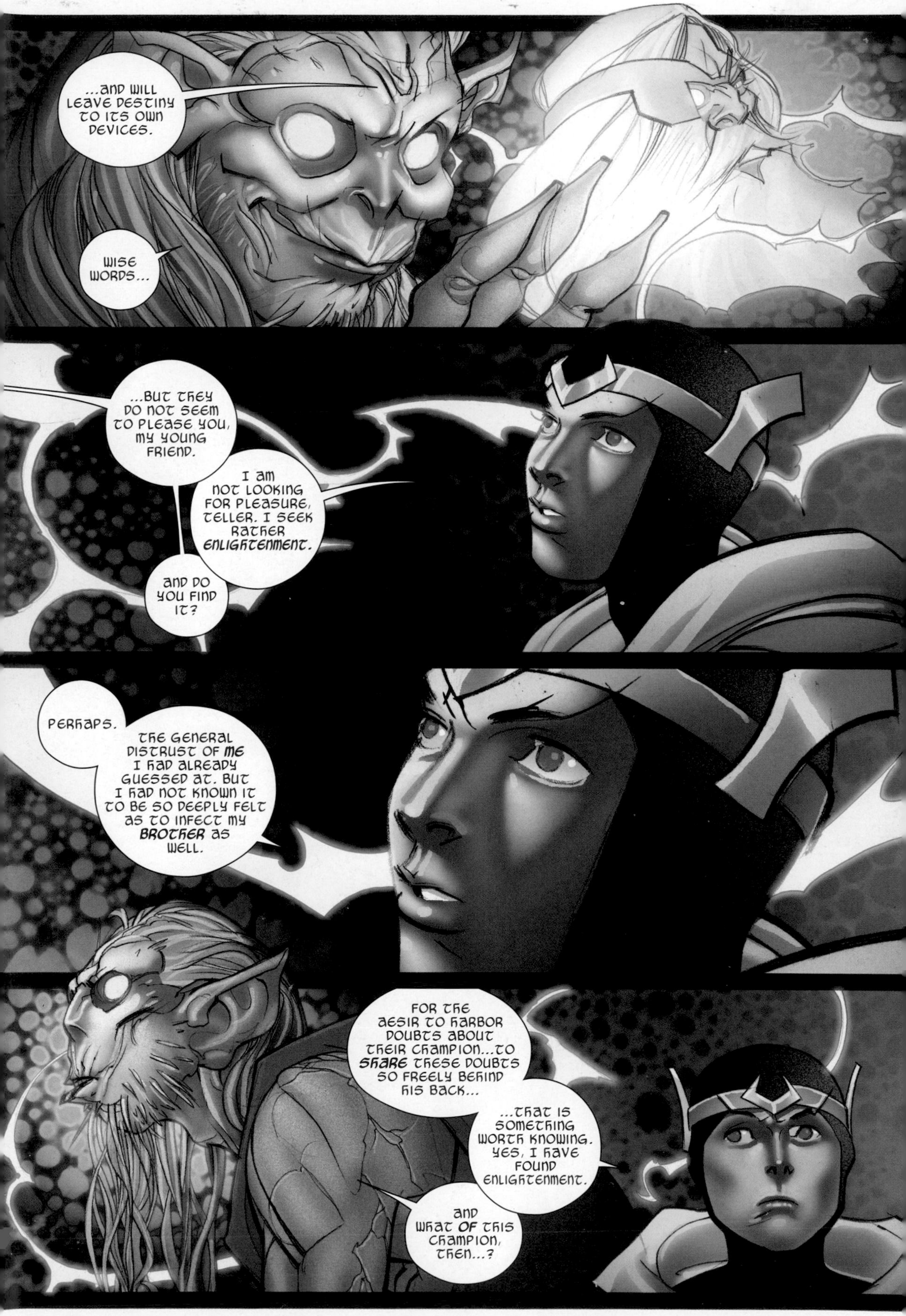
...AND WILL LEAVE DESTINY TO ITS OWN DEVICES.
WISE WORDS...
...BUT THEY DO NOT SEEM TO PLEASE YOU, MY YOUNG FRIEND.
I AM NOT LOOKING FOR PLEASURE, TELLER. I SEEK RATHER ENLIGHTENMENT.
AND DO YOU FIND IT?
PERHAPS.
THE GENERAL DISTRUST OF ME I HAD ALREADY GUESSED AT. BUT I HAD NOT KNOWN IT TO BE SO DEEPLY FELT AS TO INFECT MY BROTHER AS WELL.
FOR THE AESIR TO HARBOR DOUBTS ABOUT THEIR CHAMPION...TO SHARE THESE DOUBTS SO FREELY BEHIND HIS BACK...
...THAT IS SOMETHING WORTH KNOWING. YES, I HAVE FOUND ENLIGHTENMENT.
AND WHAT OF THIS CHAMPION, THEN...?

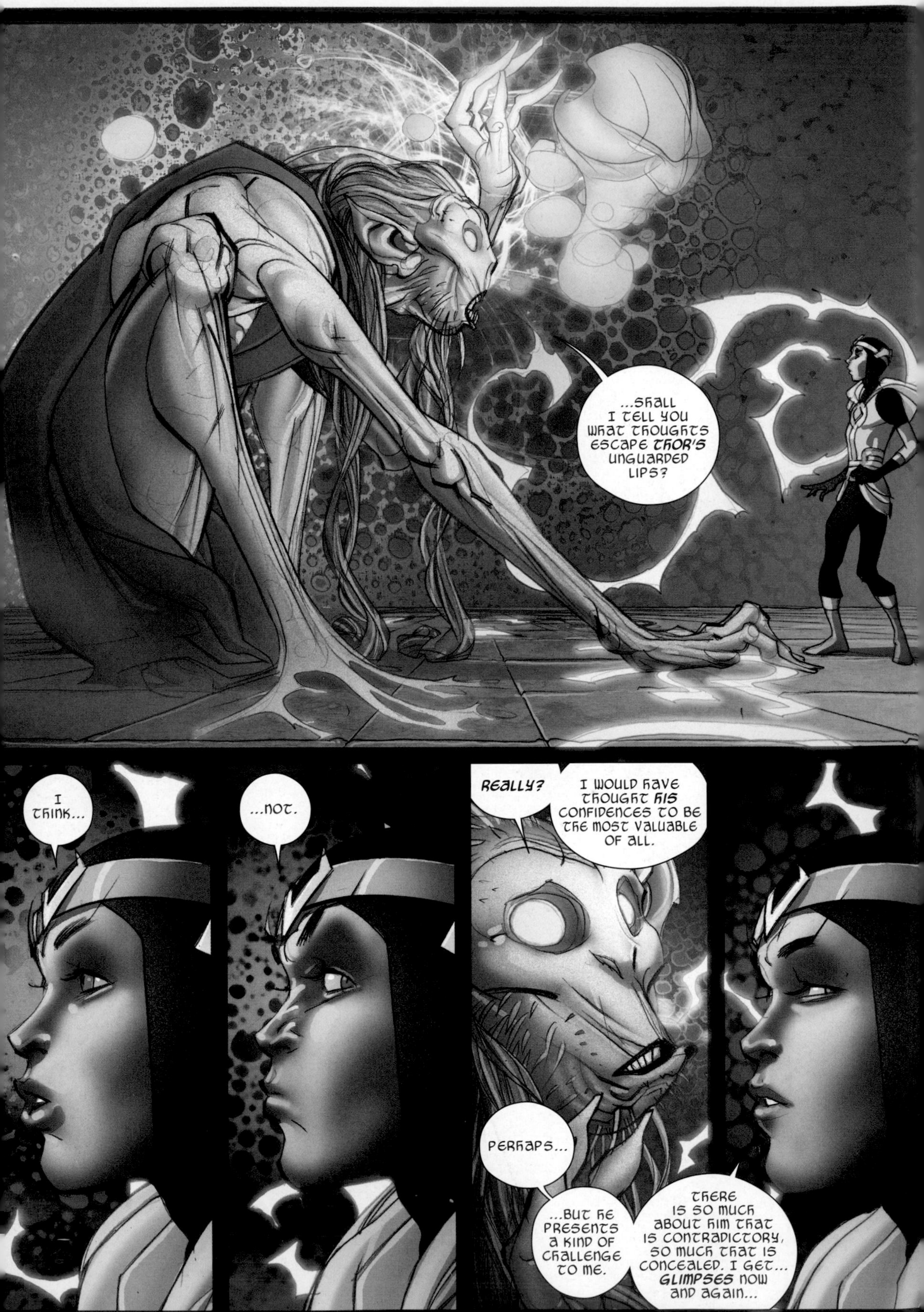
...SHALL I TELL YOU WHAT THOUGHTS ESCAPE THOR'S UNGUARDED LIPS?
I THINK...
...NOT.
REALLY?
I WOULD HAVE THOUGHT HIS CONFIDENCES TO BE THE MOST VALUABLE OF ALL.
PERHAPS...
...BUT HE PRESENTS A KIND OF CHALLENGE TO ME.
THERE IS SO MUCH ABOUT HIM THAT IS CONTRADICTORY, SO MUCH THAT IS CONCEALED. I GET... GLIMPSES NOW AND AGAIN...

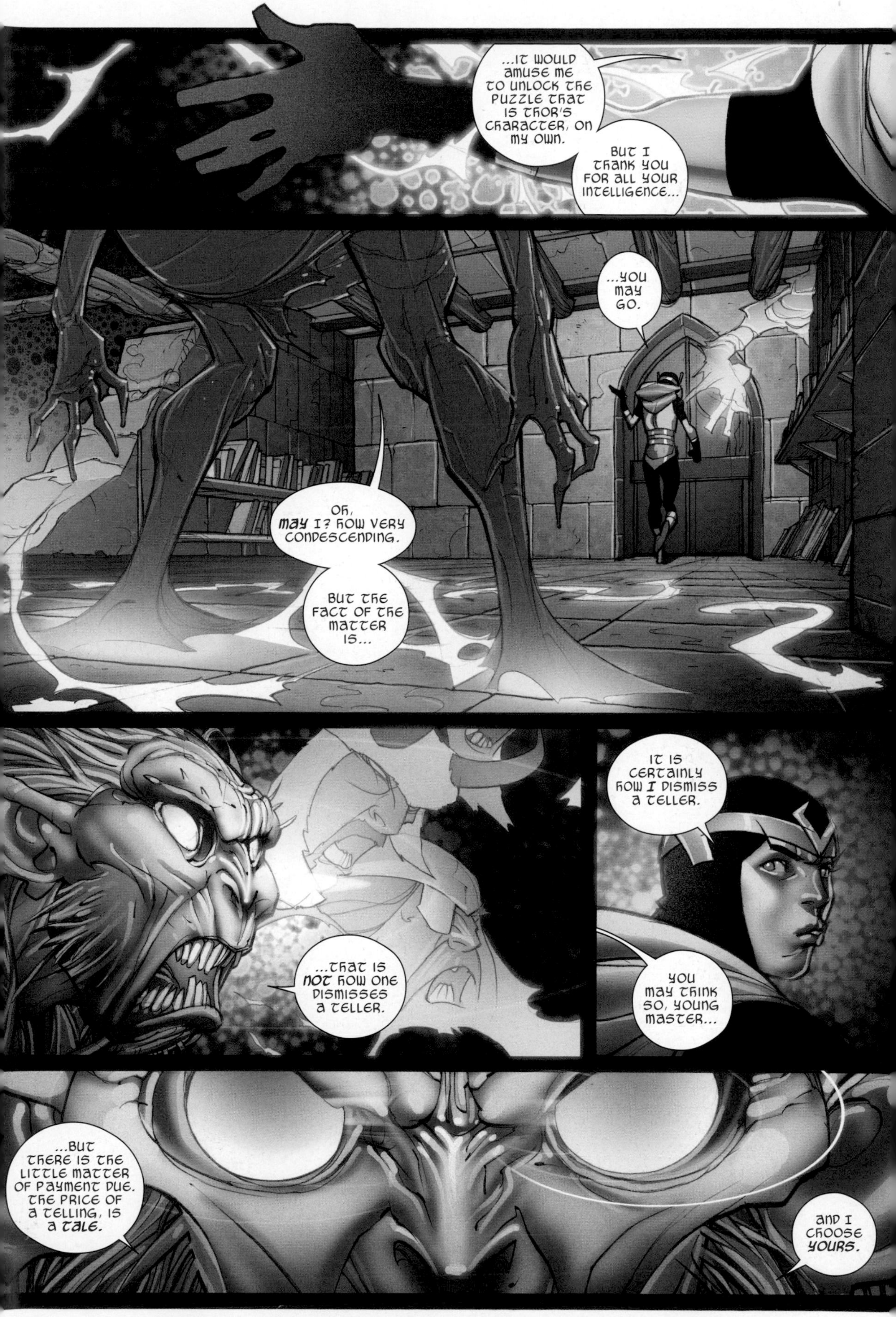
...IT WOULD AMUSE ME TO UNLOCK THE PUZZLE THAT IS THOR'S CHARACTER, ON MY OWN.
BUT I THANK YOU FOR ALL YOUR INTELLIGENCE...
...YOU MAY GO.
OH, **MAY** I? HOW VERY CONDESCENDING.
BUT THE FACT OF THE MATTER IS...
...THAT IS **NOT** HOW ONE DISMISSES A TELLER.
IT IS CERTAINLY HOW **I** DISMISS A TELLER.
YOU MAY THINK SO, YOUNG MASTER...
...BUT THERE IS THE LITTLE MATTER OF PAYMENT DUE. THE PRICE OF A TELLING, IS A **TALE.**
AND I CHOOSE **YOURS.**

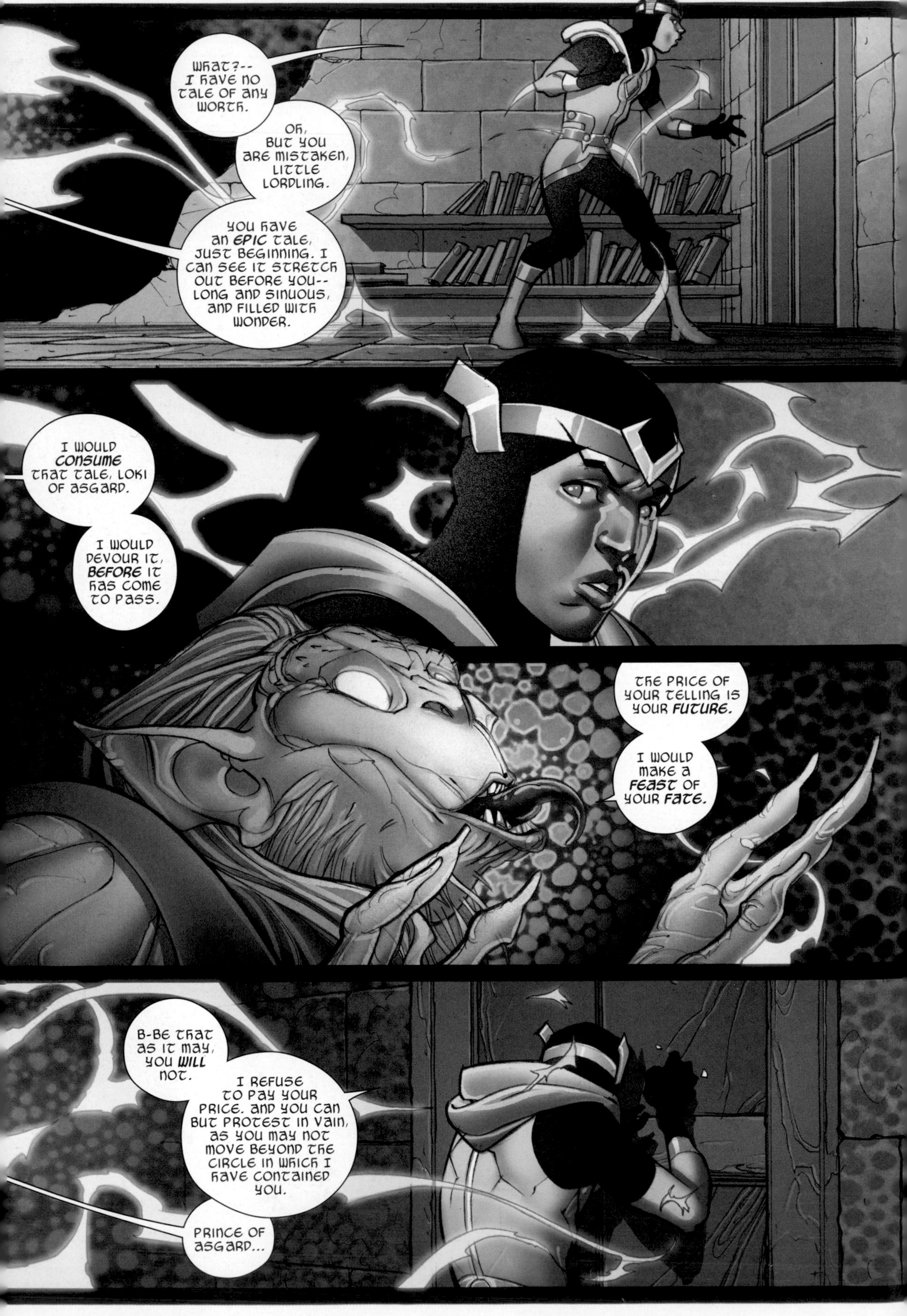
WHAT?-- I HAVE NO TALE OF ANY WORTH.
OH, BUT YOU ARE MISTAKEN, LITTLE LORDLING.
YOU HAVE AN EPIC TALE, JUST BEGINNING. I CAN SEE IT STRETCH OUT BEFORE YOU-- LONG AND SINUOUS, AND FILLED WITH WONDER.
I WOULD CONSUME THAT TALE, LOKI OF ASGARD.
I WOULD DEVOUR IT, BEFORE IT HAS COME TO PASS.
THE PRICE OF YOUR TELLING IS YOUR FUTURE.
I WOULD MAKE A FEAST OF YOUR FATE.
B-BE THAT AS IT MAY, YOU WILL NOT.
I REFUSE TO PAY YOUR PRICE. AND YOU CAN BUT PROTEST IN VAIN, AS YOU MAY NOT MOVE BEYOND THE CIRCLE IN WHICH I HAVE CONTAINED YOU.
PRINCE OF ASGARD...

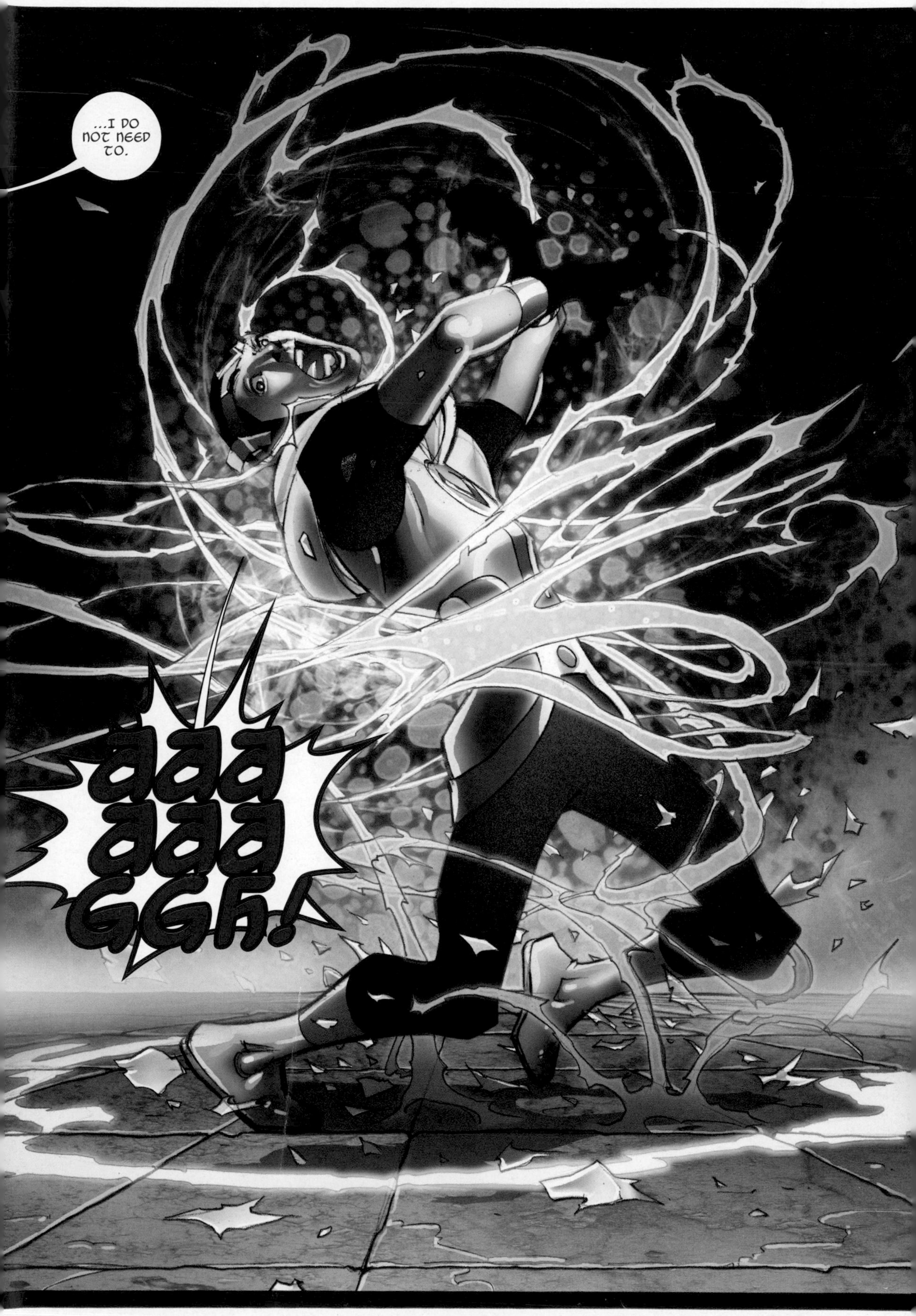
...I DO NOT NEED TO.
AAAAAAGGH!

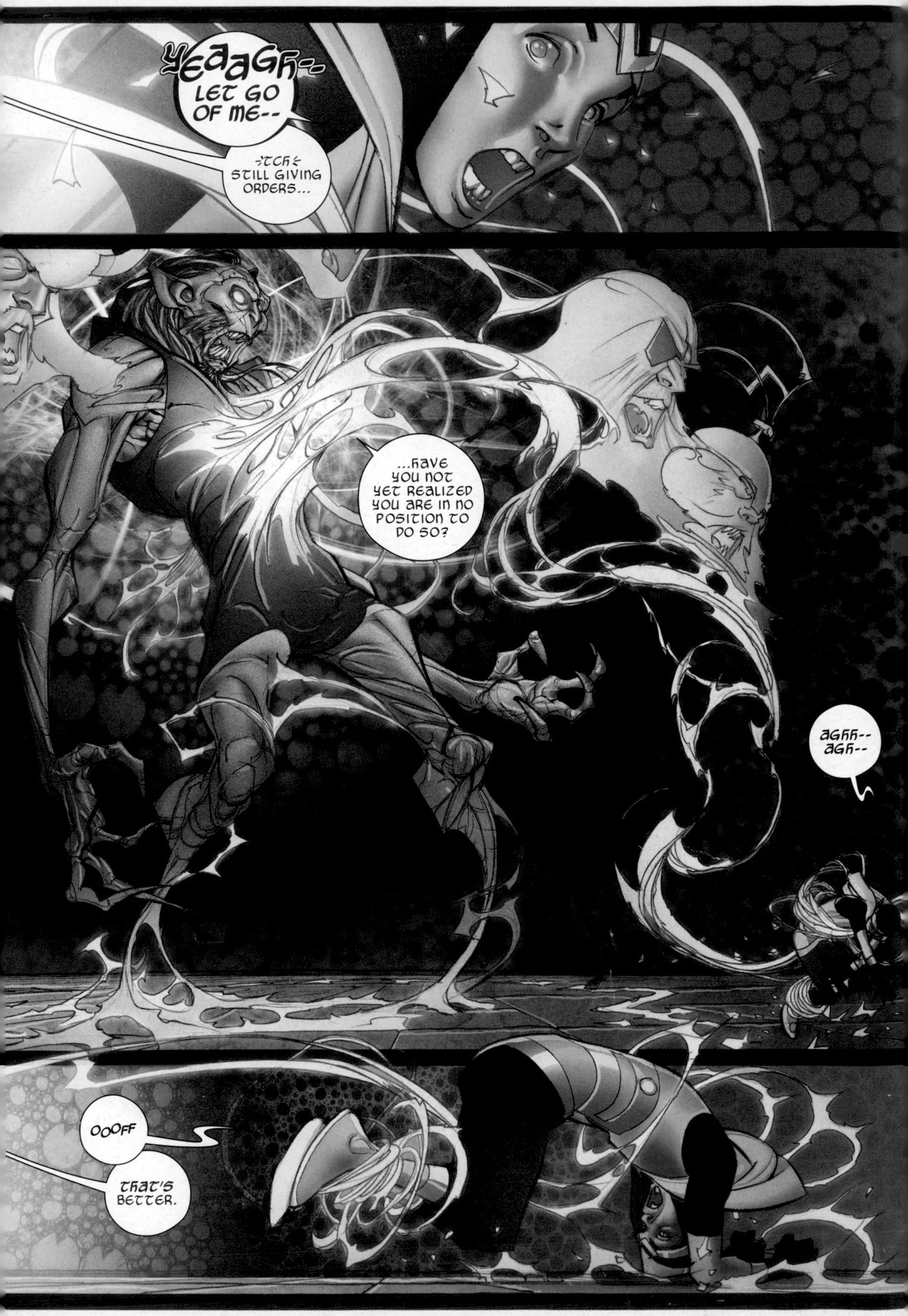
YEAAGH-- LET GO OF ME--
-TCH- STILL GIVING ORDERS...
...HAVE YOU NOT YET REALIZED YOU ARE IN NO POSITION TO DO SO?
AGHH-- AGH--
OOOFF
THAT'S BETTER.

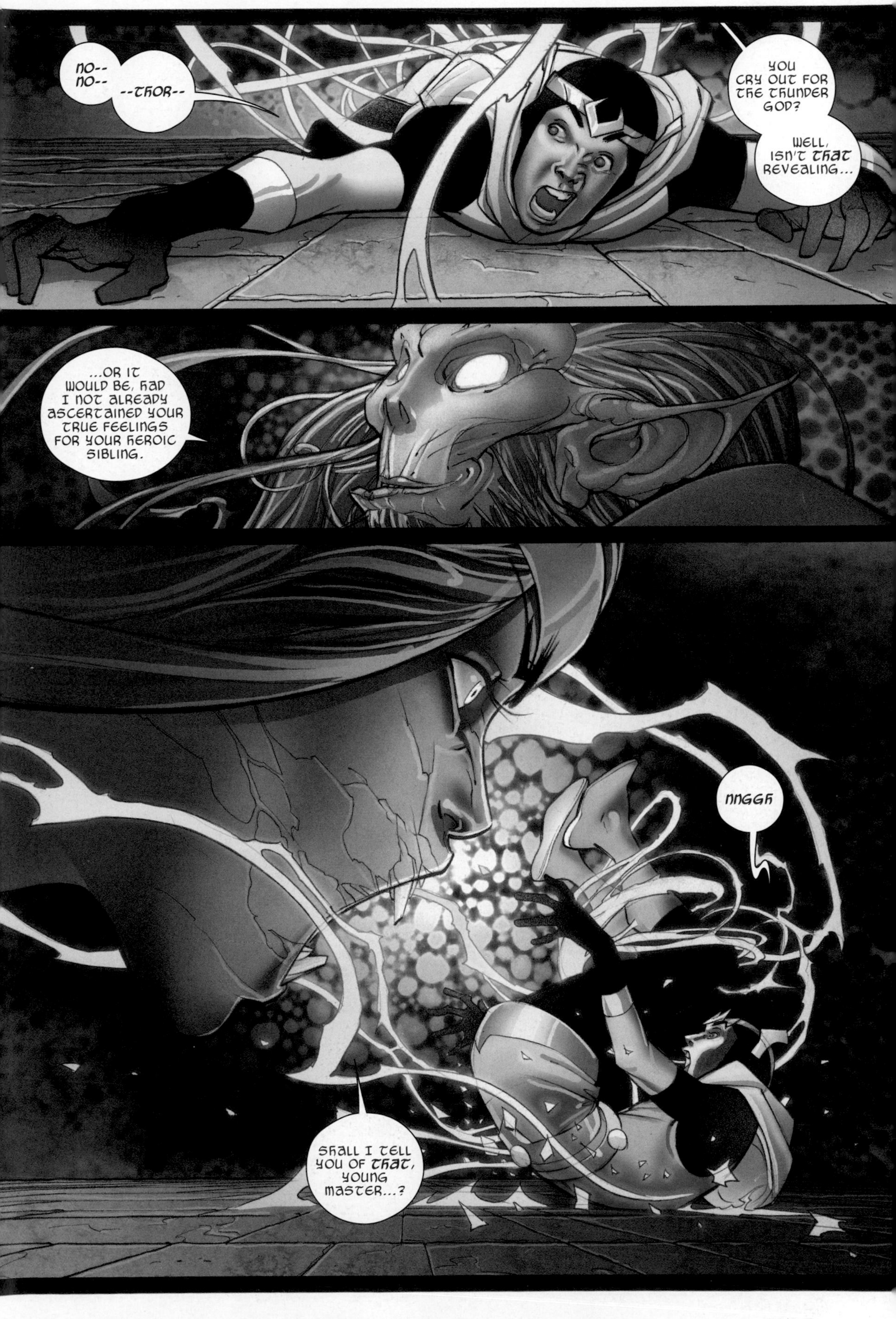

NO--
NO--
--THOR--
YOU CRY OUT FOR THE THUNDER GOD?
WELL, ISN'T THAT REVEALING...
...OR IT WOULD BE, HAD I NOT ALREADY ASCERTAINED YOUR TRUE FEELINGS FOR YOUR HEROIC SIBLING.
NNGGH
SHALL I TELL YOU OF THAT, YOUNG MASTER...?

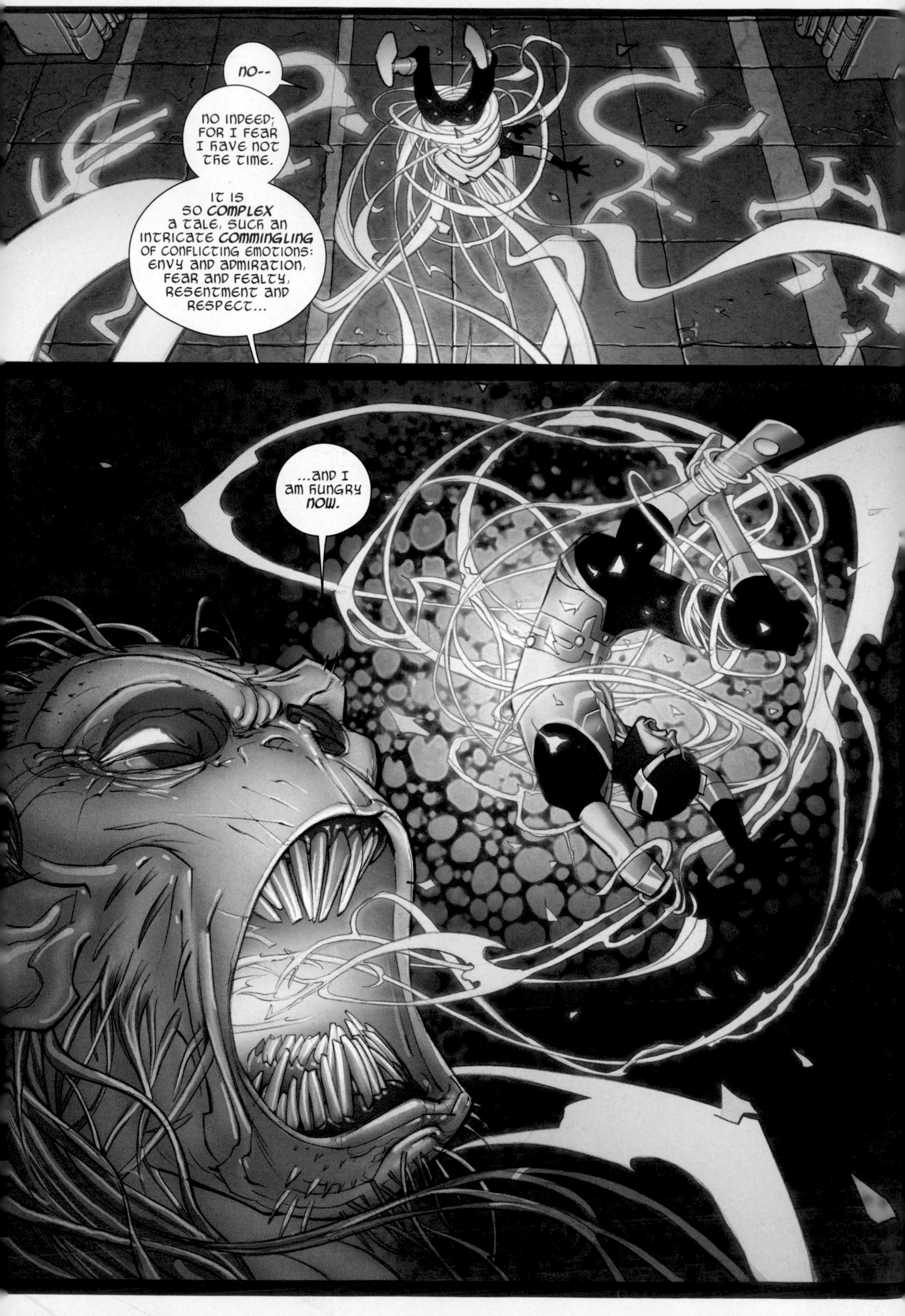
NO--
NO INDEED; FOR I FEAR I HAVE NOT THE TIME.
IT IS SO COMPLEX A TALE, SUCH AN INTRICATE COMMINGLING OF CONFLICTING EMOTIONS: ENVY AND ADMIRATION, FEAR AND FEALTY, RESENTMENT AND RESPECT...
...AND I AM HUNGRY NOW.

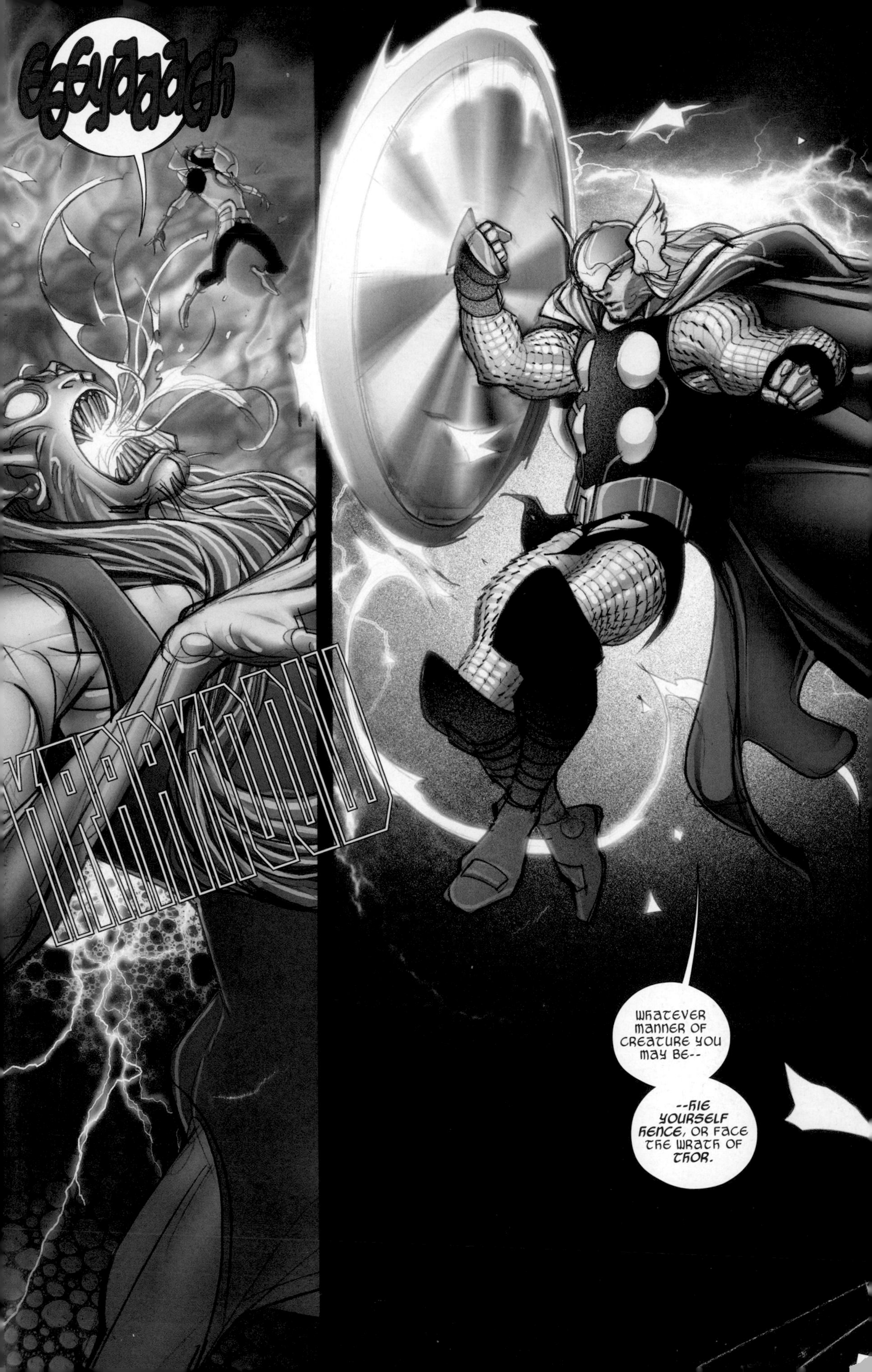
EEEYAAAGH
KRRAKAOOM
WHATEVER MANNER OF CREATURE YOU MAY BE--
--HIE YOURSELF HENCE, OR FACE THE WRATH OF THOR.

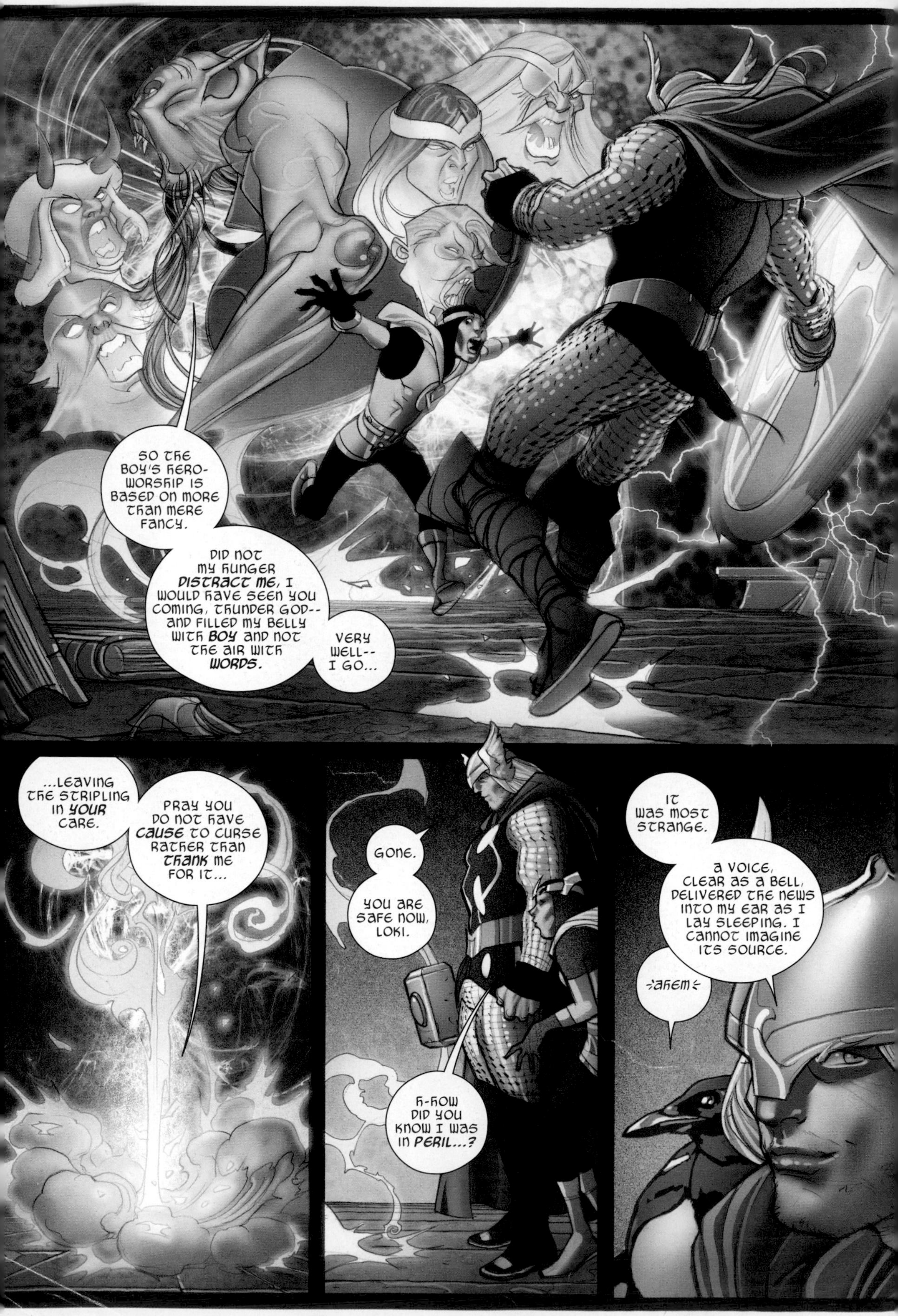
SO THE BOY'S HERO-WORSHIP IS BASED ON MORE THAN MERE FANCY.
DID NOT MY HUNGER DISTRACT ME, I WOULD HAVE SEEN YOU COMING, THUNDER GOD-- AND FILLED MY BELLY WITH BOY AND NOT THE AIR WITH WORDS.
VERY WELL-- I GO...
...LEAVING THE STRIPLING IN YOUR CARE.
PRAY YOU DO NOT HAVE CAUSE TO CURSE RATHER THAN THANK ME FOR IT...
GONE.
YOU ARE SAFE NOW, LOKI.
H-HOW DID YOU KNOW I WAS IN PERIL...?
IT WAS MOST STRANGE.
A VOICE, CLEAR AS A BELL, DELIVERED THE NEWS INTO MY EAR AS I LAY SLEEPING. I CANNOT IMAGINE ITS SOURCE.
AHEM

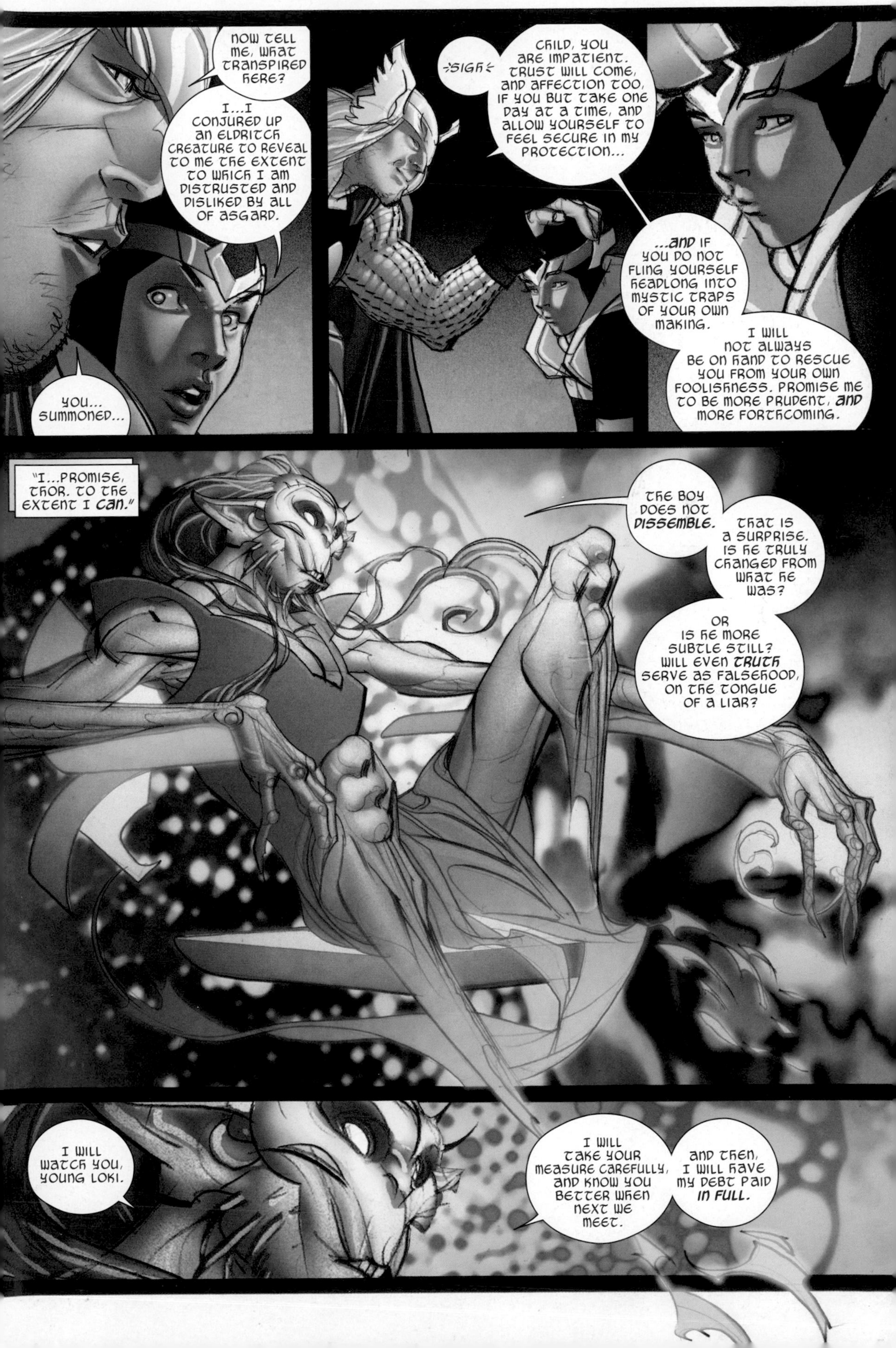

NOW TELL ME, WHAT TRANSPIRED HERE?
I...I CONJURED UP AN ELDRITCH CREATURE TO REVEAL TO ME THE EXTENT TO WHICH I AM DISTRUSTED AND DISLIKED BY ALL OF ASGARD.
YOU... SUMMONED...
SIGH
CHILD, YOU ARE IMPATIENT. TRUST WILL COME, AND AFFECTION TOO, IF YOU BUT TAKE ONE DAY AT A TIME, AND ALLOW YOURSELF TO FEEL SECURE IN MY PROTECTION...
...AND IF YOU DO NOT FLING YOURSELF HEADLONG INTO MYSTIC TRAPS OF YOUR OWN MAKING.
I WILL NOT ALWAYS BE ON HAND TO RESCUE YOU FROM YOUR OWN FOOLISHNESS. PROMISE ME TO BE MORE PRUDENT, AND MORE FORTHCOMING.
"I...PROMISE, THOR. TO THE EXTENT I CAN."
THE BOY DOES NOT DISSEMBLE.
THAT IS A SURPRISE. IS HE TRULY CHANGED FROM WHAT HE WAS?
OR IS HE MORE SUBTLE STILL? WILL EVEN TRUTH SERVE AS FALSEHOOD, ON THE TONGUE OF A LIAR?
I WILL WATCH YOU, YOUNG LOKI.
I WILL TAKE YOUR MEASURE CAREFULLY, AND KNOW YOU BETTER WHEN NEXT WE MEET.
AND THEN, I WILL HAVE MY DEBT PAID IN FULL.

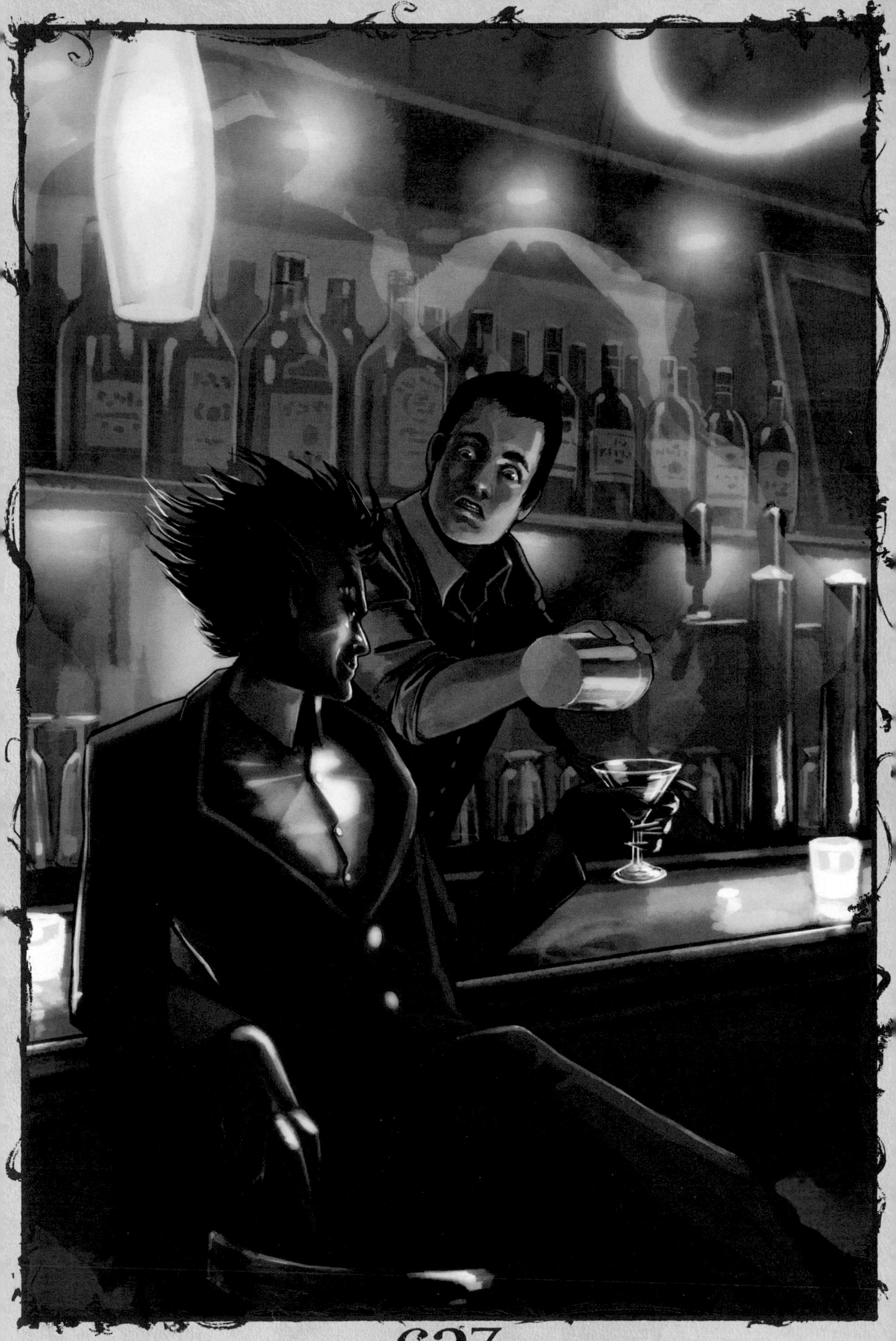

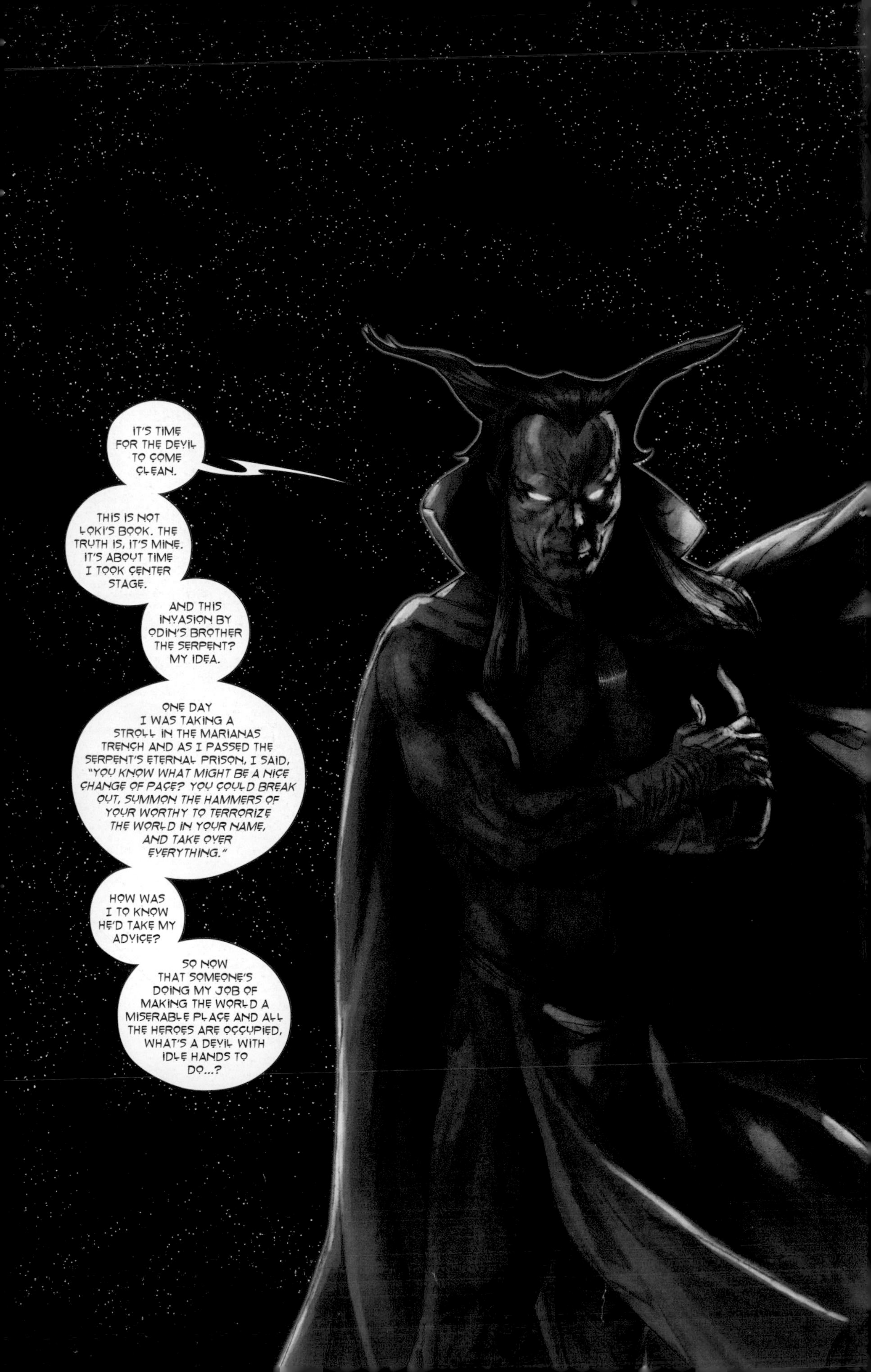
IT'S TIME FOR THE DEVIL TO COME CLEAN.
THIS IS NOT LOKI'S BOOK. THE TRUTH IS, IT'S MINE. IT'S ABOUT TIME I TOOK CENTER STAGE.
AND THIS INVASION BY ODIN'S BROTHER THE SERPENT? MY IDEA.
ONE DAY I WAS TAKING A STROLL IN THE MARIANAS TRENCH AND AS I PASSED THE SERPENT'S ETERNAL PRISON, I SAID, *"YOU KNOW WHAT MIGHT BE A NICE CHANGE OF PACE? YOU COULD BREAK OUT, SUMMON THE HAMMERS OF YOUR WORTHY TO TERRORIZE THE WORLD IN YOUR NAME, AND TAKE OVER EVERYTHING."*
HOW WAS I TO KNOW HE'D TAKE MY ADVICE?
SO NOW THAT SOMEONE'S DOING MY JOB OF MAKING THE WORLD A MISERABLE PLACE AND ALL THE HEROES ARE OCCUPIED, WHAT'S A DEVIL WITH IDLE HANDS TO DO...?

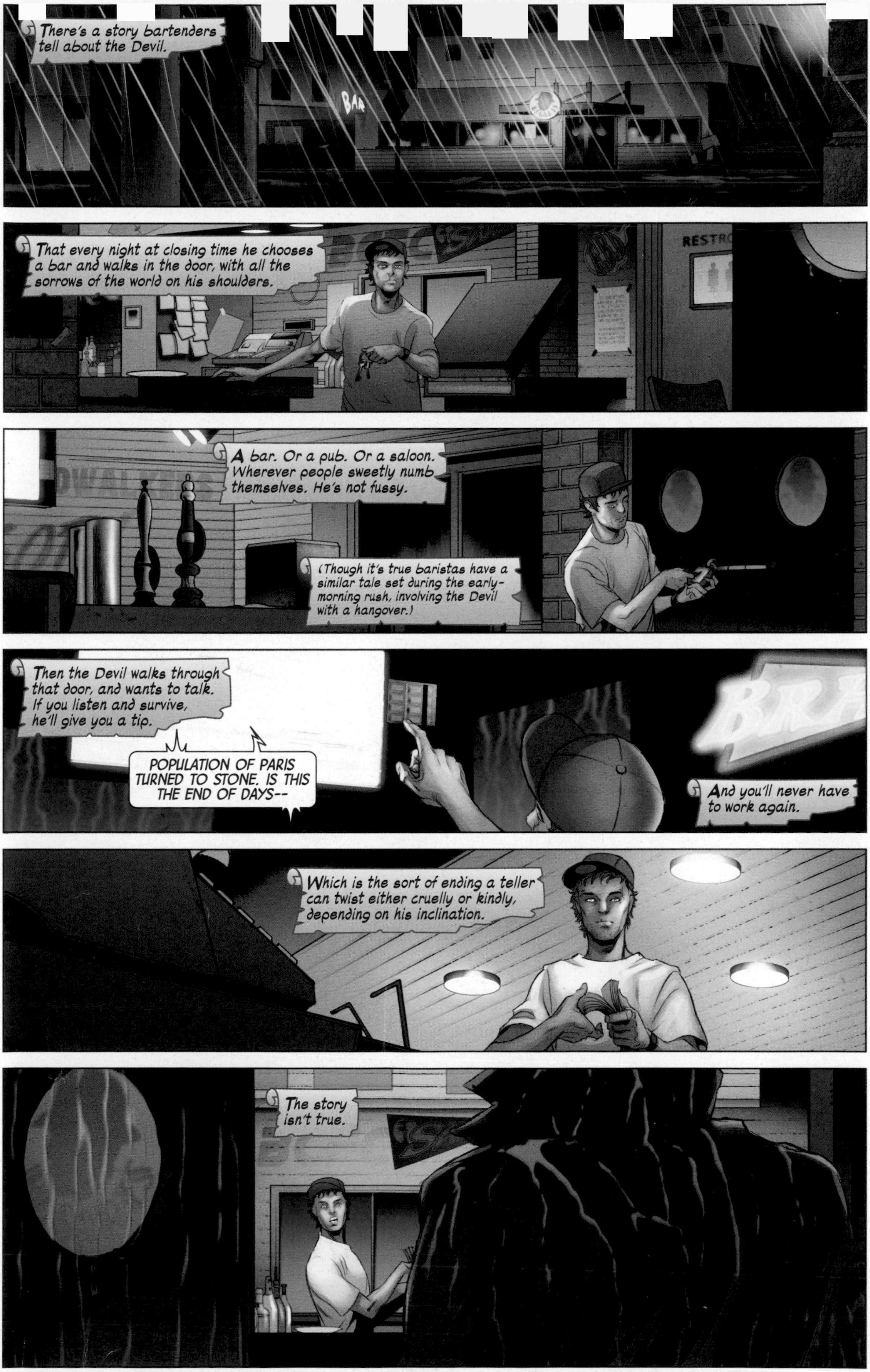
There's a story bartenders tell about the Devil.
BAR
That every night at closing time he chooses a bar and walks in the door, with all the sorrows of the world on his shoulders.
RESTRO
A bar. Or a pub. Or a saloon. Wherever people sweetly numb themselves. He's not fussy.
(Though it's true baristas have a similar tale set during the early-morning rush, involving the Devil with a hangover.)
Then the Devil walks through that door, and wants to talk. If you listen and survive, he'll give you a tip.
POPULATION OF PARIS TURNED TO STONE. IS THIS THE END OF DAYS--
And you'll never have to work again.
Which is the sort of ending a teller can twist either cruelly or kindly, depending on his inclination.
The story isn't true.

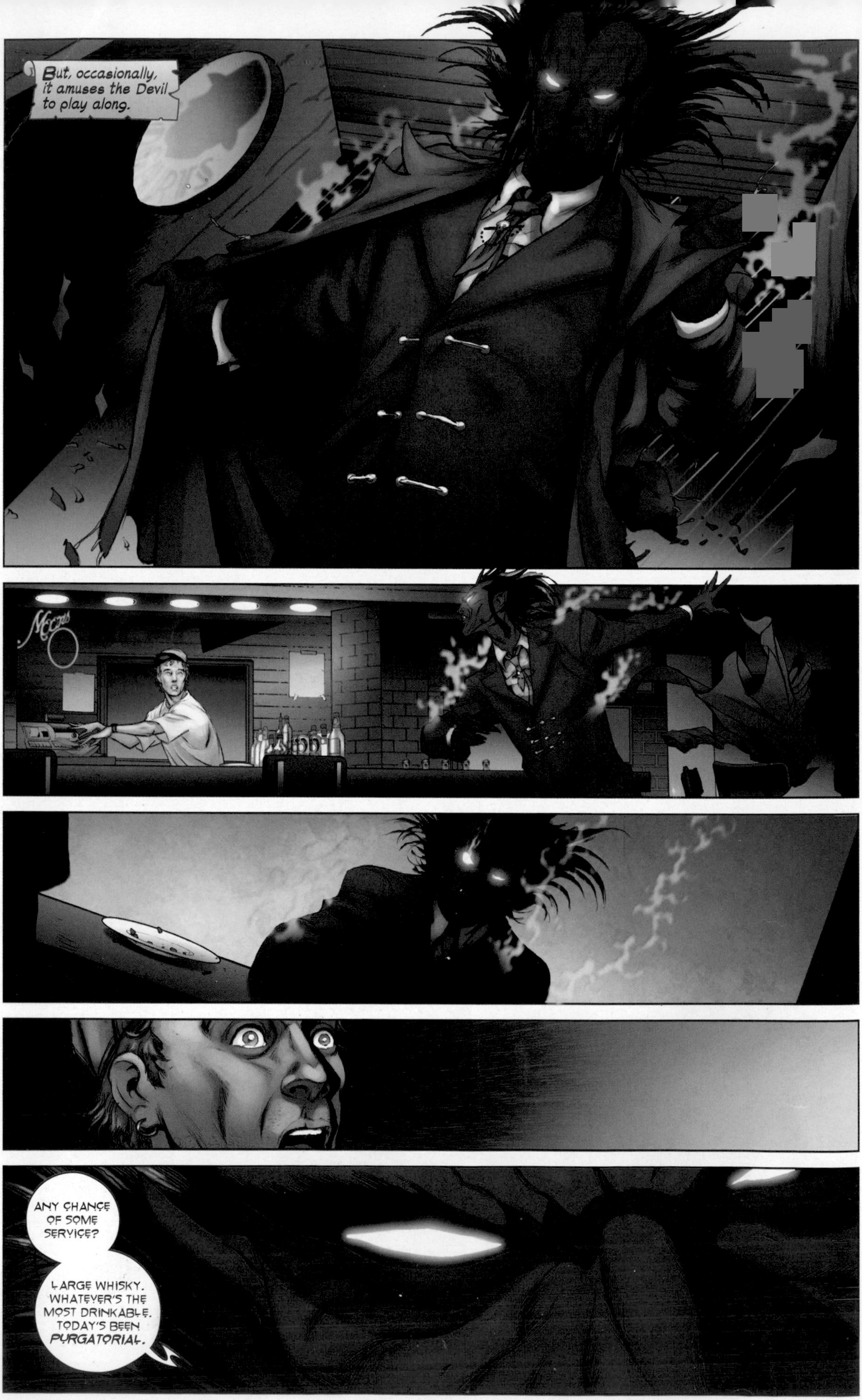
But, occasionally, it amuses the Devil to play along.
ANY CHANCE OF SOME SERVICE?
LARGE WHISKY. WHATEVER'S THE MOST DRINKABLE. TODAY'S BEEN PURGATORIAL.

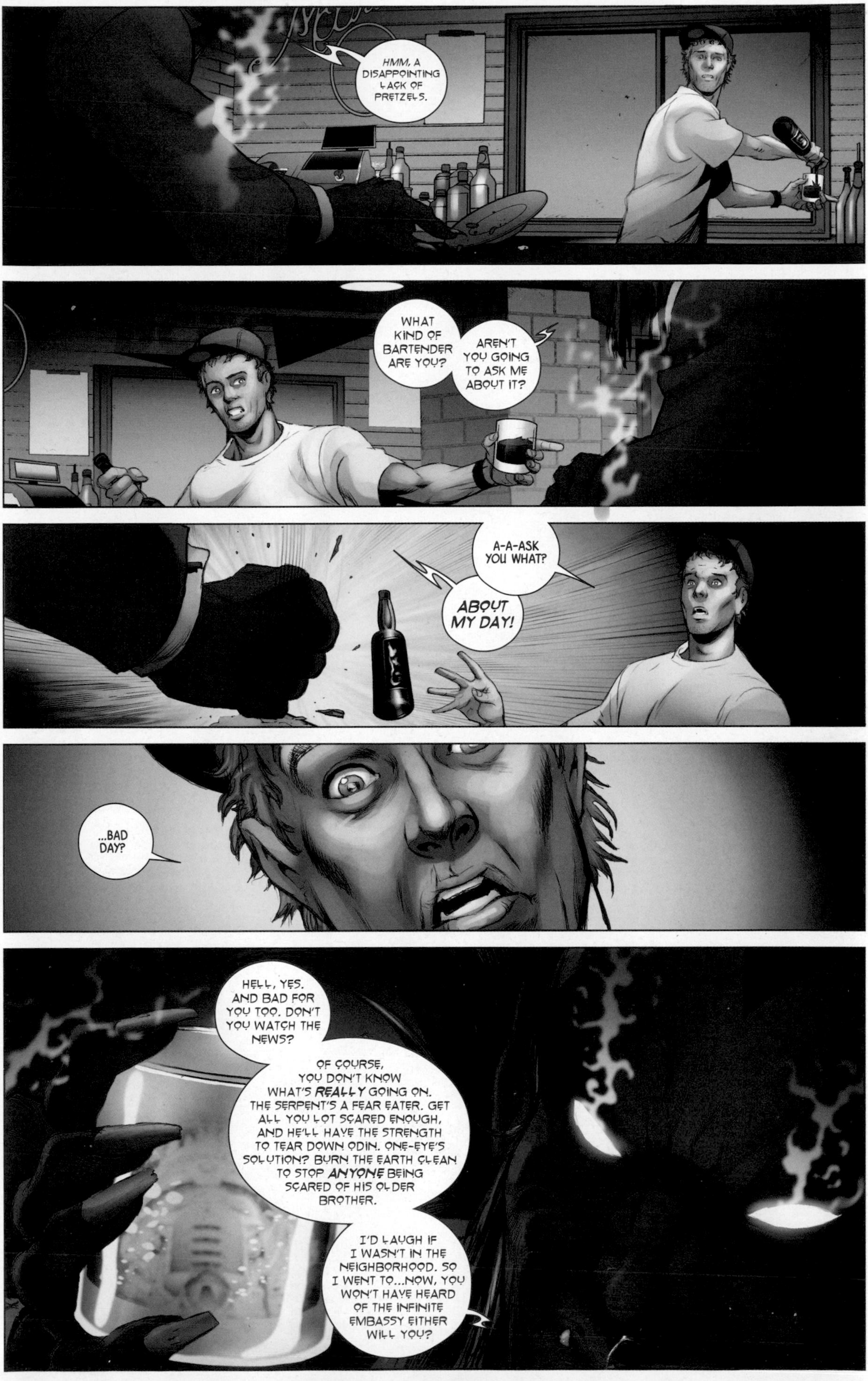
HMM, A DISAPPOINTING LACK OF PRETZELS.
WHAT KIND OF BARTENDER ARE YOU?
AREN'T YOU GOING TO ASK ME ABOUT IT?
A-A-ASK YOU WHAT?
ABOUT MY DAY!
...BAD DAY?
HELL, YES. AND BAD FOR YOU TOO. DON'T YOU WATCH THE NEWS?
OF COURSE, YOU DON'T KNOW WHAT'S REALLY GOING ON. THE SERPENT'S A FEAR EATER. GET ALL YOU LOT SCARED ENOUGH, AND HE'LL HAVE THE STRENGTH TO TEAR DOWN ODIN. ONE-EYE'S SOLUTION? BURN THE EARTH CLEAN TO STOP ANYONE BEING SCARED OF HIS OLDER BROTHER.
I'D LAUGH IF I WASN'T IN THE NEIGHBORHOOD. SO I WENT TO...NOW, YOU WON'T HAVE HEARD OF THE INFINITE EMBASSY EITHER WILL YOU?

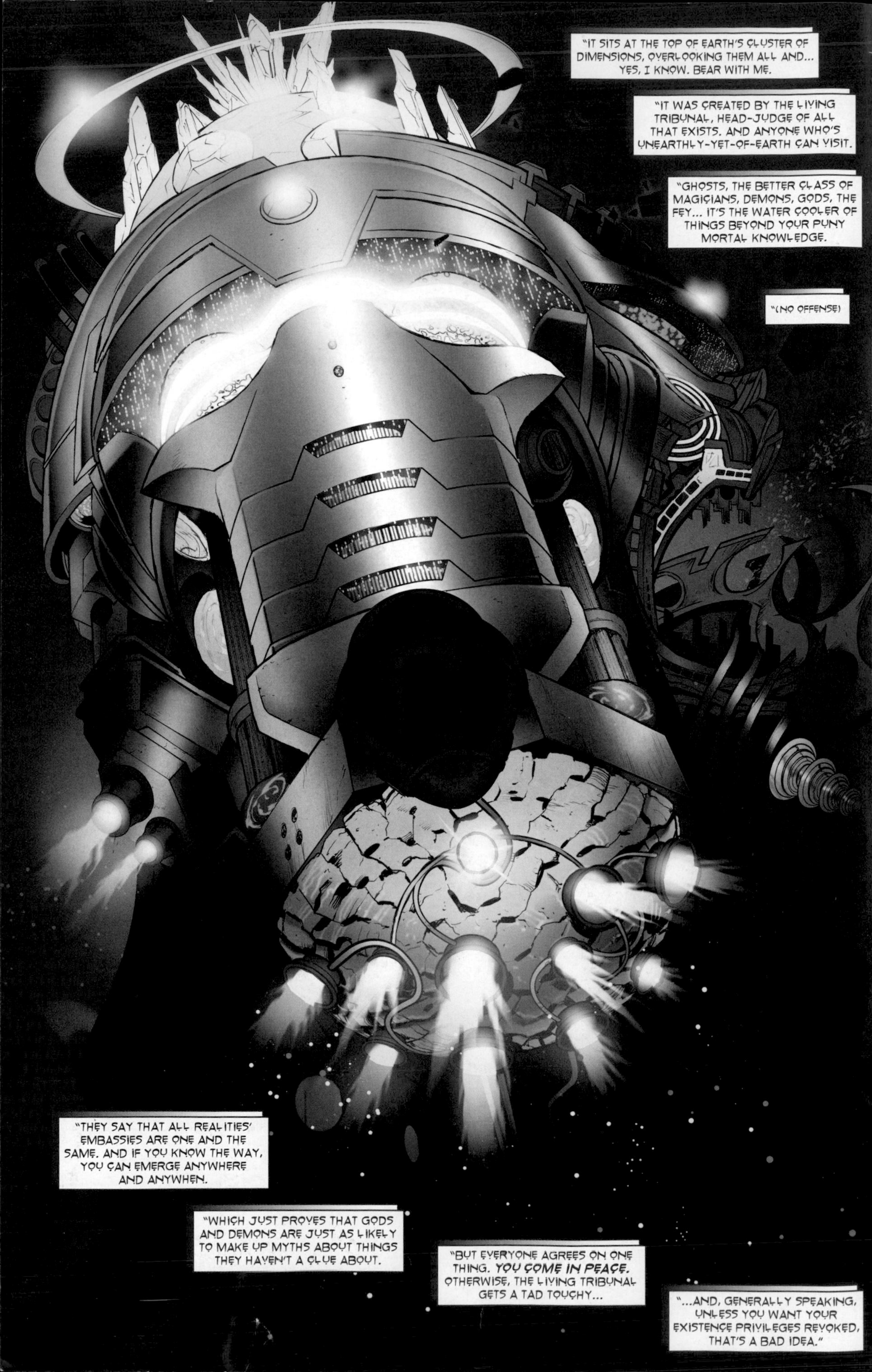
"IT SITS AT THE TOP OF EARTH'S CLUSTER OF DIMENSIONS, OVERLOOKING THEM ALL AND... YES, I KNOW. BEAR WITH ME.
"IT WAS CREATED BY THE LIVING TRIBUNAL, HEAD-JUDGE OF ALL THAT EXISTS. AND ANYONE WHO'S UNEARTHLY-YET-OF-EARTH CAN VISIT.
"GHOSTS, THE BETTER CLASS OF MAGICIANS, DEMONS, GODS, THE FEY... IT'S THE WATER COOLER OF THINGS BEYOND YOUR PUNY MORTAL KNOWLEDGE.
"(NO OFFENSE)
"THEY SAY THAT ALL REALITIES' EMBASSIES ARE ONE AND THE SAME. AND IF YOU KNOW THE WAY, YOU CAN EMERGE ANYWHERE AND ANYWHEN.
"WHICH JUST PROVES THAT GODS AND DEMONS ARE JUST AS LIKELY TO MAKE UP MYTHS ABOUT THINGS THEY HAVEN'T A CLUE ABOUT.
"BUT EVERYONE AGREES ON ONE THING. *YOU COME IN PEACE.* OTHERWISE, THE LIVING TRIBUNAL GETS A TAD TOUCHY...
"...AND, GENERALLY SPEAKING, UNLESS YOU WANT YOUR EXISTENCE PRIVILEGES REVOKED, THAT'S A BAD IDEA."

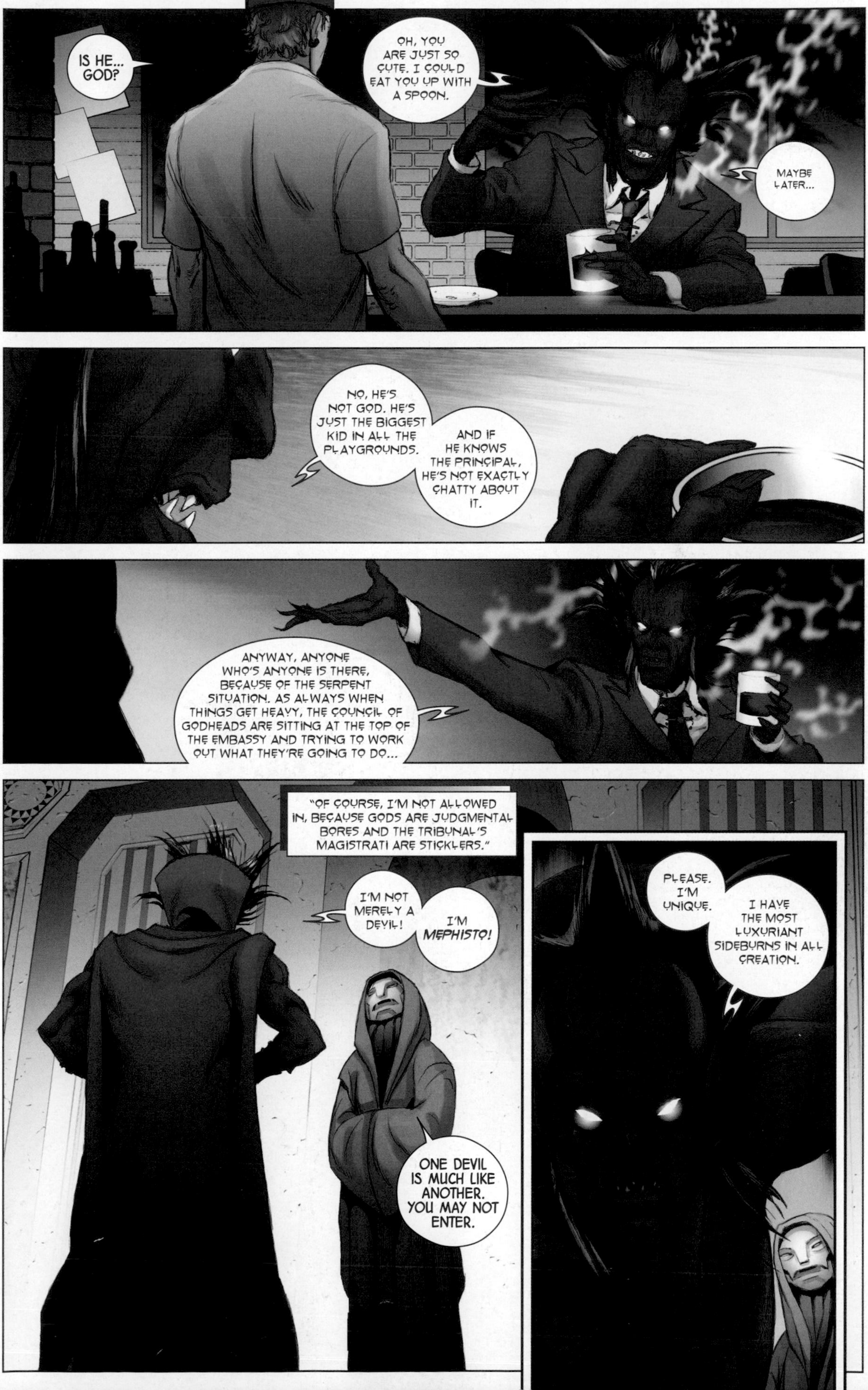
IS HE... GOD?
OH, YOU ARE JUST SO CUTE. I COULD EAT YOU UP WITH A SPOON.
MAYBE LATER...
NO, HE'S NOT GOD. HE'S JUST THE BIGGEST KID IN ALL THE PLAYGROUNDS.
AND IF HE KNOWS THE PRINCIPAL, HE'S NOT EXACTLY CHATTY ABOUT IT.
ANYWAY, ANYONE WHO'S ANYONE IS THERE, BECAUSE OF THE SERPENT SITUATION. AS ALWAYS WHEN THINGS GET HEAVY, THE COUNCIL OF GODHEADS ARE SITTING AT THE TOP OF THE EMBASSY AND TRYING TO WORK OUT WHAT THEY'RE GOING TO DO...
"OF COURSE, I'M NOT ALLOWED IN, BECAUSE GODS ARE JUDGMENTAL BORES AND THE TRIBUNAL'S MAGISTRATI ARE STICKLERS."
I'M NOT MERELY A DEVIL!
I'M MEPHISTO!
ONE DEVIL IS MUCH LIKE ANOTHER. YOU MAY NOT ENTER.
PLEASE. I'M UNIQUE.
I HAVE THE MOST LUXURIANT SIDEBURNS IN ALL CREATION.

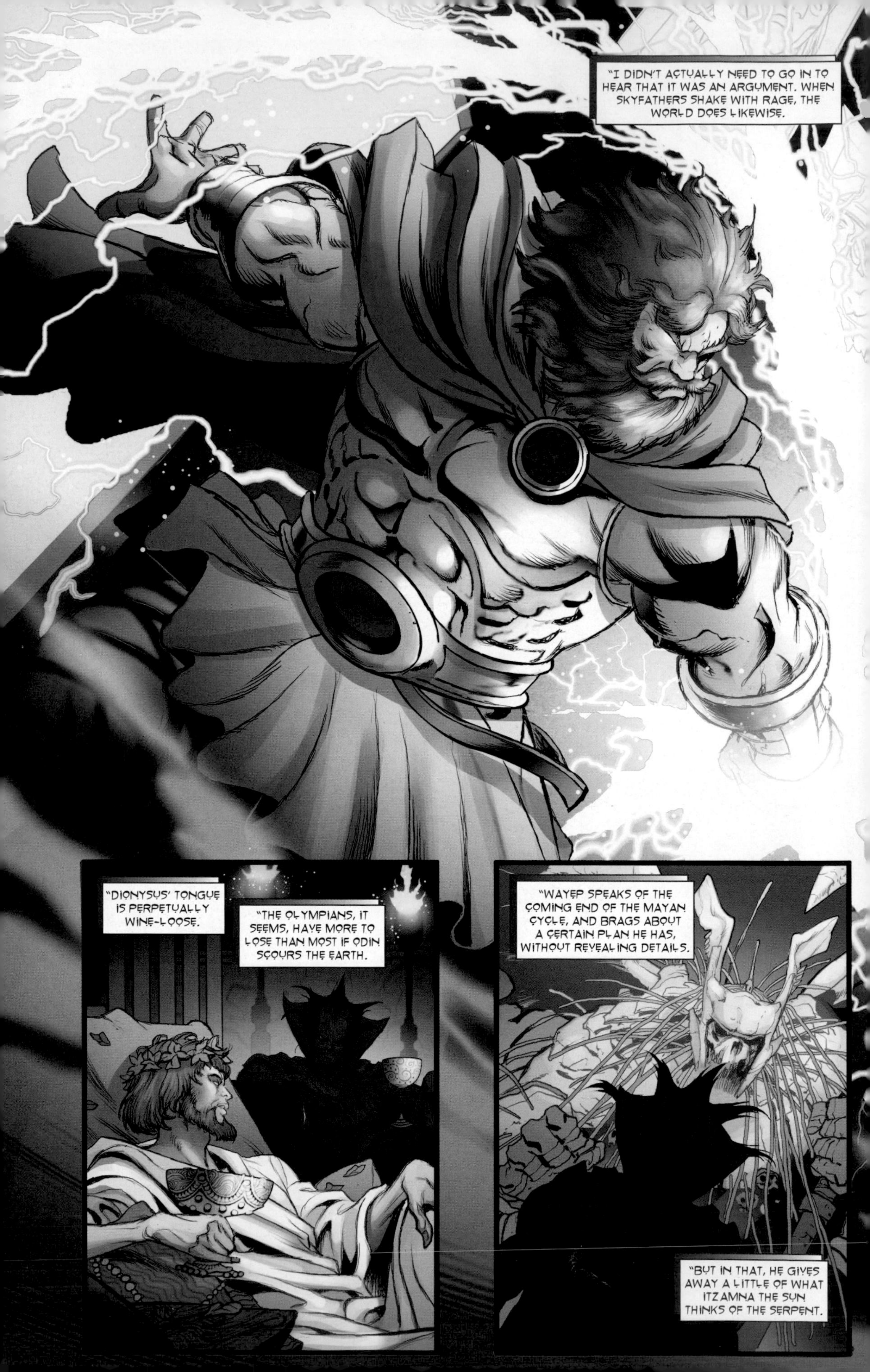
"I DIDN'T ACTUALLY NEED TO GO IN TO HEAR THAT IT WAS AN ARGUMENT. WHEN SKYFATHERS SHAKE WITH RAGE, THE WORLD DOES LIKEWISE.
"DIONYSUS' TONGUE IS PERPETUALLY WINE-LOOSE.
"THE OLYMPIANS, IT SEEMS, HAVE MORE TO LOSE THAN MOST IF ODIN SCOURS THE EARTH.
"WAYEP SPEAKS OF THE COMING END OF THE MAYAN CYCLE, AND BRAGS ABOUT A CERTAIN PLAN HE HAS, WITHOUT REVEALING DETAILS.
"BUT IN THAT, HE GIVES AWAY A LITTLE OF WHAT ITZAMNA THE SUN THINKS OF THE SERPENT.

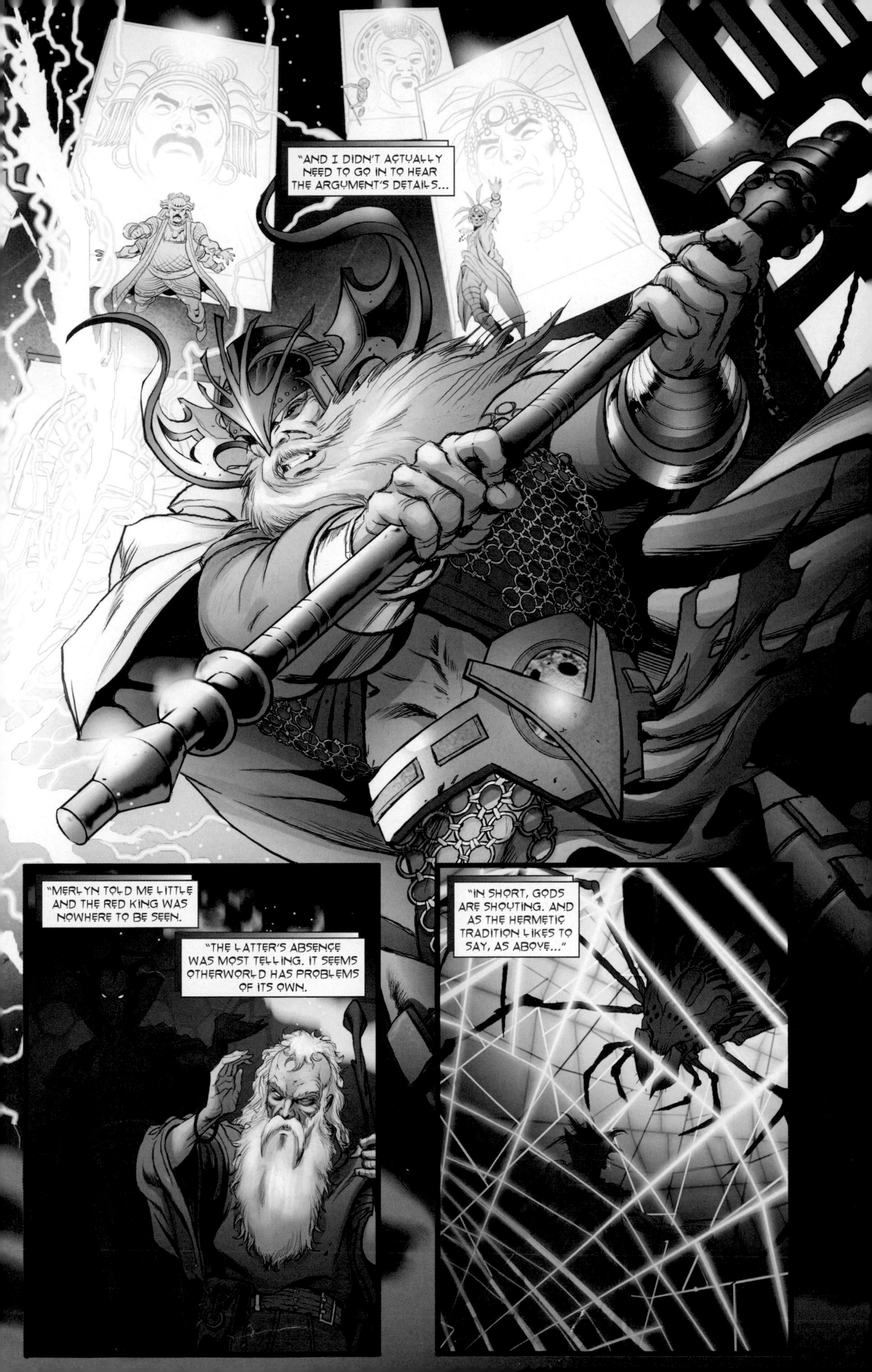
"AND I DIDN'T ACTUALLY NEED TO GO IN TO HEAR THE ARGUMENT'S DETAILS...
"MERLYN TOLD ME LITTLE AND THE RED KING WAS NOWHERE TO BE SEEN.
"THE LATTER'S ABSENCE WAS MOST TELLING. IT SEEMS OTHERWORLD HAS PROBLEMS OF ITS OWN.
"IN SHORT, GODS ARE SHOUTING. AND AS THE HERMETIC TRADITION LIKES TO SAY, AS ABOVE..."

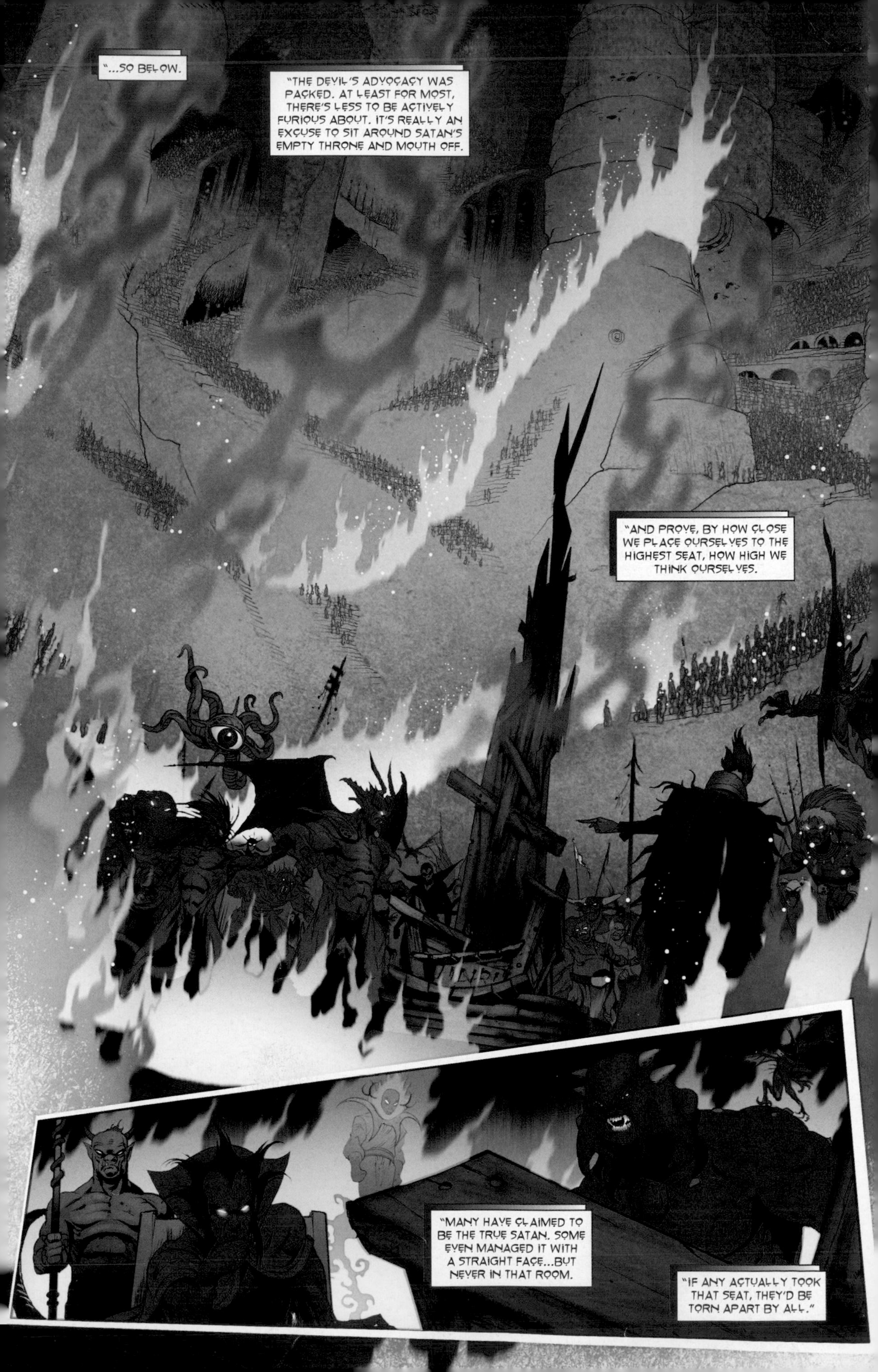
"...SO BELOW.
"THE DEVIL'S ADVOCACY WAS PACKED. AT LEAST FOR MOST, THERE'S LESS TO BE ACTIVELY FURIOUS ABOUT. IT'S REALLY AN EXCUSE TO SIT AROUND SATAN'S EMPTY THRONE AND MOUTH OFF.
"AND PROVE, BY HOW CLOSE WE PLACE OURSELVES TO THE HIGHEST SEAT, HOW HIGH WE THINK OURSELVES.
"MANY HAVE CLAIMED TO BE THE TRUE SATAN. SOME EVEN MANAGED IT WITH A STRAIGHT FACE...BUT NEVER IN THAT ROOM.
"IF ANY ACTUALLY TOOK THAT SEAT, THEY'D BE TORN APART BY ALL."

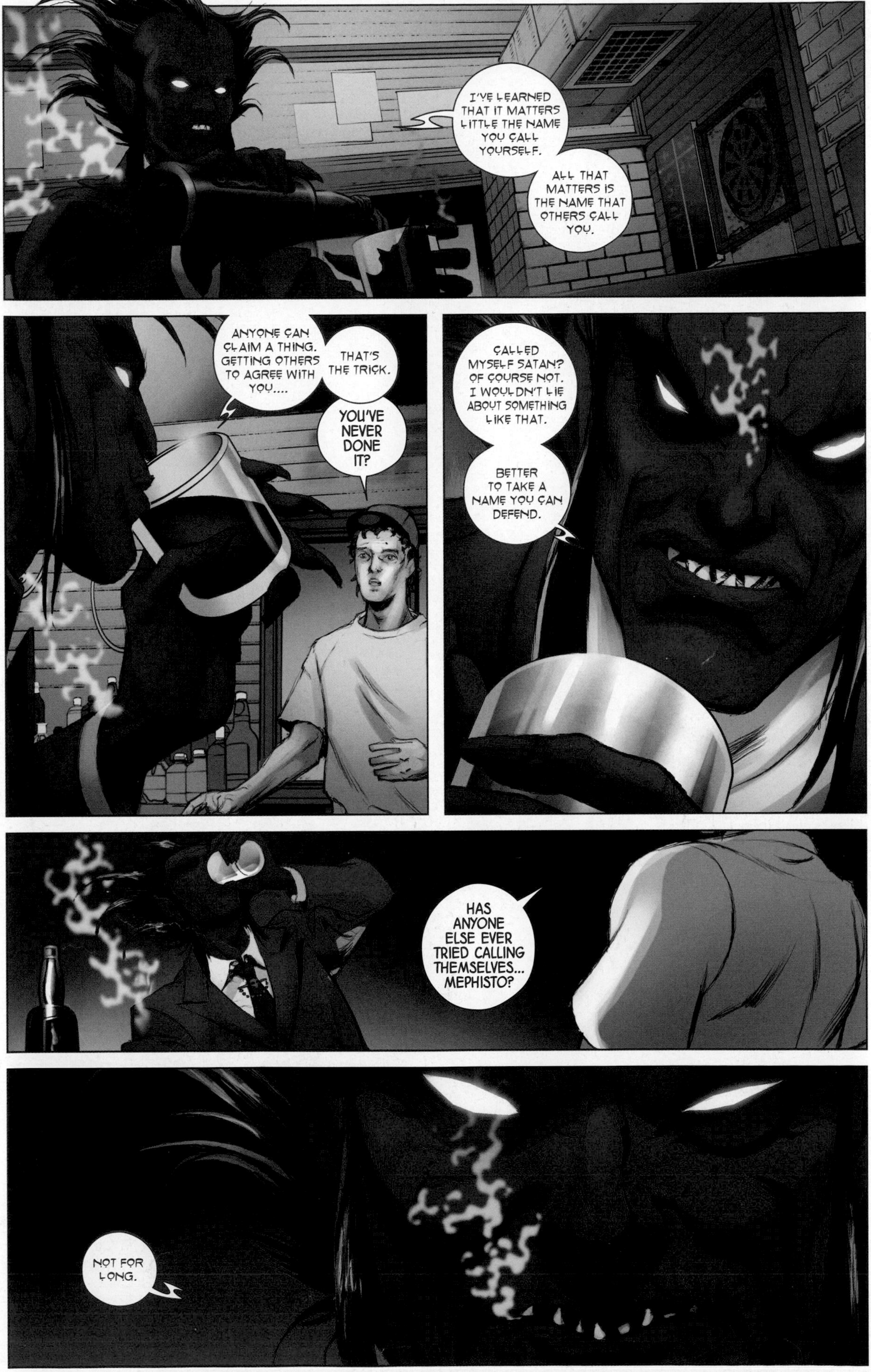
I'VE LEARNED THAT IT MATTERS LITTLE THE NAME YOU CALL YOURSELF.
ALL THAT MATTERS IS THE NAME THAT OTHERS CALL YOU.
ANYONE CAN CLAIM A THING. GETTING OTHERS TO AGREE WITH YOU....
THAT'S THE TRICK.
YOU'VE NEVER DONE IT?
CALLED MYSELF SATAN? OF COURSE NOT. I WOULDN'T LIE ABOUT SOMETHING LIKE THAT.
BETTER TO TAKE A NAME YOU CAN DEFEND.
HAS ANYONE ELSE EVER TRIED CALLING THEMSELVES... MEPHISTO?
NOT FOR LONG.

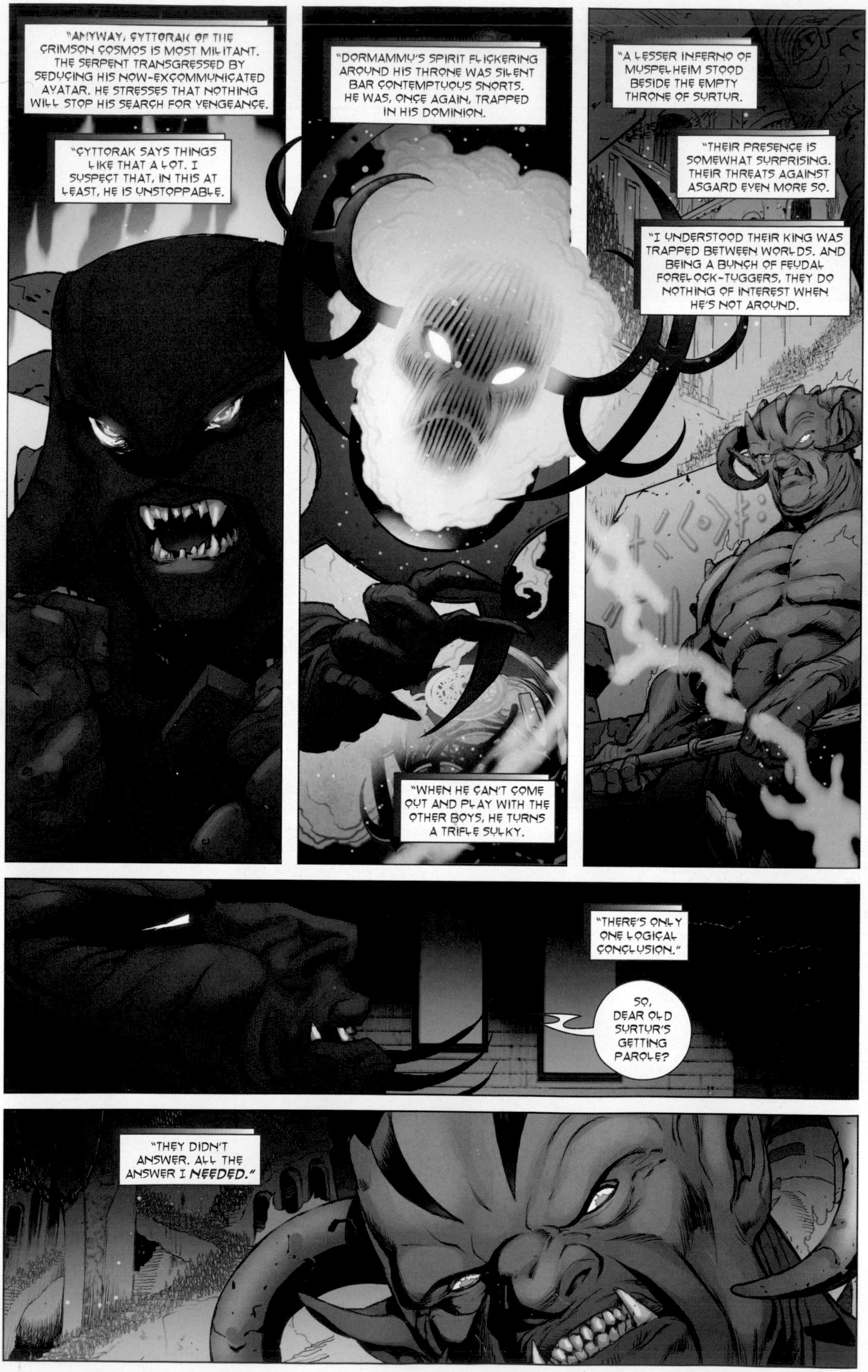
"ANYWAY, CYTTORAK OF THE CRIMSON COSMOS IS MOST MILITANT. THE SERPENT TRANSGRESSED BY SEDUCING HIS NOW-EXCOMMUNICATED AVATAR. HE STRESSES THAT NOTHING WILL STOP HIS SEARCH FOR VENGEANCE.
"CYTTORAK SAYS THINGS LIKE THAT A LOT. I SUSPECT THAT, IN THIS AT LEAST, HE IS UNSTOPPABLE.
"DORMAMMU'S SPIRIT FLICKERING AROUND HIS THRONE WAS SILENT BAR CONTEMPTUOUS SNORTS. HE WAS, ONCE AGAIN, TRAPPED IN HIS DOMINION.
"WHEN HE CAN'T COME OUT AND PLAY WITH THE OTHER BOYS, HE TURNS A TRIFLE SULKY.
"A LESSER INFERNO OF MUSPELHEIM STOOD BESIDE THE EMPTY THRONE OF SURTUR.
"THEIR PRESENCE IS SOMEWHAT SURPRISING. THEIR THREATS AGAINST ASGARD EVEN MORE SO.
"I UNDERSTOOD THEIR KING WAS TRAPPED BETWEEN WORLDS. AND BEING A BUNCH OF FEUDAL FORELOCK-TUGGERS, THEY DO NOTHING OF INTEREST WHEN HE'S NOT AROUND.
"THERE'S ONLY ONE LOGICAL CONCLUSION."
SO, DEAR OLD SURTUR'S GETTING PAROLE?
"THEY DIDN'T ANSWER. ALL THE ANSWER I NEEDED."

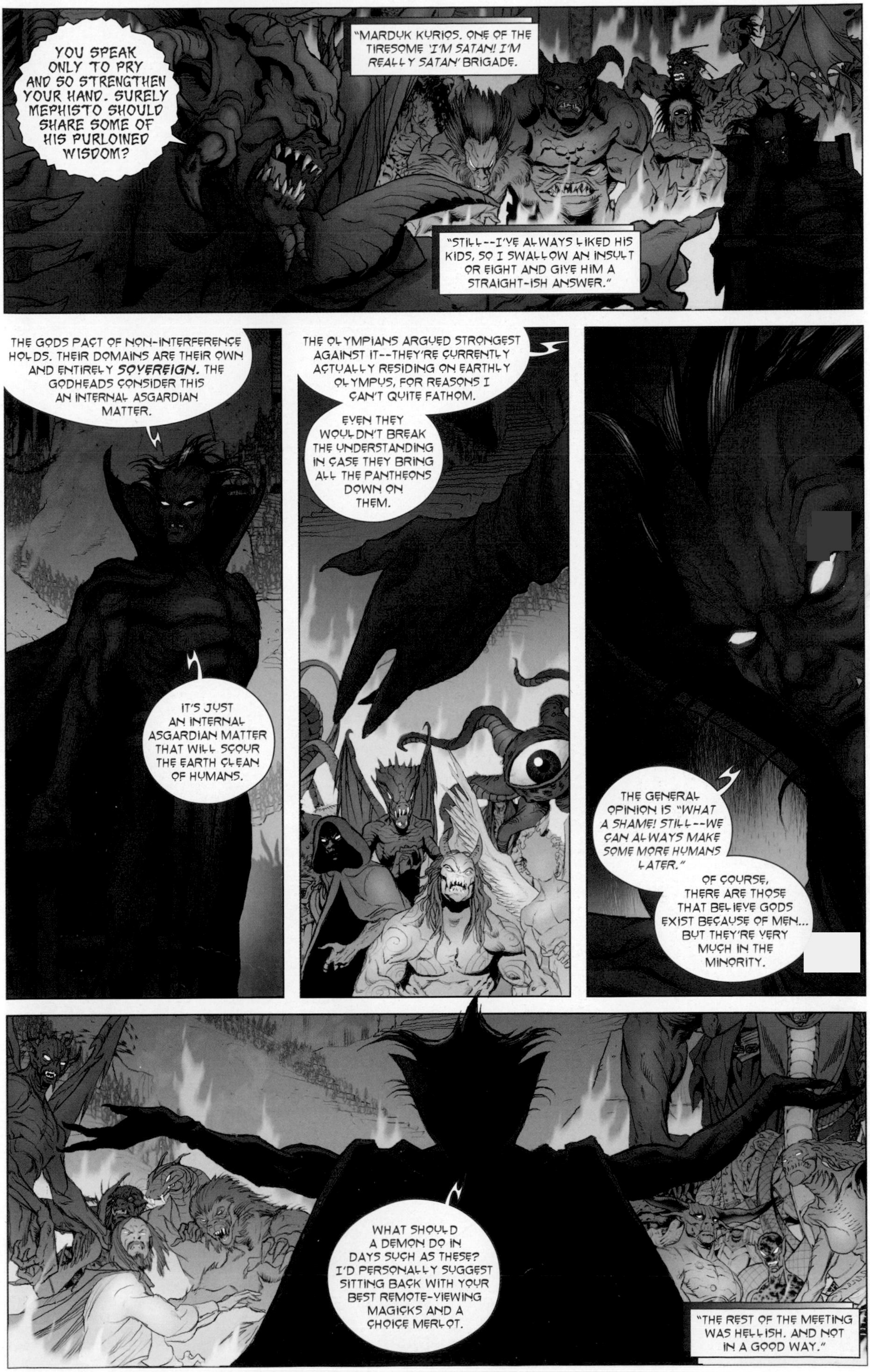
YOU SPEAK ONLY TO PRY AND SO STRENGTHEN YOUR HAND. SURELY MEPHISTO SHOULD SHARE SOME OF HIS PURLOINED WISDOM?
"MARDUK KURIOS. ONE OF THE TIRESOME 'I'M SATAN! I'M REALLY SATAN' BRIGADE.
"STILL--I'VE ALWAYS LIKED HIS KIDS, SO I SWALLOW AN INSULT OR EIGHT AND GIVE HIM A STRAIGHT-ISH ANSWER."
THE GODS PACT OF NON-INTERFERENCE HOLDS. THEIR DOMAINS ARE THEIR OWN AND ENTIRELY SOVEREIGN. THE GODHEADS CONSIDER THIS AN INTERNAL ASGARDIAN MATTER.
IT'S JUST AN INTERNAL ASGARDIAN MATTER THAT WILL SCOUR THE EARTH CLEAN OF HUMANS.
THE OLYMPIANS ARGUED STRONGEST AGAINST IT--THEY'RE CURRENTLY ACTUALLY RESIDING ON EARTHLY OLYMPUS, FOR REASONS I CAN'T QUITE FATHOM.
EVEN THEY WOULDN'T BREAK THE UNDERSTANDING IN CASE THEY BRING ALL THE PANTHEONS DOWN ON THEM.
THE GENERAL OPINION IS "WHAT A SHAME! STILL--WE CAN ALWAYS MAKE SOME MORE HUMANS LATER."
OF COURSE, THERE ARE THOSE THAT BELIEVE GODS EXIST BECAUSE OF MEN... BUT THEY'RE VERY MUCH IN THE MINORITY.
WHAT SHOULD A DEMON DO IN DAYS SUCH AS THESE? I'D PERSONALLY SUGGEST SITTING BACK WITH YOUR BEST REMOTE-VIEWING MAGICKS AND A CHOICE MERLOT.
"THE REST OF THE MEETING WAS HELLISH. AND NOT IN A GOOD WAY."

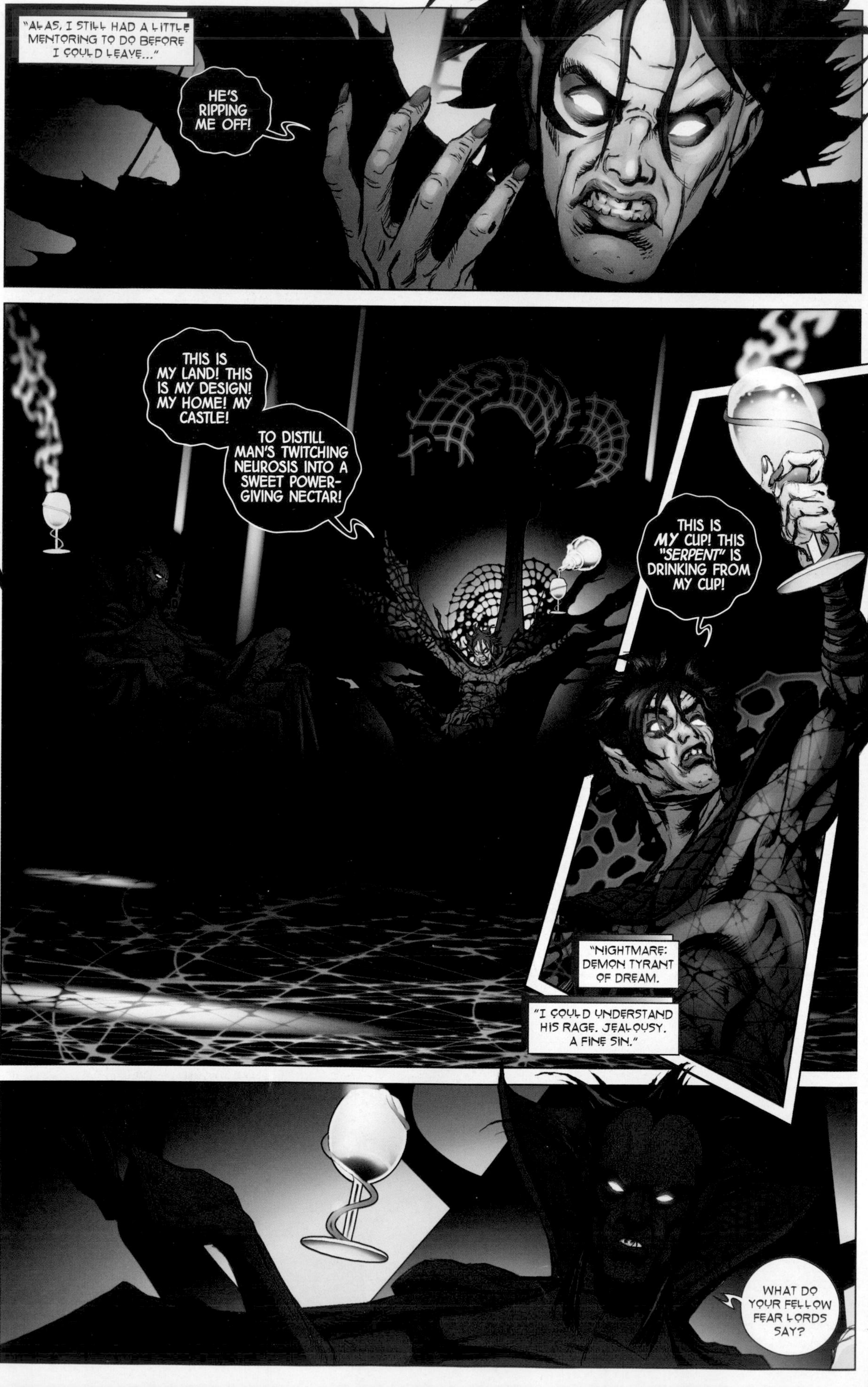
"ALAS, I STILL HAD A LITTLE MENTORING TO DO BEFORE I COULD LEAVE..."
HE'S RIPPING ME OFF!
THIS IS MY LAND! THIS IS MY DESIGN! MY HOME! MY CASTLE!
TO DISTILL MAN'S TWITCHING NEUROSIS INTO A SWEET POWER-GIVING NECTAR!
THIS IS MY CUP! THIS "SERPENT" IS DRINKING FROM MY CUP!
"NIGHTMARE: DEMON TYRANT OF DREAM.
"I COULD UNDERSTAND HIS RAGE. JEALOUSY. A FINE SIN."
WHAT DO YOUR FELLOW FEAR LORDS SAY?

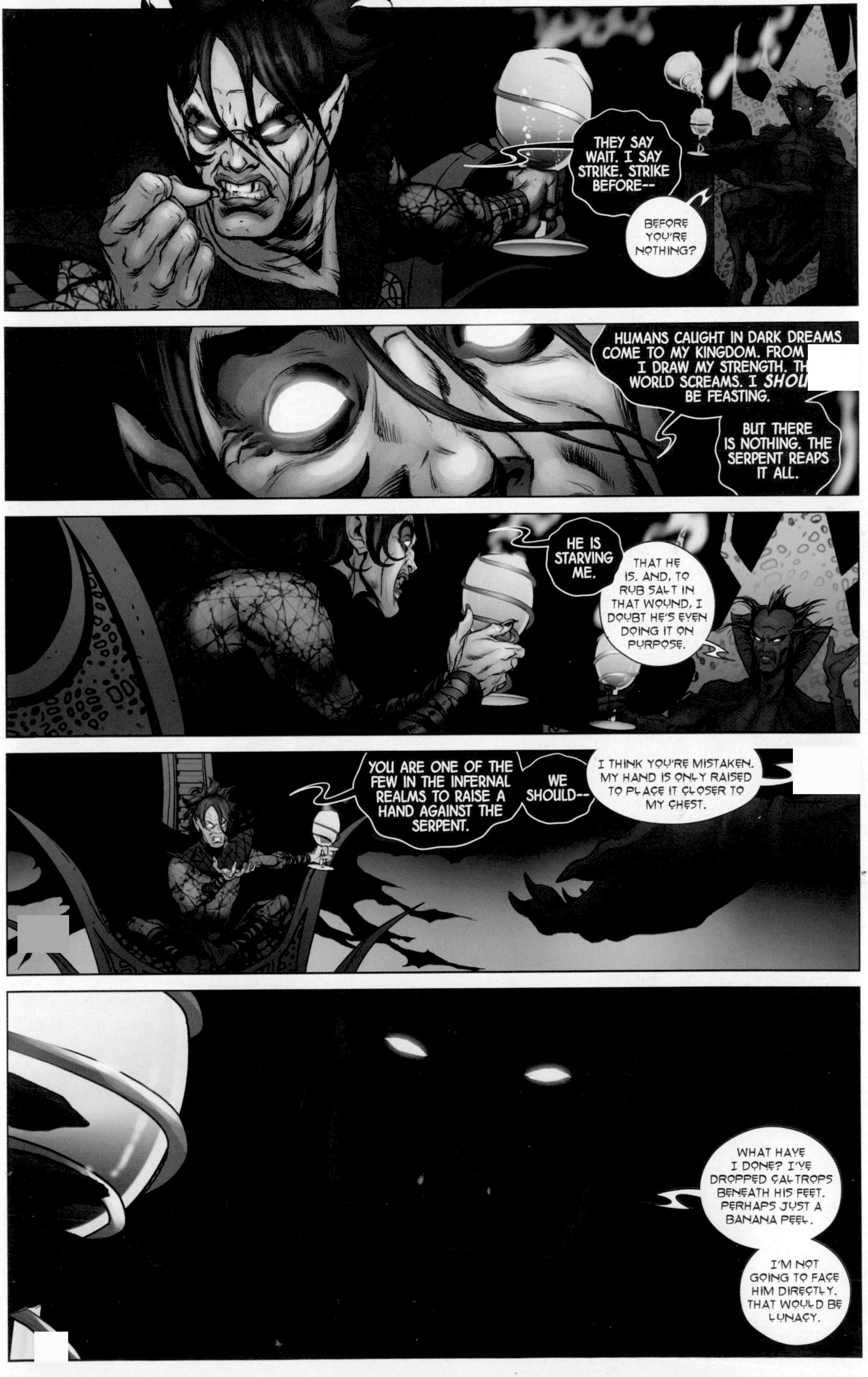
THEY SAY WAIT. I SAY STRIKE. STRIKE BEFORE--
BEFORE YOU'RE NOTHING?
HUMANS CAUGHT IN DARK DREAMS COME TO MY KINGDOM. FROM I DRAW MY STRENGTH. TH WORLD SCREAMS. I SHOU BE FEASTING.
BUT THERE IS NOTHING. THE SERPENT REAPS IT ALL.
HE IS STARVING ME.
THAT HE IS. AND, TO RUB SALT IN THAT WOUND, I DOUBT HE'S EVEN DOING IT ON PURPOSE.
YOU ARE ONE OF THE FEW IN THE INFERNAL REALMS TO RAISE A HAND AGAINST THE SERPENT.
WE SHOULD--
I THINK YOU'RE MISTAKEN. MY HAND IS ONLY RAISED TO PLACE IT CLOSER TO MY CHEST.
WHAT HAVE I DONE? I'VE DROPPED CALTROPS BENEATH HIS FEET. PERHAPS JUST A BANANA PEEL.
I'M NOT GOING TO FACE HIM DIRECTLY. THAT WOULD BE LUNACY.

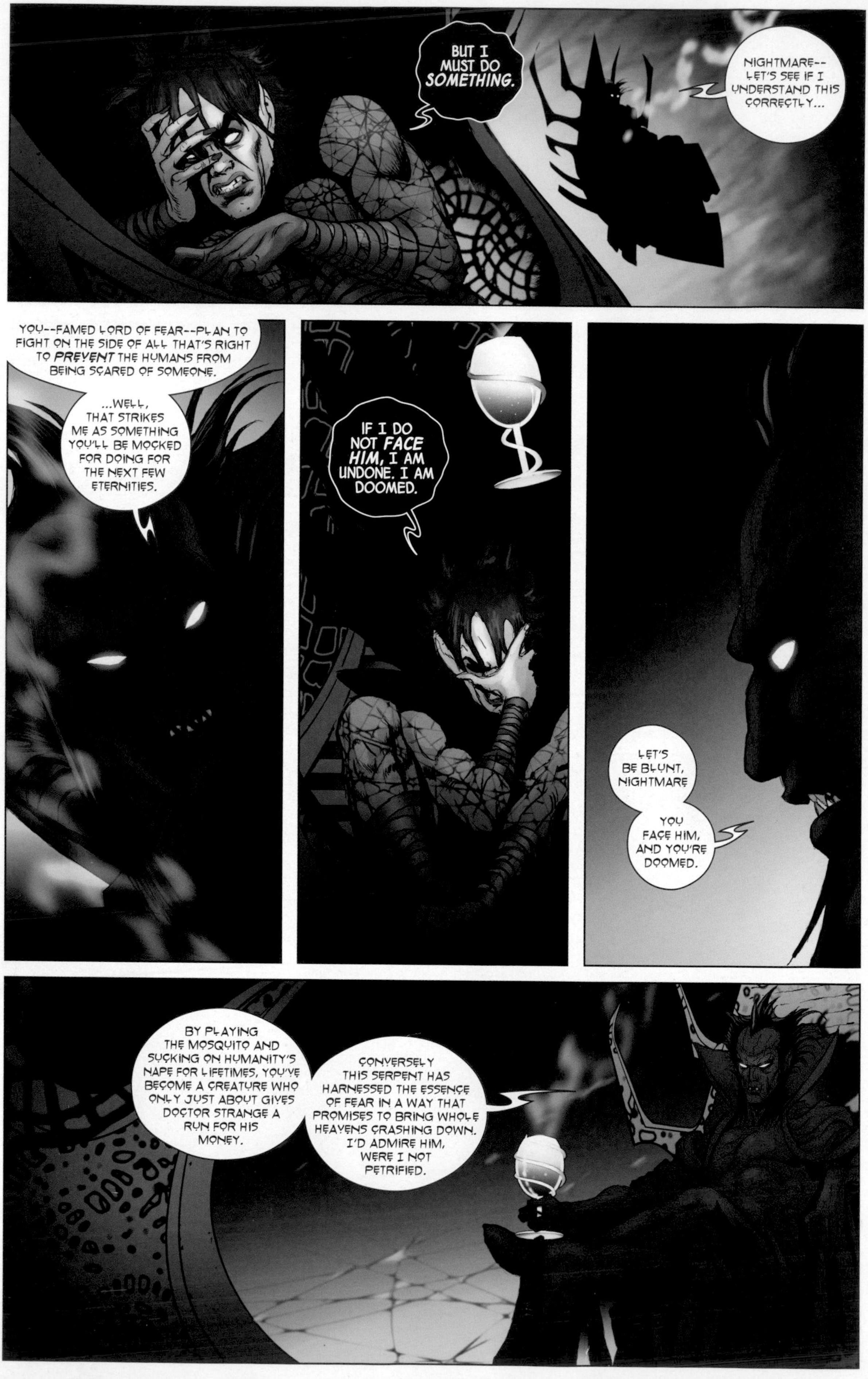
BUT I MUST DO SOMETHING.
NIGHTMARE-- LET'S SEE IF I UNDERSTAND THIS CORRECTLY...
YOU--FAMED LORD OF FEAR--PLAN TO FIGHT ON THE SIDE OF ALL THAT'S RIGHT TO PREVENT THE HUMANS FROM BEING SCARED OF SOMEONE.
...WELL, THAT STRIKES ME AS SOMETHING YOU'LL BE MOCKED FOR DOING FOR THE NEXT FEW ETERNITIES.
IF I DO NOT FACE HIM, I AM UNDONE. I AM DOOMED.
LET'S BE BLUNT, NIGHTMARE
YOU FACE HIM, AND YOU'RE DOOMED.
BY PLAYING THE MOSQUITO AND SUCKING ON HUMANITY'S NAPE FOR LIFETIMES, YOU'VE BECOME A CREATURE WHO ONLY JUST ABOUT GIVES DOCTOR STRANGE A RUN FOR HIS MONEY.
CONVERSELY THIS SERPENT HAS HARNESSED THE ESSENCE OF FEAR IN A WAY THAT PROMISES TO BRING WHOLE HEAVENS CRASHING DOWN. I'D ADMIRE HIM, WERE I NOT PETRIFIED.

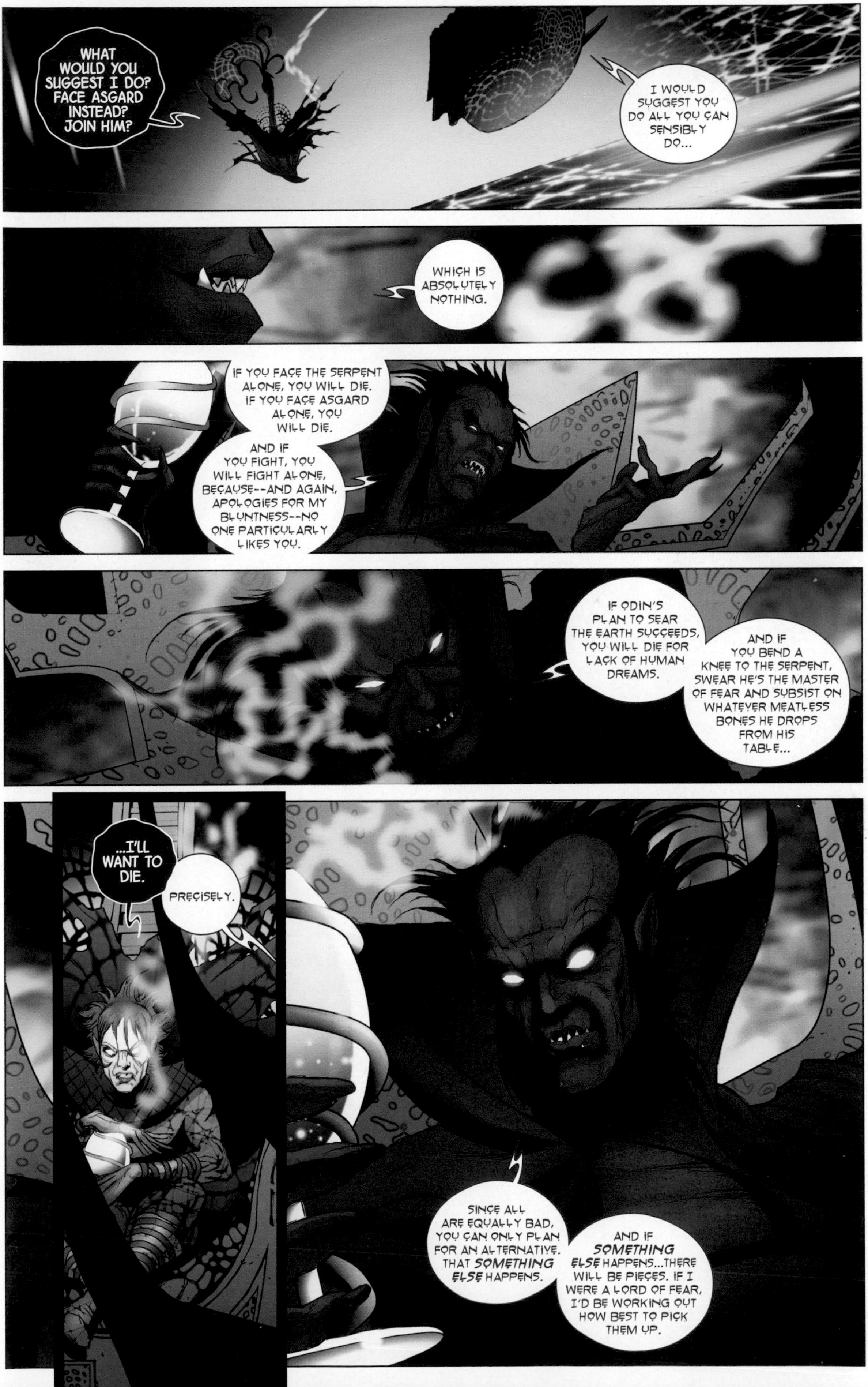
WHAT WOULD YOU SUGGEST I DO? FACE ASGARD INSTEAD? JOIN HIM?
I WOULD SUGGEST YOU DO ALL YOU CAN SENSIBLY DO...
WHICH IS ABSOLUTELY NOTHING.
IF YOU FACE THE SERPENT ALONE, YOU WILL DIE. IF YOU FACE ASGARD ALONE, YOU WILL DIE.
AND IF YOU FIGHT, YOU WILL FIGHT ALONE, BECAUSE--AND AGAIN, APOLOGIES FOR MY BLUNTNESS--NO ONE PARTICULARLY LIKES YOU.
IF ODIN'S PLAN TO SEAR THE EARTH SUCCEEDS, YOU WILL DIE FOR LACK OF HUMAN DREAMS.
AND IF YOU BEND A KNEE TO THE SERPENT, SWEAR HE'S THE MASTER OF FEAR AND SUBSIST ON WHATEVER MEATLESS BONES HE DROPS FROM HIS TABLE...
...I'LL WANT TO DIE.
PRECISELY.
SINCE ALL ARE EQUALLY BAD, YOU CAN ONLY PLAN FOR AN ALTERNATIVE. THAT *SOMETHING ELSE* HAPPENS.
AND IF *SOMETHING ELSE* HAPPENS...THERE WILL BE PIECES. IF I WERE A LORD OF FEAR, I'D BE WORKING OUT HOW BEST TO PICK THEM UP.

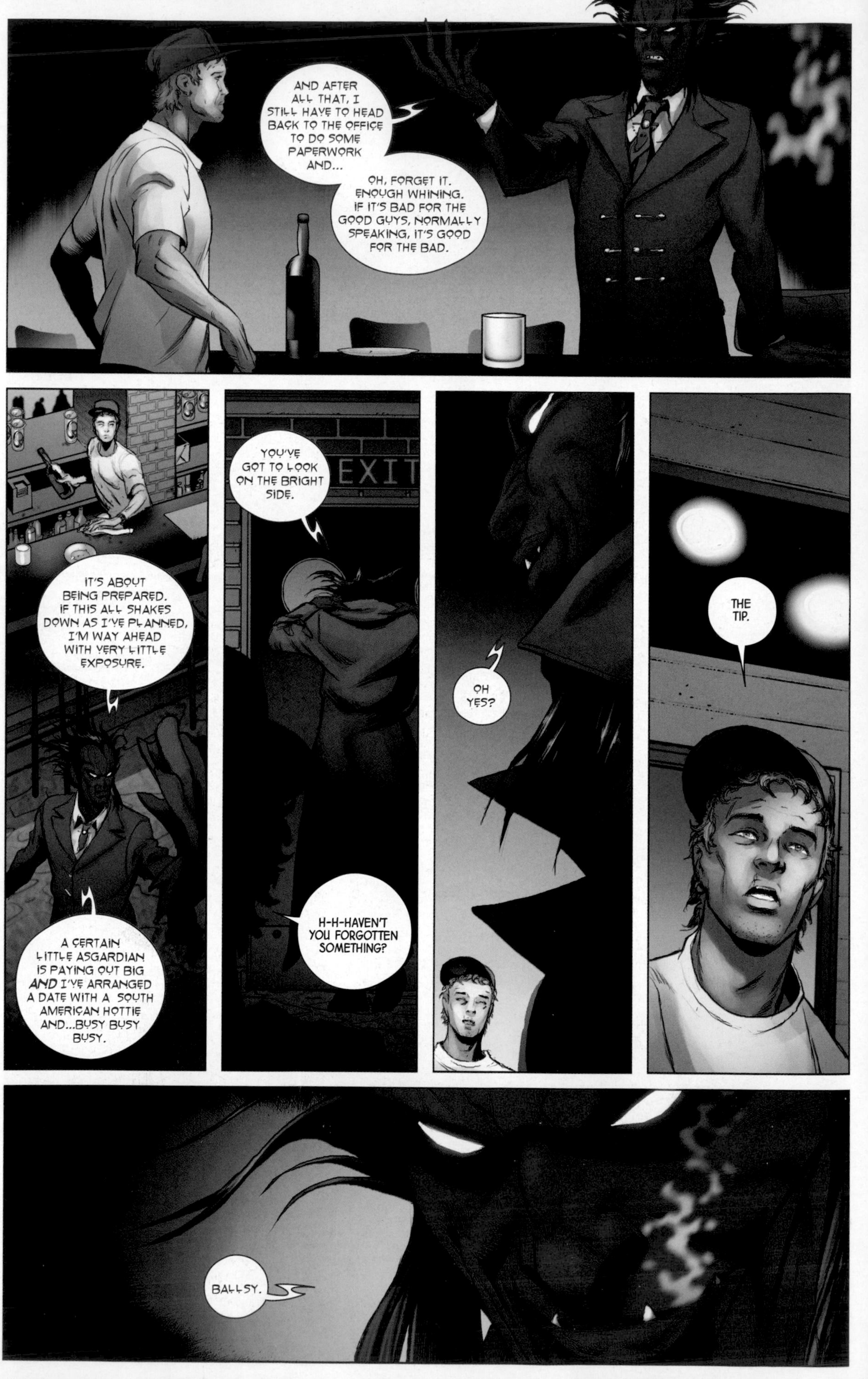
AND AFTER ALL THAT, I STILL HAVE TO HEAD BACK TO THE OFFICE TO DO SOME PAPERWORK AND...
OH, FORGET IT. ENOUGH WHINING. IF IT'S BAD FOR THE GOOD GUYS, NORMALLY SPEAKING, IT'S GOOD FOR THE BAD.
IT'S ABOUT BEING PREPARED. IF THIS ALL SHAKES DOWN AS I'VE PLANNED, I'M WAY AHEAD WITH VERY LITTLE EXPOSURE.
A CERTAIN LITTLE ASGARDIAN IS PAYING OUT BIG AND I'VE ARRANGED A DATE WITH A SOUTH AMERICAN HOTTIE AND...BUSY BUSY BUSY.
EXIT
YOU'VE GOT TO LOOK ON THE BRIGHT SIDE.
H-H-HAVEN'T YOU FORGOTTEN SOMETHING?
OH YES?
THE TIP.
BALLSY.

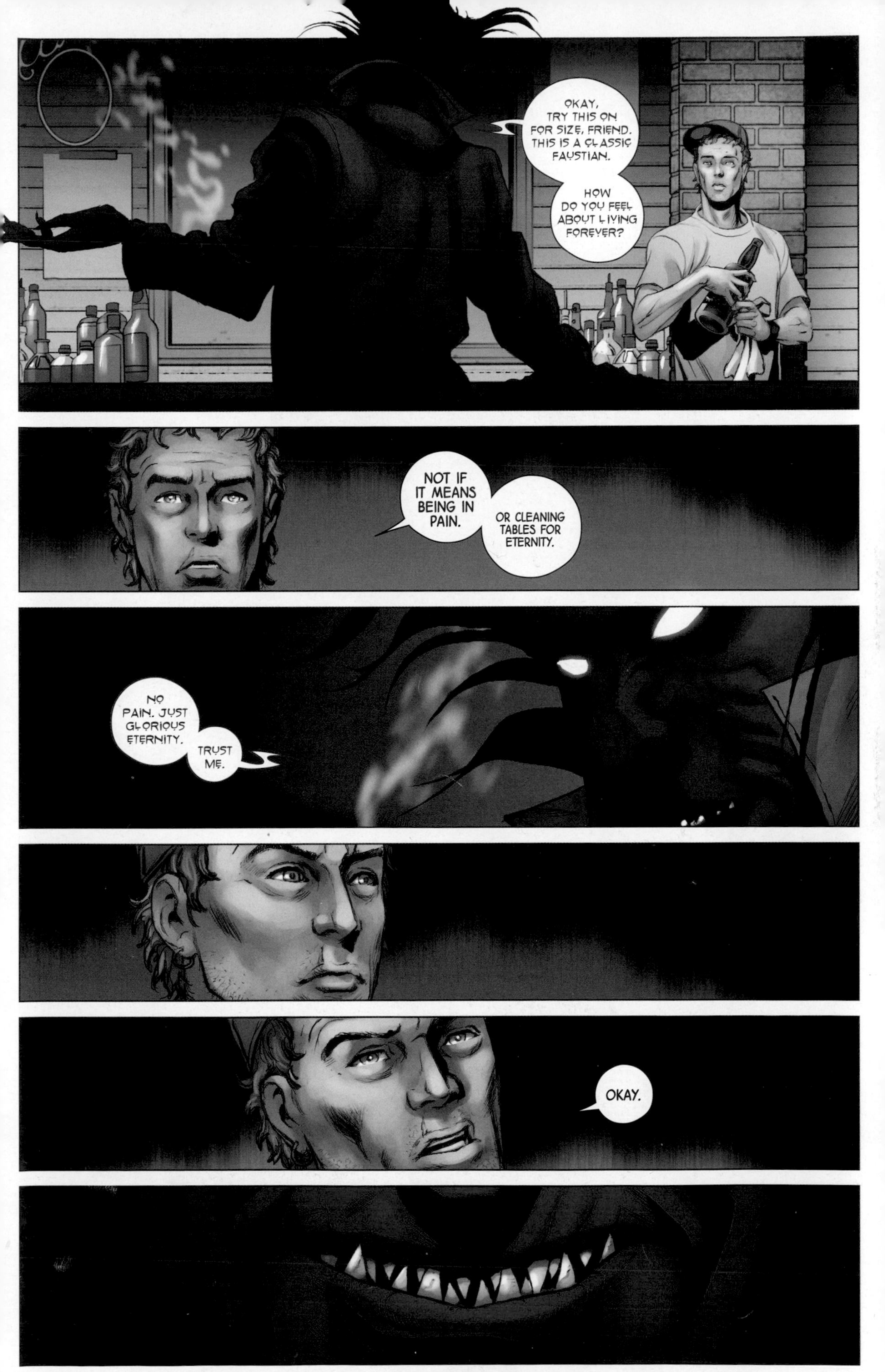
OKAY, TRY THIS ON FOR SIZE, FRIEND. THIS IS A CLASSIC FAUSTIAN.
HOW DO YOU FEEL ABOUT LIVING FOREVER?
NOT IF IT MEANS BEING IN PAIN.
OR CLEANING TABLES FOR ETERNITY.
NO PAIN. JUST GLORIOUS ETERNITY.
TRUST ME.
OKAY.

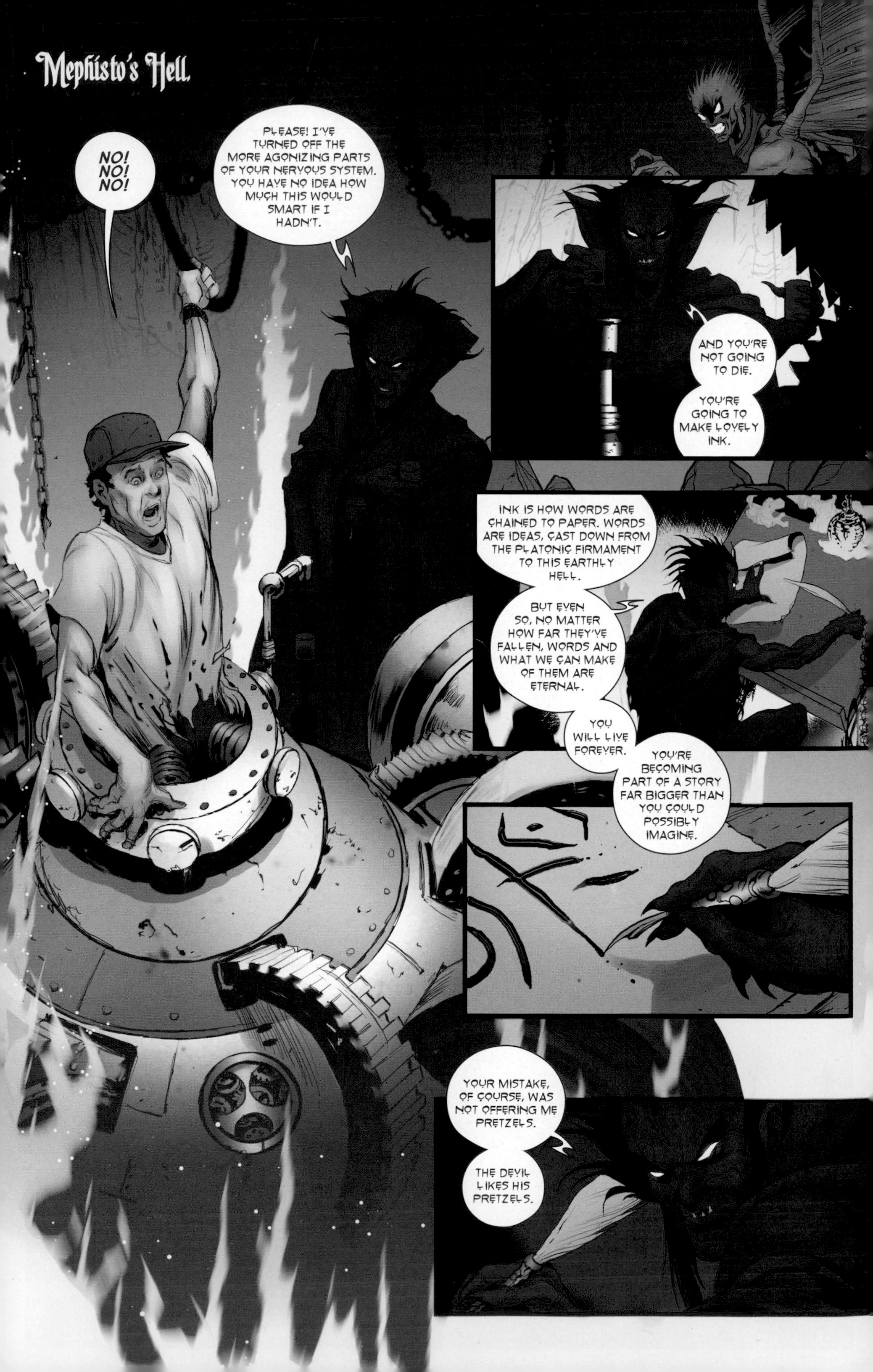
Mephisto's Hell.
NO! NO! NO!
PLEASE! I'VE TURNED OFF THE MORE AGONIZING PARTS OF YOUR NERVOUS SYSTEM. YOU HAVE NO IDEA HOW MUCH THIS WOULD SMART IF I HADN'T.
AND YOU'RE NOT GOING TO DIE.
YOU'RE GOING TO MAKE LOVELY INK.
INK IS HOW WORDS ARE CHAINED TO PAPER. WORDS ARE IDEAS, CAST DOWN FROM THE PLATONIC FIRMAMENT TO THIS EARTHLY HELL.
BUT EVEN SO, NO MATTER HOW FAR THEY'VE FALLEN, WORDS AND WHAT WE CAN MAKE OF THEM ARE ETERNAL.
YOU WILL LIVE FOREVER.
YOU'RE BECOMING PART OF A STORY FAR BIGGER THAN YOU COULD POSSIBLY IMAGINE.
YOUR MISTAKE, OF COURSE, WAS NOT OFFERING ME PRETZELS.
THE DEVIL LIKES HIS PRETZELS.

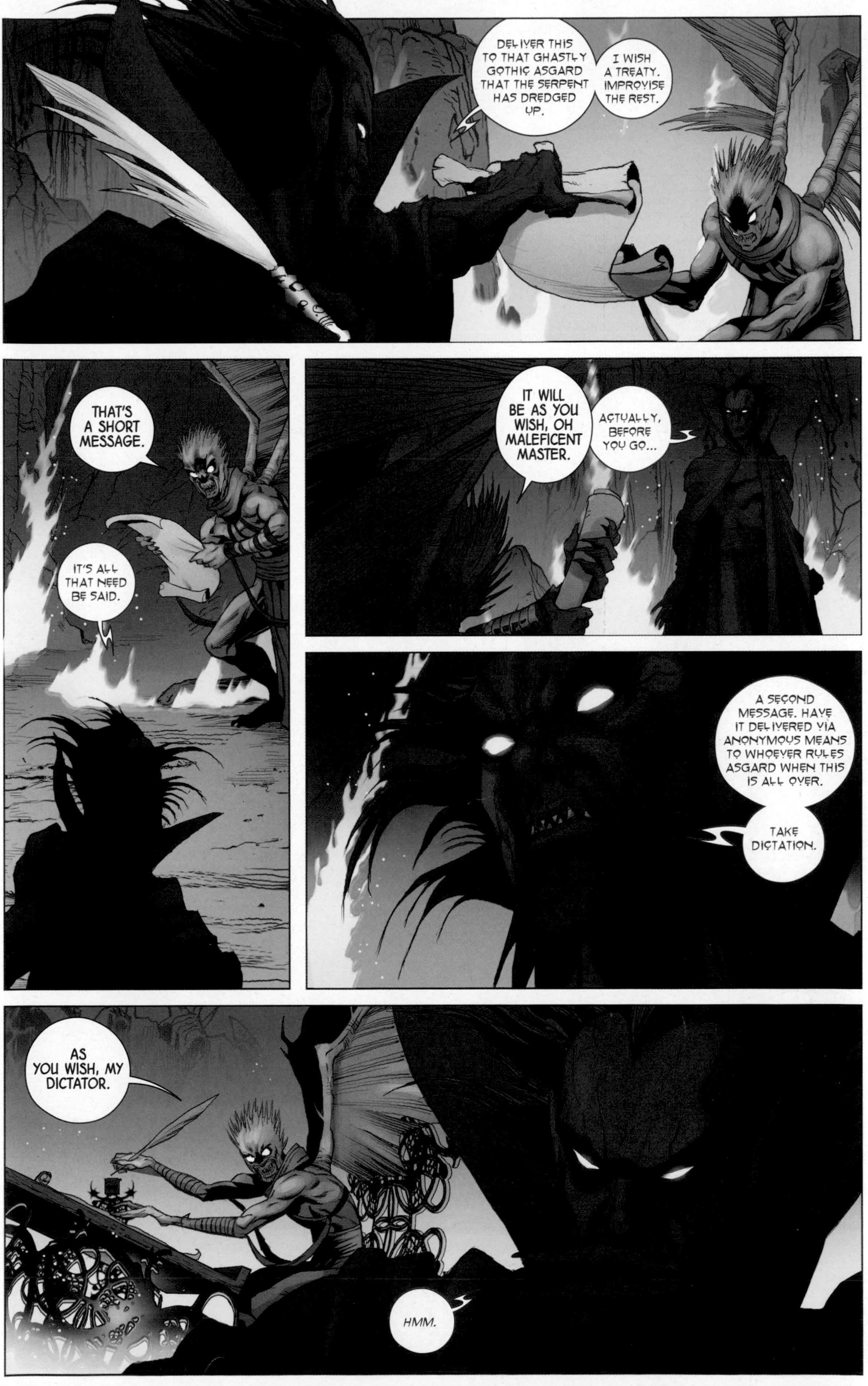
DELIVER THIS TO THAT GHASTLY GOTHIC ASGARD THAT THE SERPENT HAS DREDGED UP.
I WISH A TREATY. IMPROVISE THE REST.
THAT'S A SHORT MESSAGE.
IT'S ALL THAT NEED BE SAID.
IT WILL BE AS YOU WISH, OH MALEFICENT MASTER.
ACTUALLY, BEFORE YOU GO...
A SECOND MESSAGE. HAVE IT DELIVERED VIA ANONYMOUS MEANS TO WHOEVER RULES ASGARD WHEN THIS IS ALL OVER.
TAKE DICTATION.
AS YOU WISH, MY DICTATOR.
HMM.

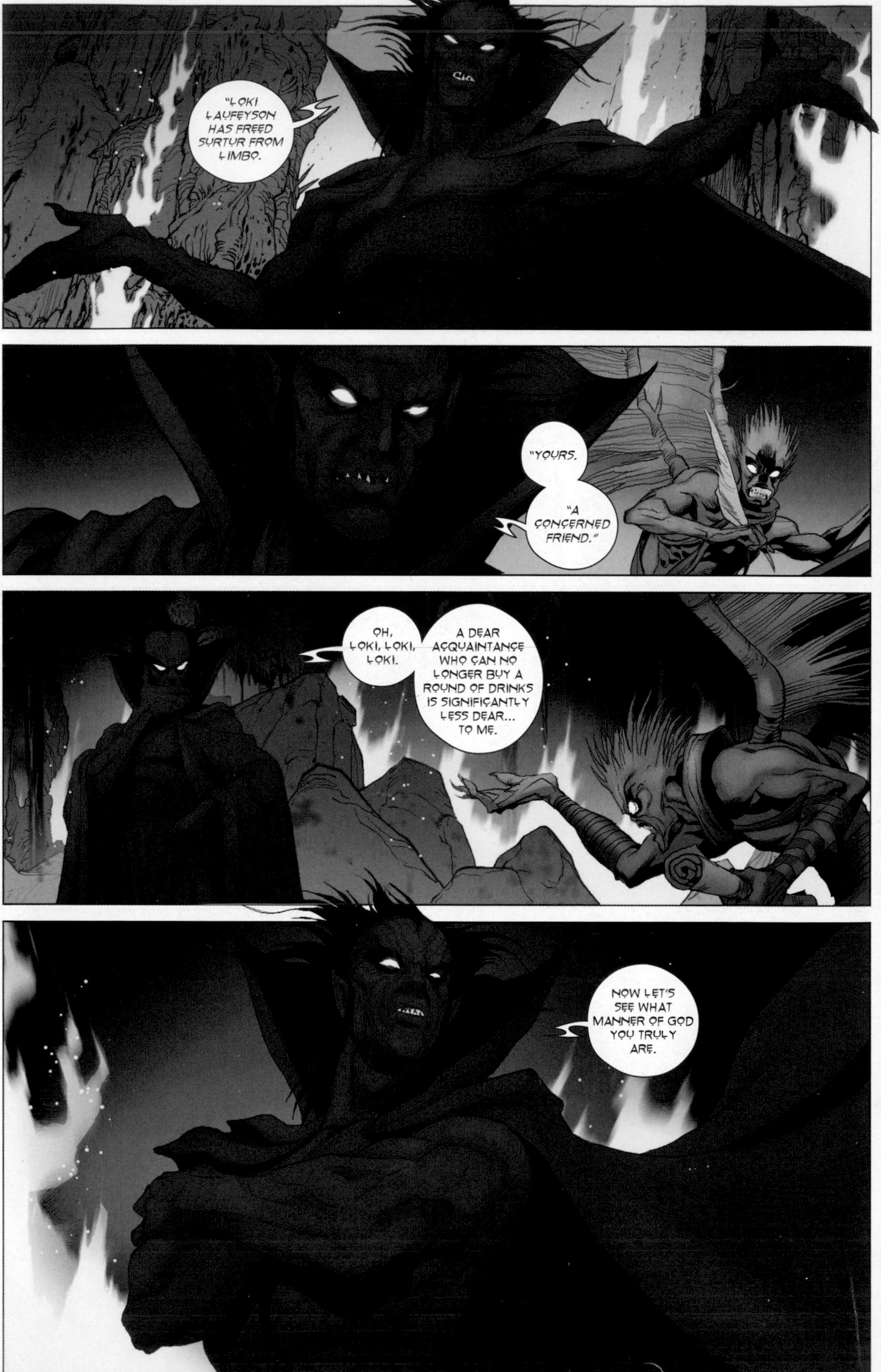
"LOKI LAUFEYSON HAS FREED SURTUR FROM LIMBO.
"YOURS.
"A CONCERNED FRIEND."
OH, LOKI, LOKI, LOKI.
A DEAR ACQUAINTANCE WHO CAN NO LONGER BUY A ROUND OF DRINKS IS SIGNIFICANTLY LESS DEAR... TO ME.
NOW LET'S SEE WHAT MANNER OF GOD YOU TRULY ARE.

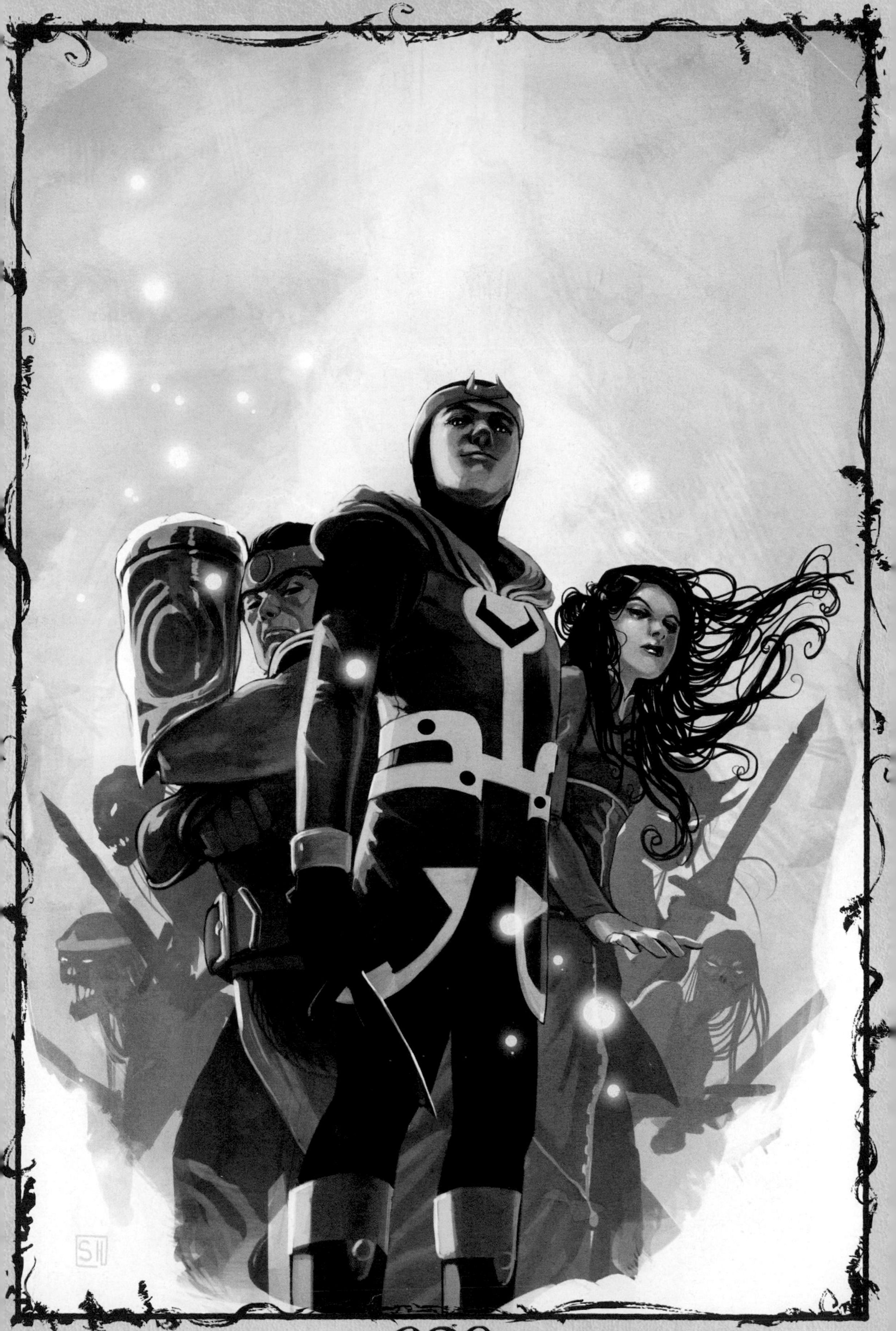

628

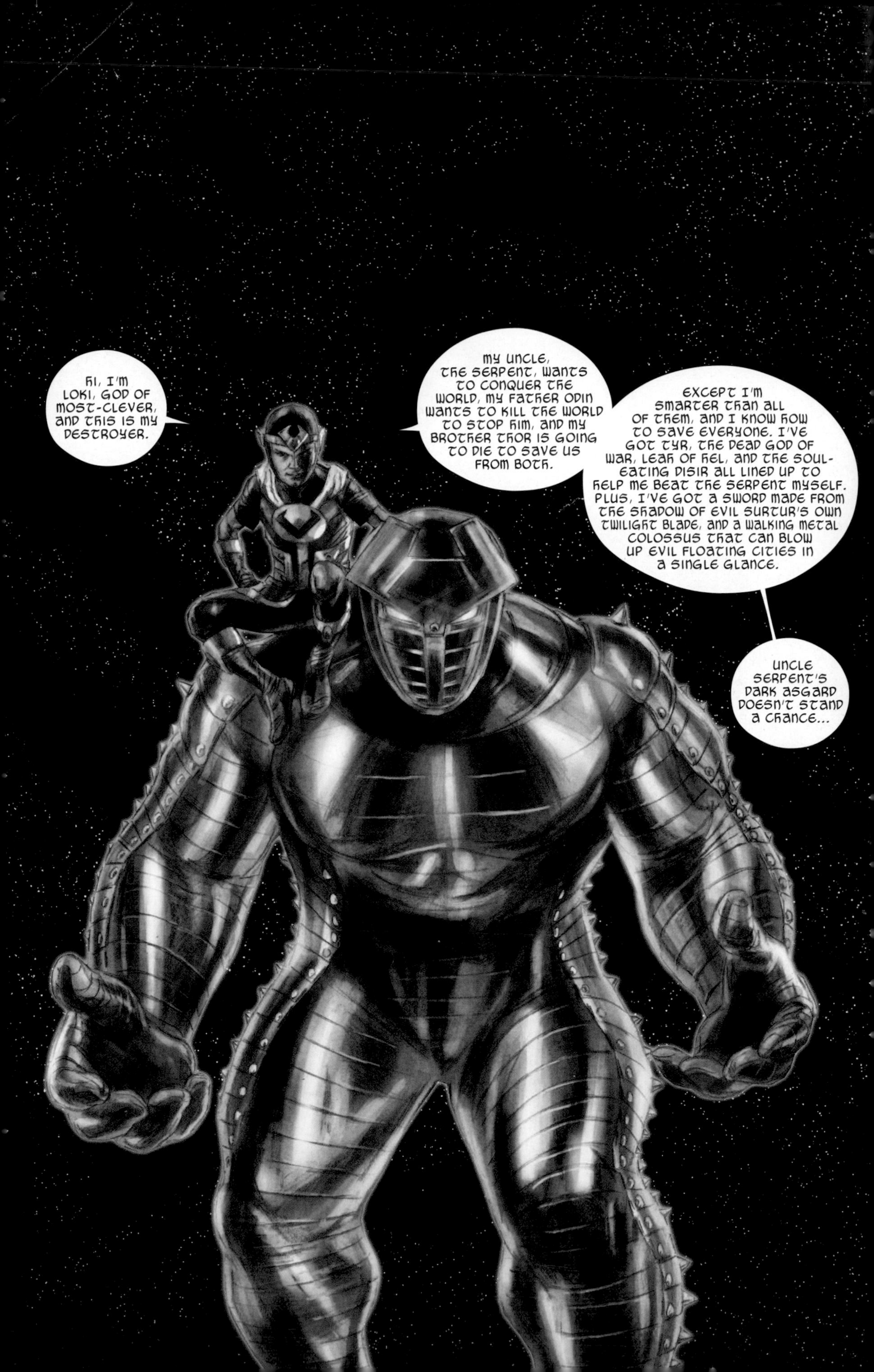
HI, I'M LOKI, GOD OF MOST-CLEVER, AND THIS IS MY DESTROYER.
MY UNCLE, THE SERPENT, WANTS TO CONQUER THE WORLD, MY FATHER ODIN WANTS TO KILL THE WORLD TO STOP HIM, AND MY BROTHER THOR IS GOING TO DIE TO SAVE US FROM BOTH.
EXCEPT I'M SMARTER THAN ALL OF THEM, AND I KNOW HOW TO SAVE EVERYONE. I'VE GOT TYR, THE DEAD GOD OF WAR, LEAH OF HEL, AND THE SOUL-EATING DISIR ALL LINED UP TO HELP ME BEAT THE SERPENT MYSELF. PLUS, I'VE GOT A SWORD MADE FROM THE SHADOW OF EVIL SURTUR'S OWN TWILIGHT BLADE, AND A WALKING METAL COLOSSUS THAT CAN BLOW UP EVIL FLOATING CITIES IN A SINGLE GLANCE.
UNCLE SERPENT'S DARK ASGARD DOESN'T STAND A CHANCE...

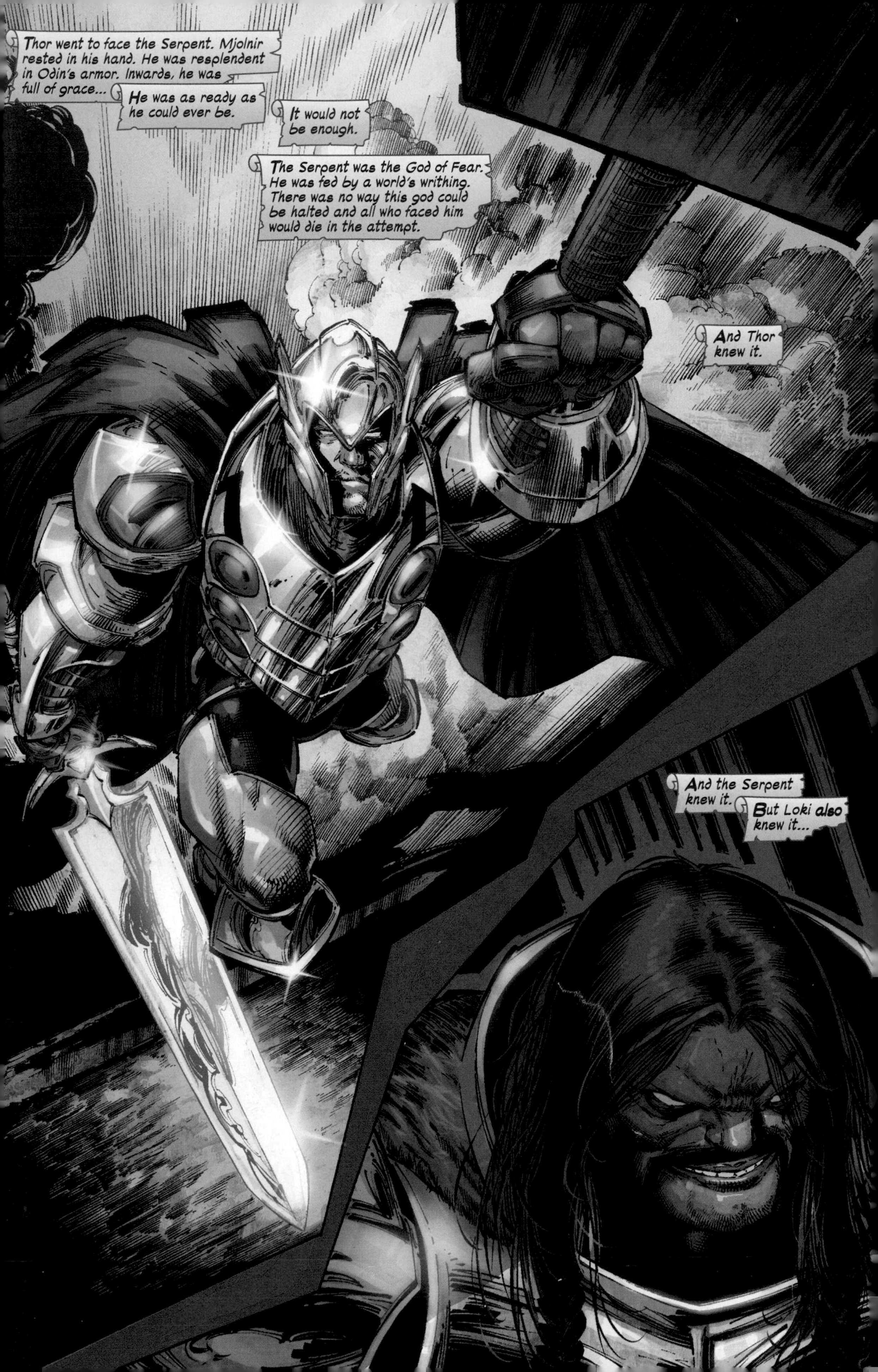
Thor went to face the Serpent. Mjolnir rested in his hand. He was resplendent in Odin's armor. Inwards, he was full of grace...
He was as ready as he could ever be.
It would not be enough.
The Serpent was the God of Fear. He was fed by a world's writhing. There was no way this god could be halted and all who faced him would die in the attempt.
And Thor knew it.
And the Serpent knew it.
But Loki also knew it...

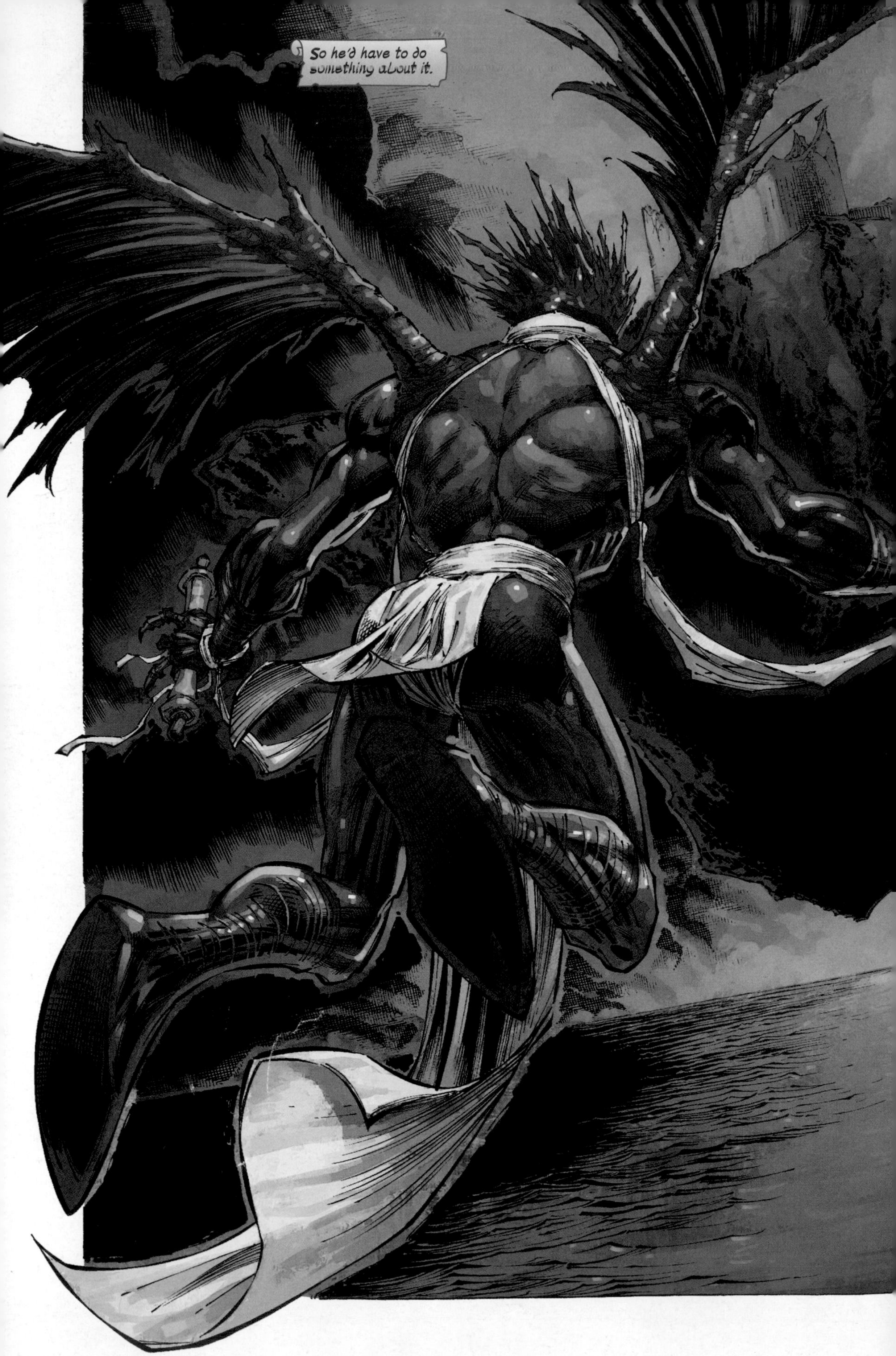
So he'd have to do something about it.

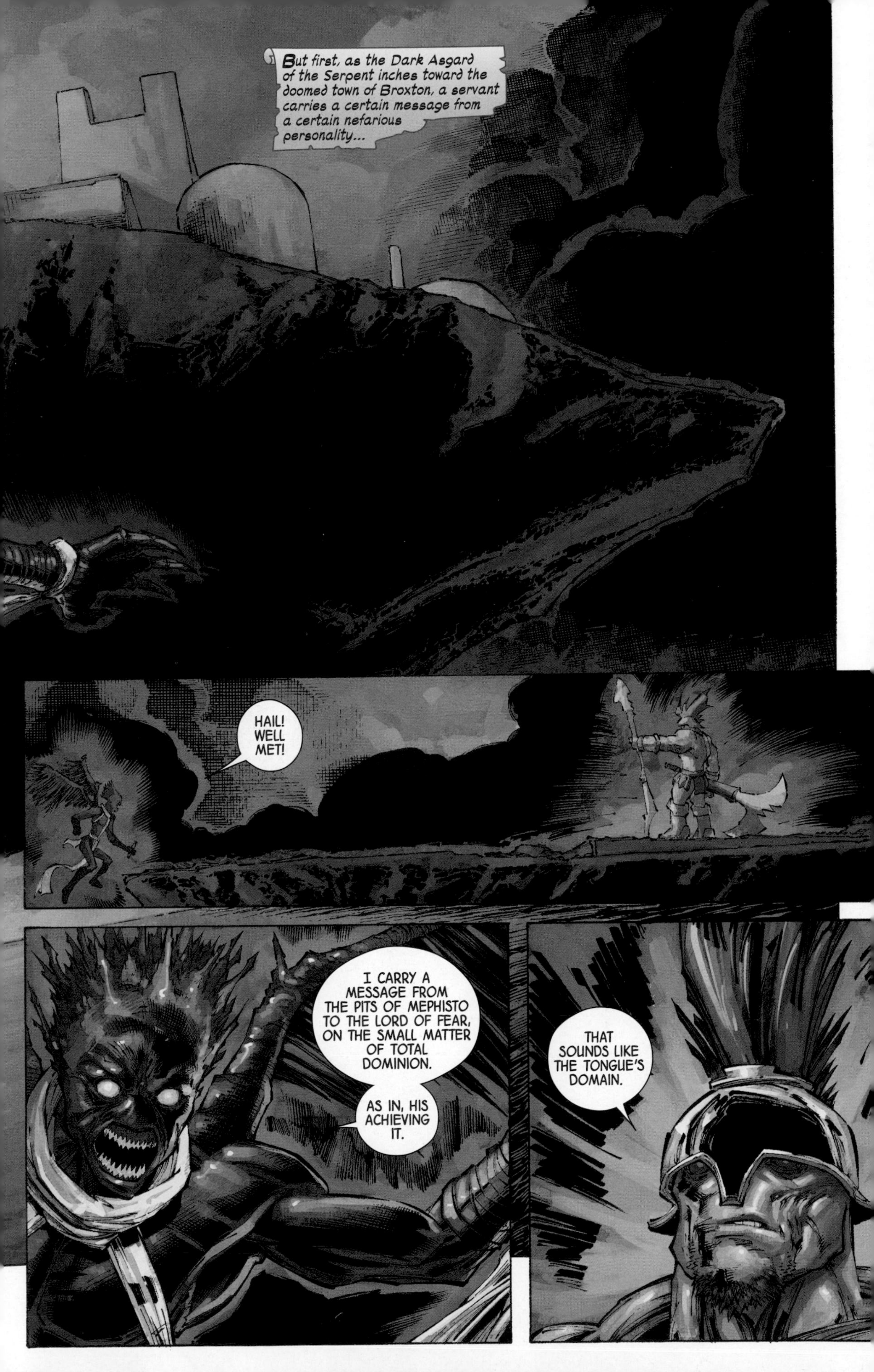
But first, as the Dark Asgard of the Serpent inches toward the doomed town of Broxton, a servant carries a certain message from a certain nefarious personality...
HAIL! WELL MET!
I CARRY A MESSAGE FROM THE PITS OF MEPHISTO TO THE LORD OF FEAR, ON THE SMALL MATTER OF TOTAL DOMINION.
AS IN, HIS ACHIEVING IT.
THAT SOUNDS LIKE THE TONGUE'S DOMAIN.

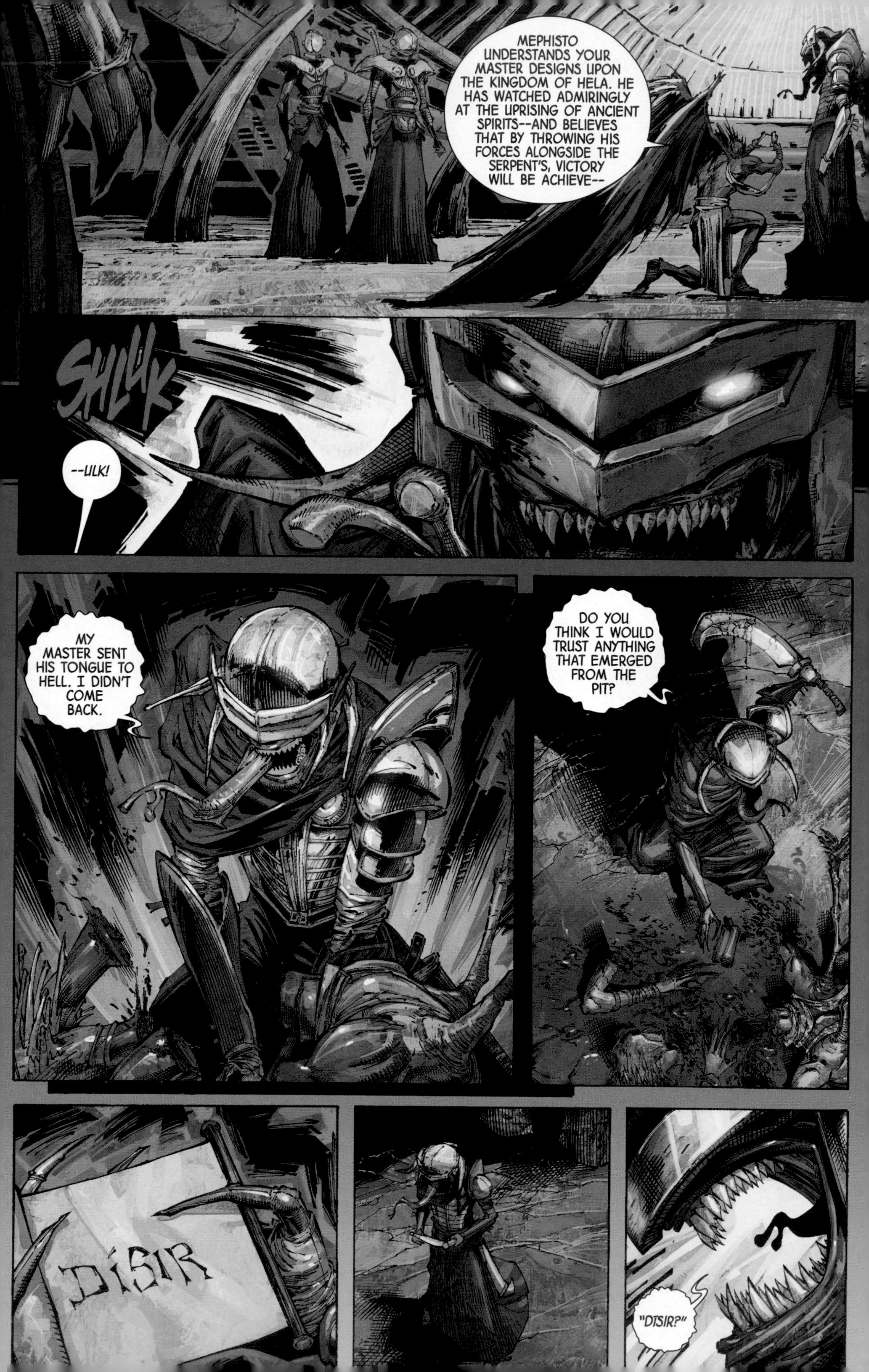
MEPHISTO UNDERSTANDS YOUR MASTER DESIGNS UPON THE KINGDOM OF HELA. HE HAS WATCHED ADMIRINGLY AT THE UPRISING OF ANCIENT SPIRITS--AND BELIEVES THAT BY THROWING HIS FORCES ALONGSIDE THE SERPENT'S, VICTORY WILL BE ACHIEVE--
SHLUK
--ULK!
MY MASTER SENT HIS TONGUE TO HELL. I DIDN'T COME BACK.
DO YOU THINK I WOULD TRUST ANYTHING THAT EMERGED FROM THE PIT?
DÍSIR
"DISIR?"

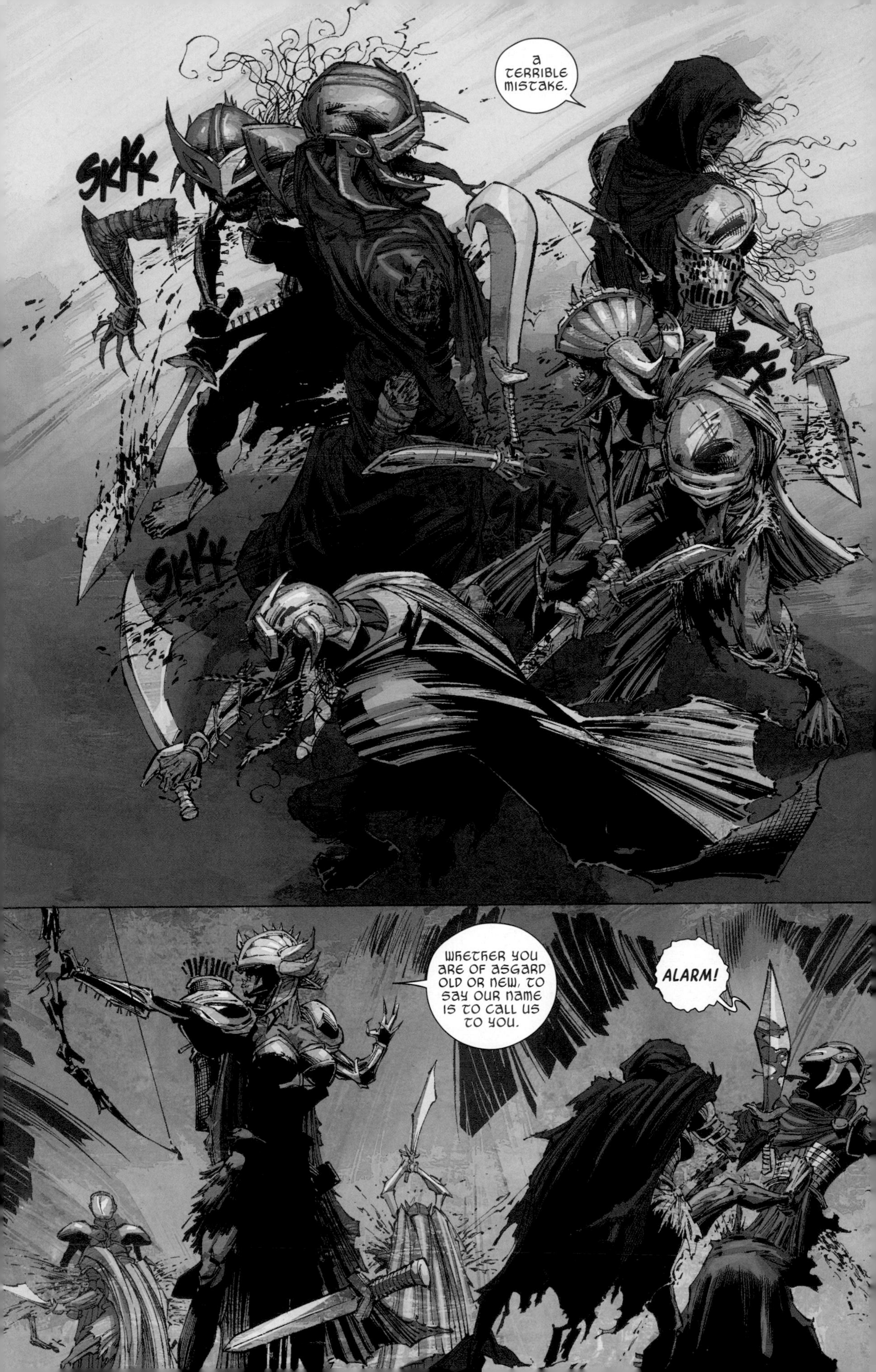

SKKK
A TERRIBLE MISTAKE.
SKKK
SKKK
SKKK
WHETHER YOU ARE OF ASGARD OLD OR NEW, TO SAY OUR NAME IS TO CALL US TO YOU.
ALARM!

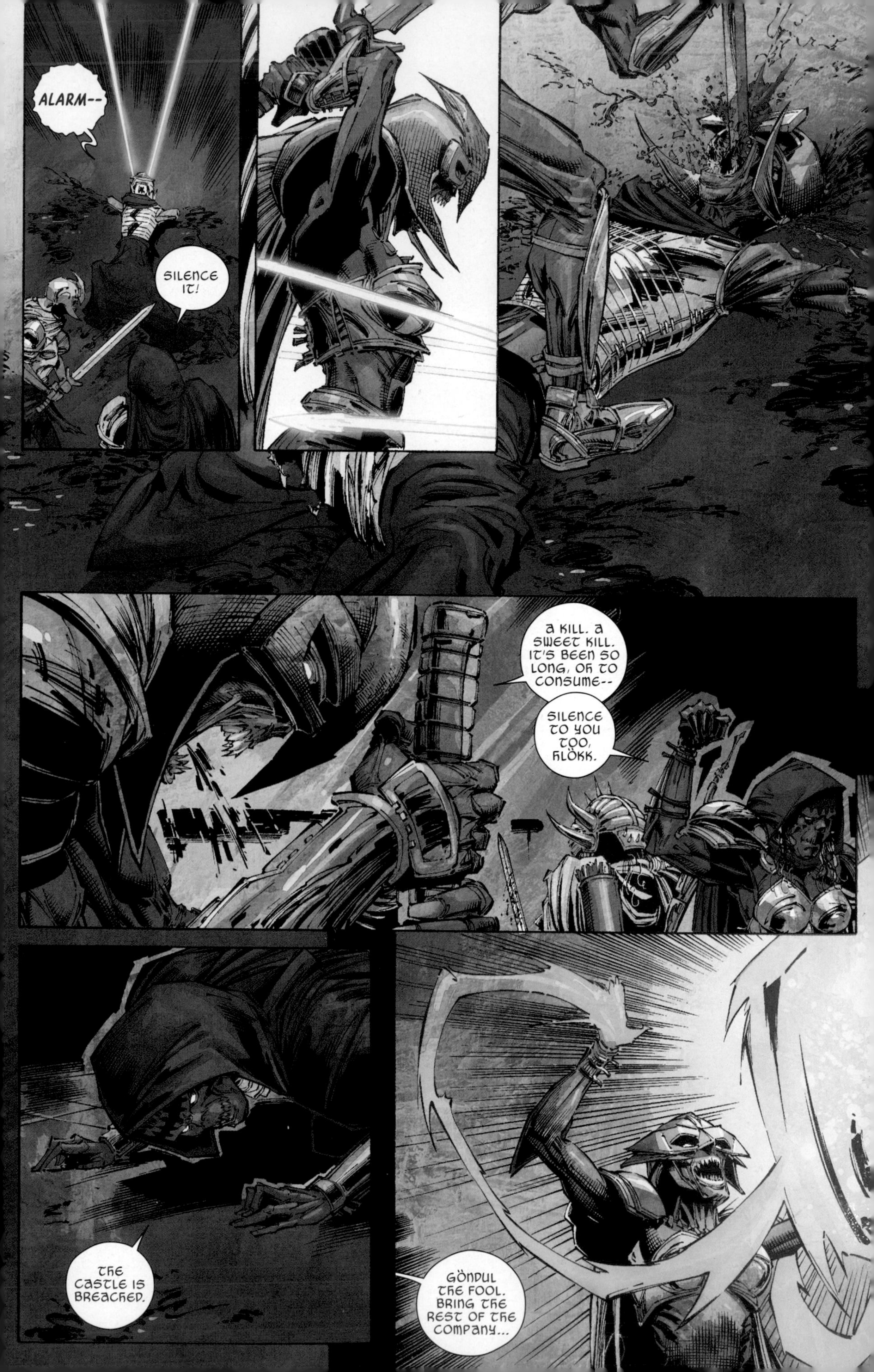
ALARM--
SILENCE IT!
A KILL. A SWEET KILL. IT'S BEEN SO LONG, OH TO CONSUME--
SILENCE TO YOU TOO, HLÖKK.
THE CASTLE IS BREACHED.
GÖNDUL THE FOOL. BRING THE REST OF THE COMPANY...

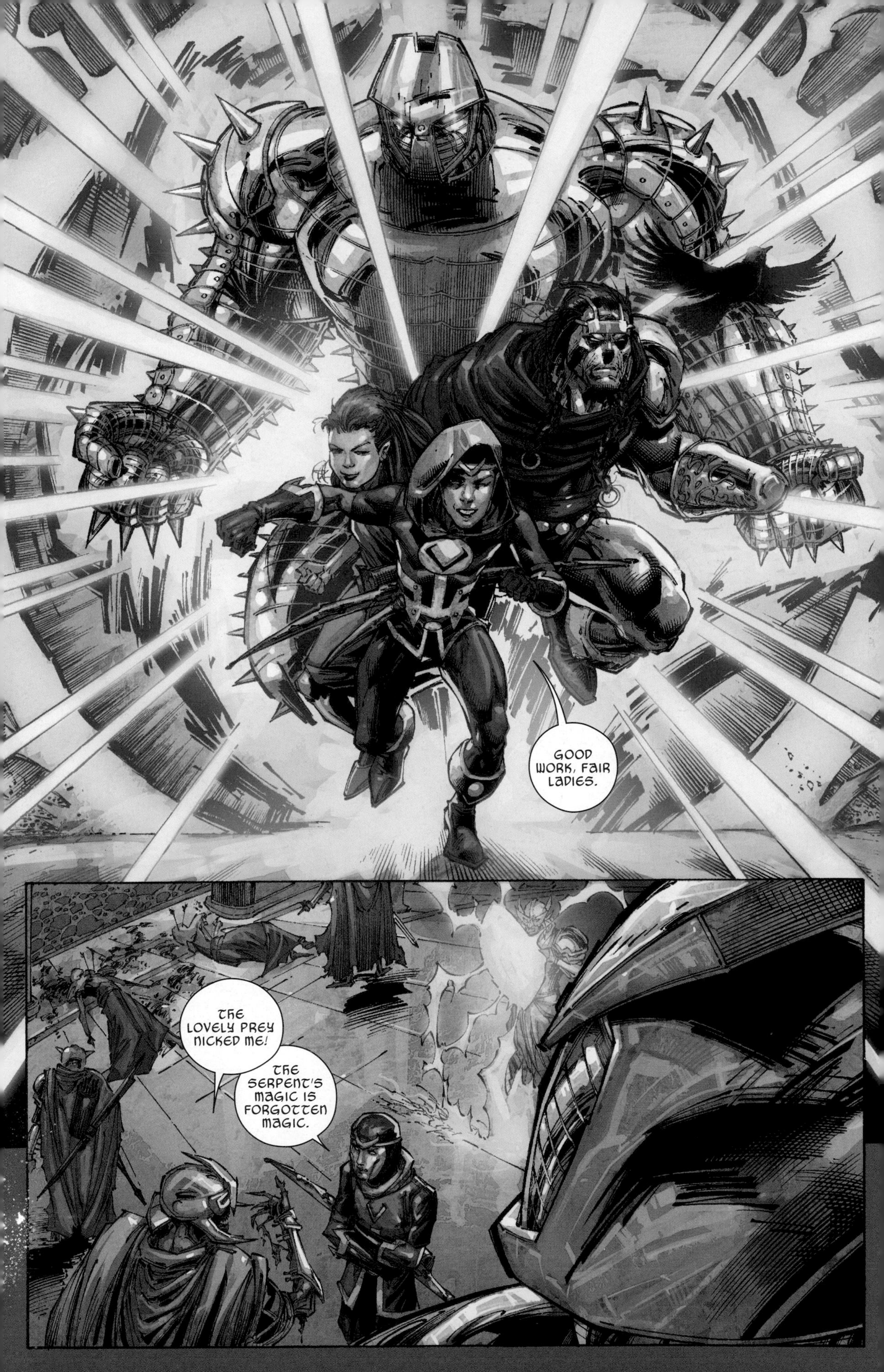
GOOD WORK, FAIR LADIES.
THE LOVELY PREY NICKED ME!
THE SERPENT'S MAGIC IS FORGOTTEN MAGIC.

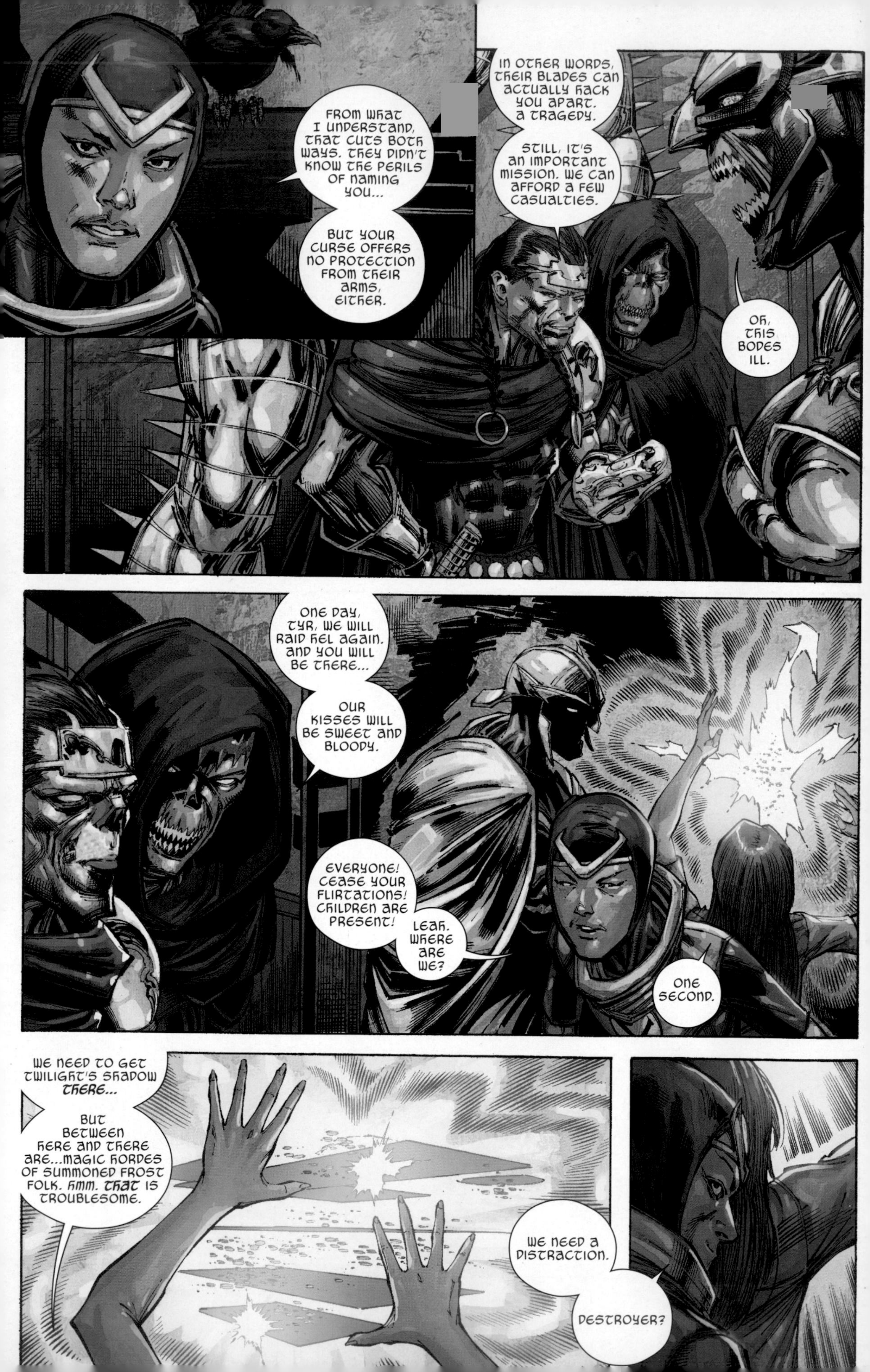
FROM WHAT I UNDERSTAND, THAT CUTS BOTH WAYS. THEY DIDN'T KNOW THE PERILS OF NAMING YOU...
BUT YOUR CURSE OFFERS NO PROTECTION FROM THEIR ARMS, EITHER.
IN OTHER WORDS, THEIR BLADES CAN ACTUALLY HACK YOU APART. A TRAGEDY.
STILL, IT'S AN IMPORTANT MISSION. WE CAN AFFORD A FEW CASUALTIES.
OH, THIS BODES ILL.
ONE DAY, TYR, WE WILL RAID HEL AGAIN. AND YOU WILL BE THERE...
OUR KISSES WILL BE SWEET AND BLOODY.
EVERYONE! CEASE YOUR FLIRTATIONS! CHILDREN ARE PRESENT!
LEAH. WHERE ARE WE?
ONE SECOND.
WE NEED TO GET TWILIGHT'S SHADOW *THERE*...
BUT BETWEEN HERE AND THERE ARE...MAGIC HORDES OF SUMMONED FROST FOLK. *HMM. THAT* IS TROUBLESOME.
WE NEED A DISTRACTION.
DESTROYER?

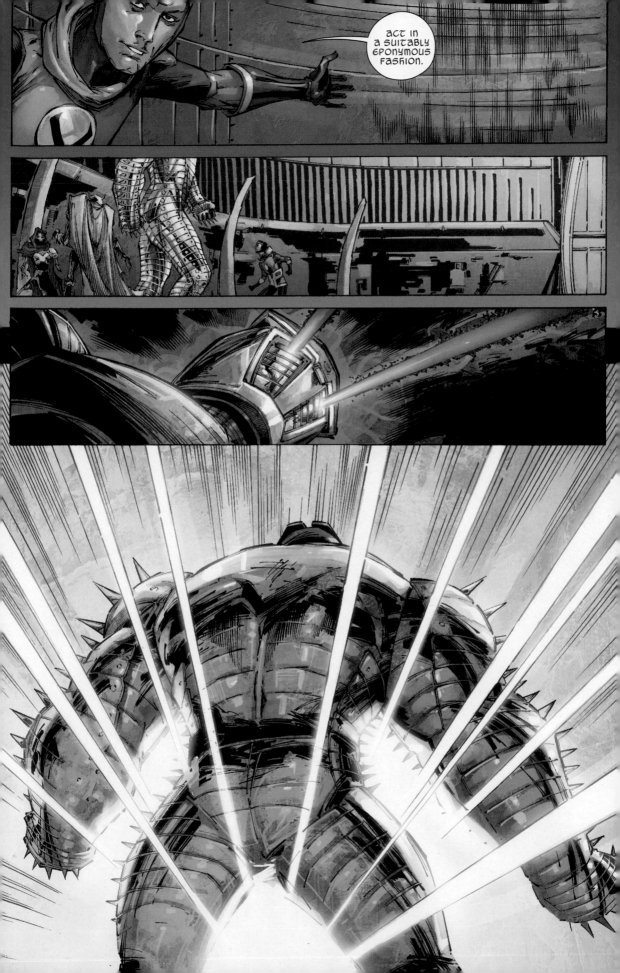

ACT IN A SUITABLY EPONYMOUS FASHION.

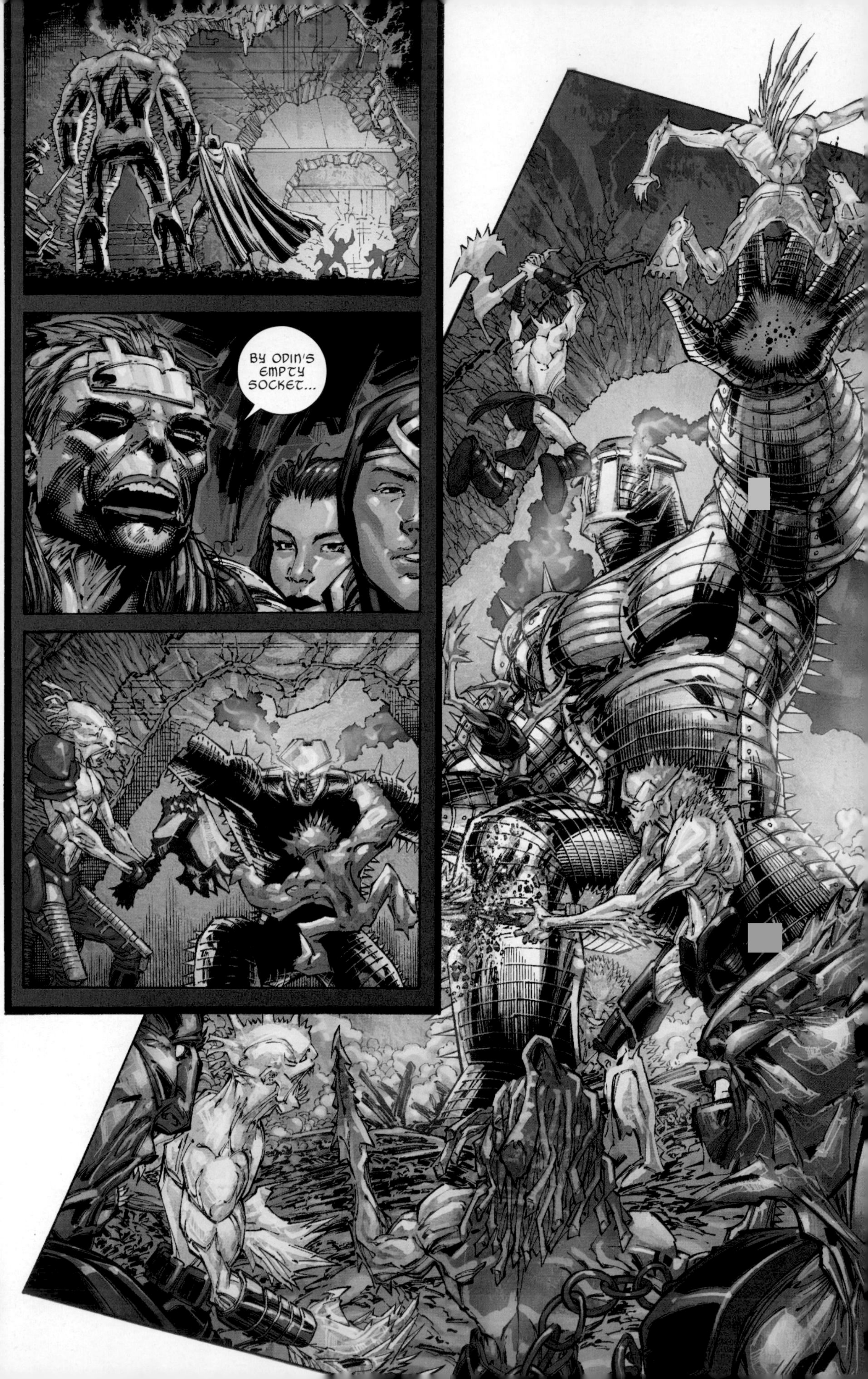
BY ODIN'S EMPTY SOCKET...

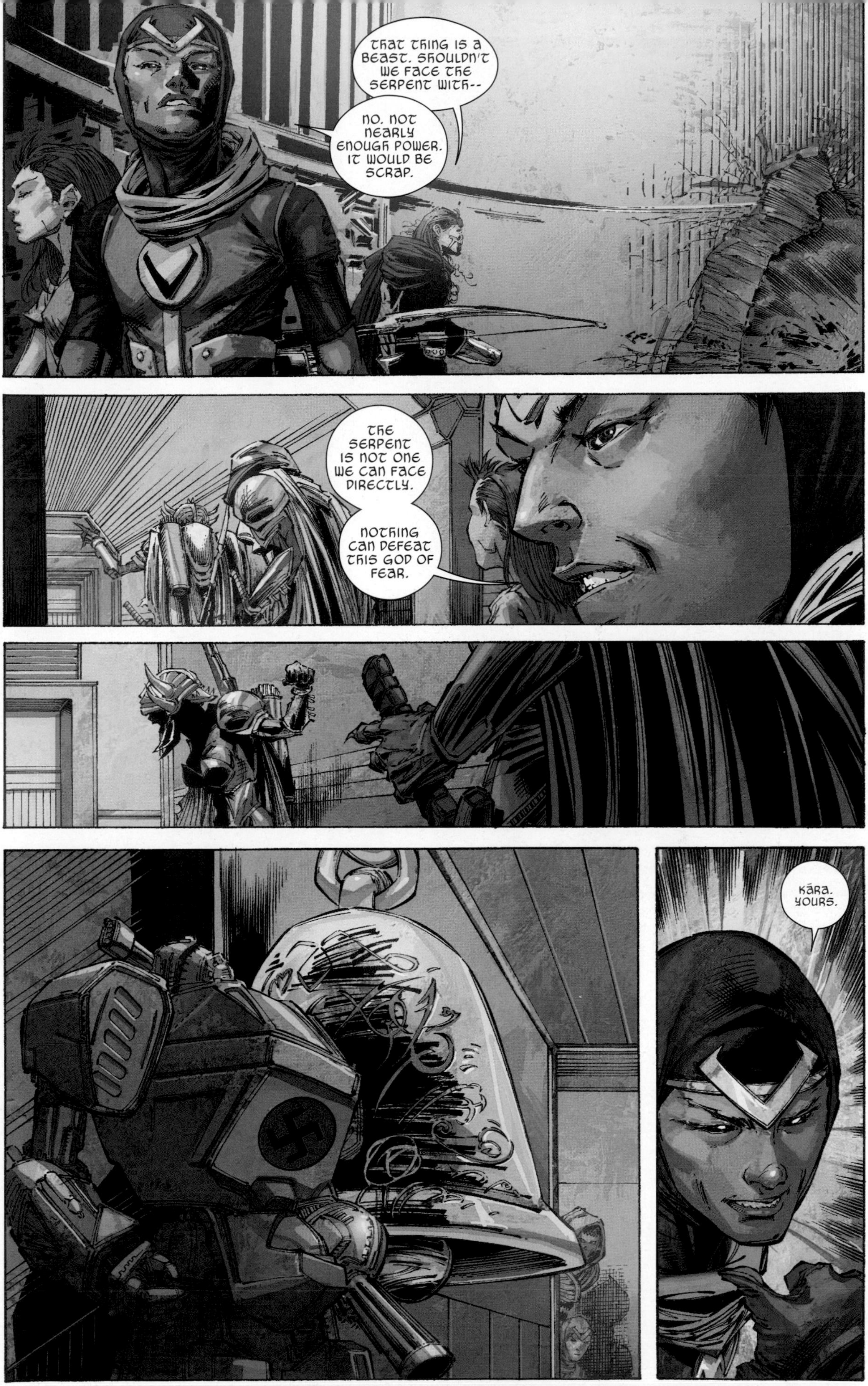
THAT THING IS A BEAST. SHOULDN'T WE FACE THE SERPENT WITH--
NO. NOT NEARLY ENOUGH POWER. IT WOULD BE SCRAP.
THE SERPENT IS NOT ONE WE CAN FACE DIRECTLY.
NOTHING CAN DEFEAT THIS GOD OF FEAR.
KÁRA. YOURS.

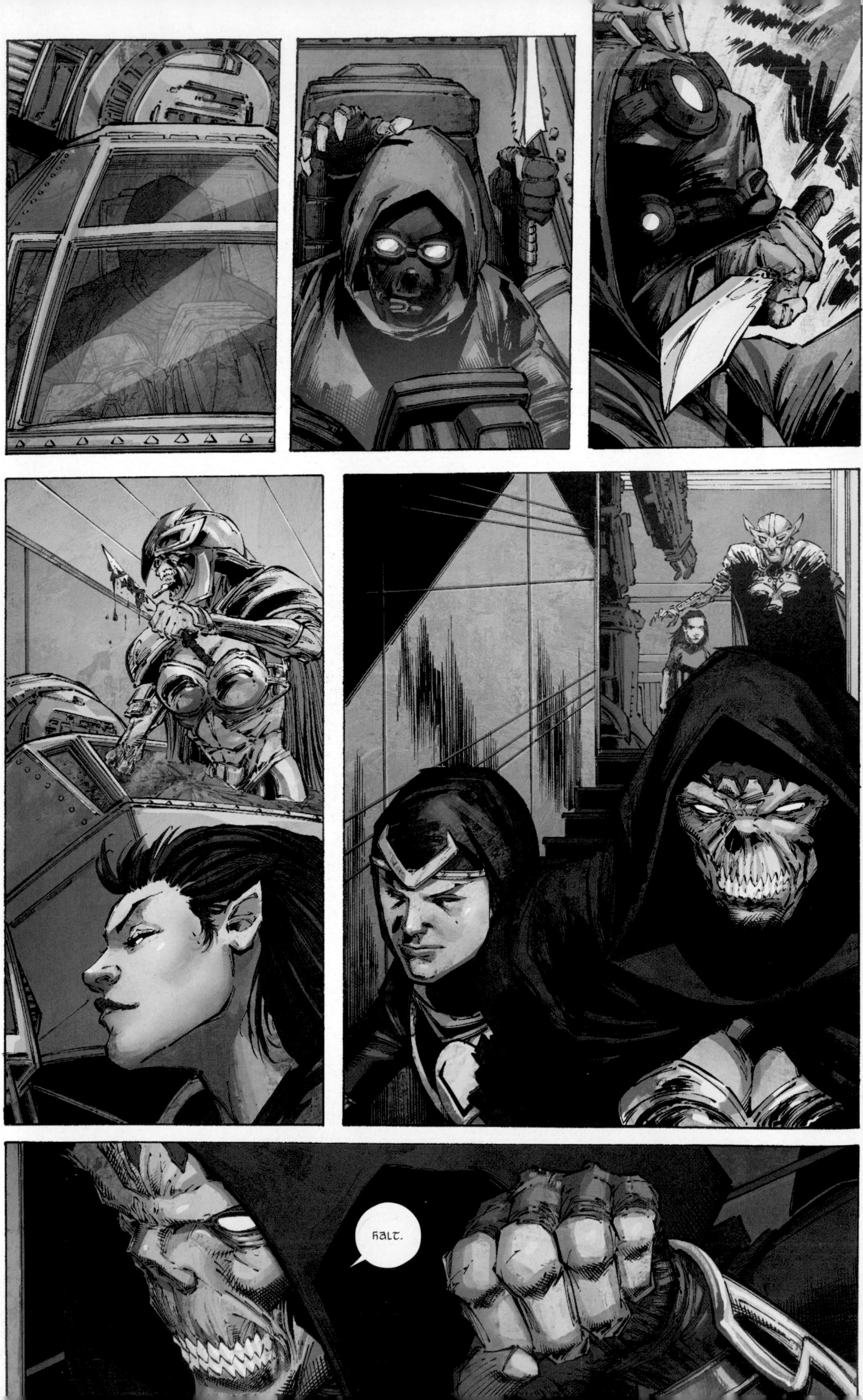
HALT.

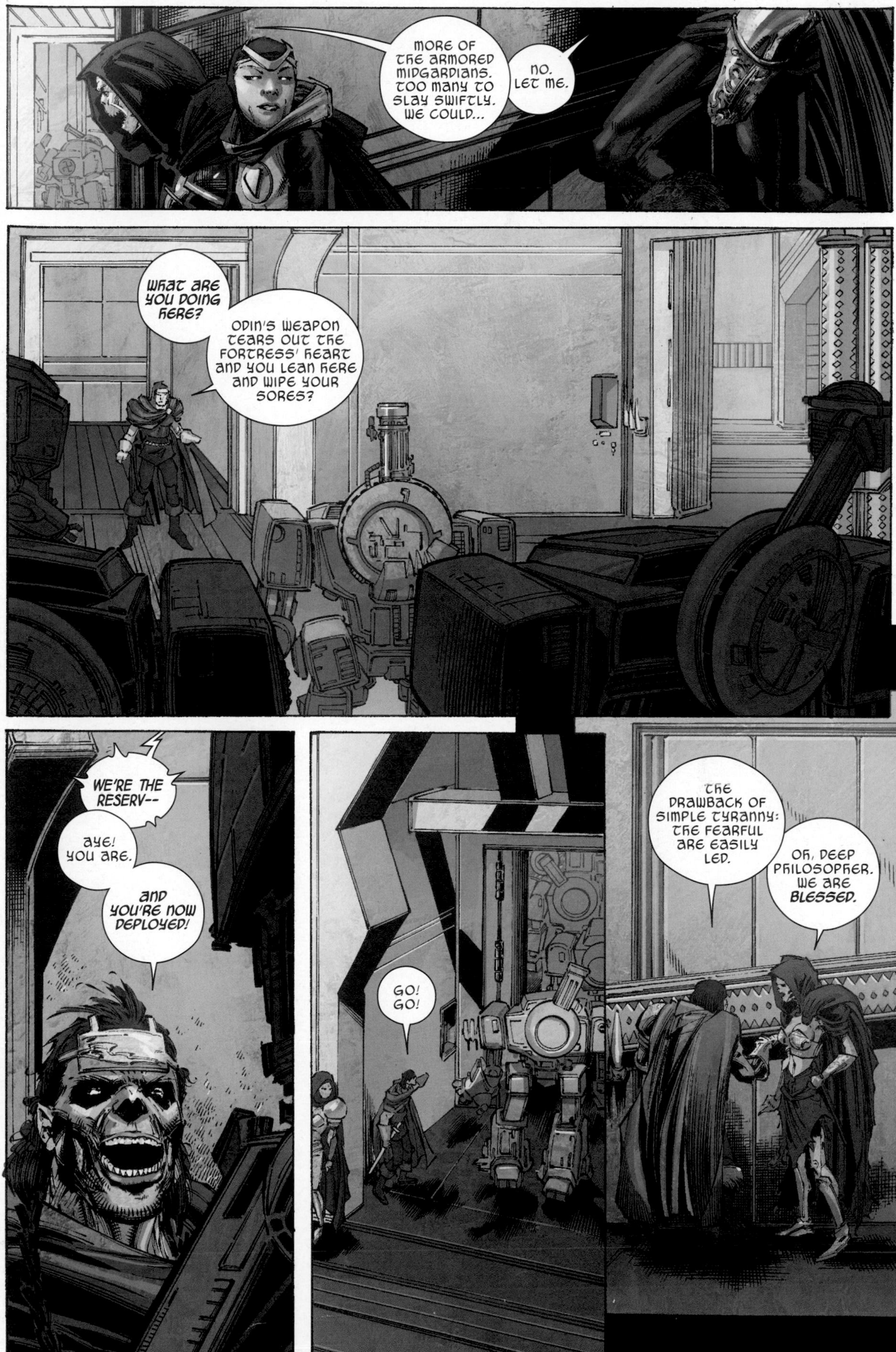

MORE OF THE ARMORED MIDGARDIANS. TOO MANY TO SLAY SWIFTLY. WE COULD...
NO. LET ME.
WHAT ARE YOU DOING HERE?
ODIN'S WEAPON TEARS OUT THE FORTRESS' HEART AND YOU LEAN HERE AND WIPE YOUR SORES?
WE'RE THE RESERV--
AYE! YOU ARE.
AND YOU'RE NOW DEPLOYED!
GO! GO!
THE DRAWBACK OF SIMPLE TYRANNY: THE FEARFUL ARE EASILY LED.
OH, DEEP PHILOSOPHER. WE ARE BLESSED.

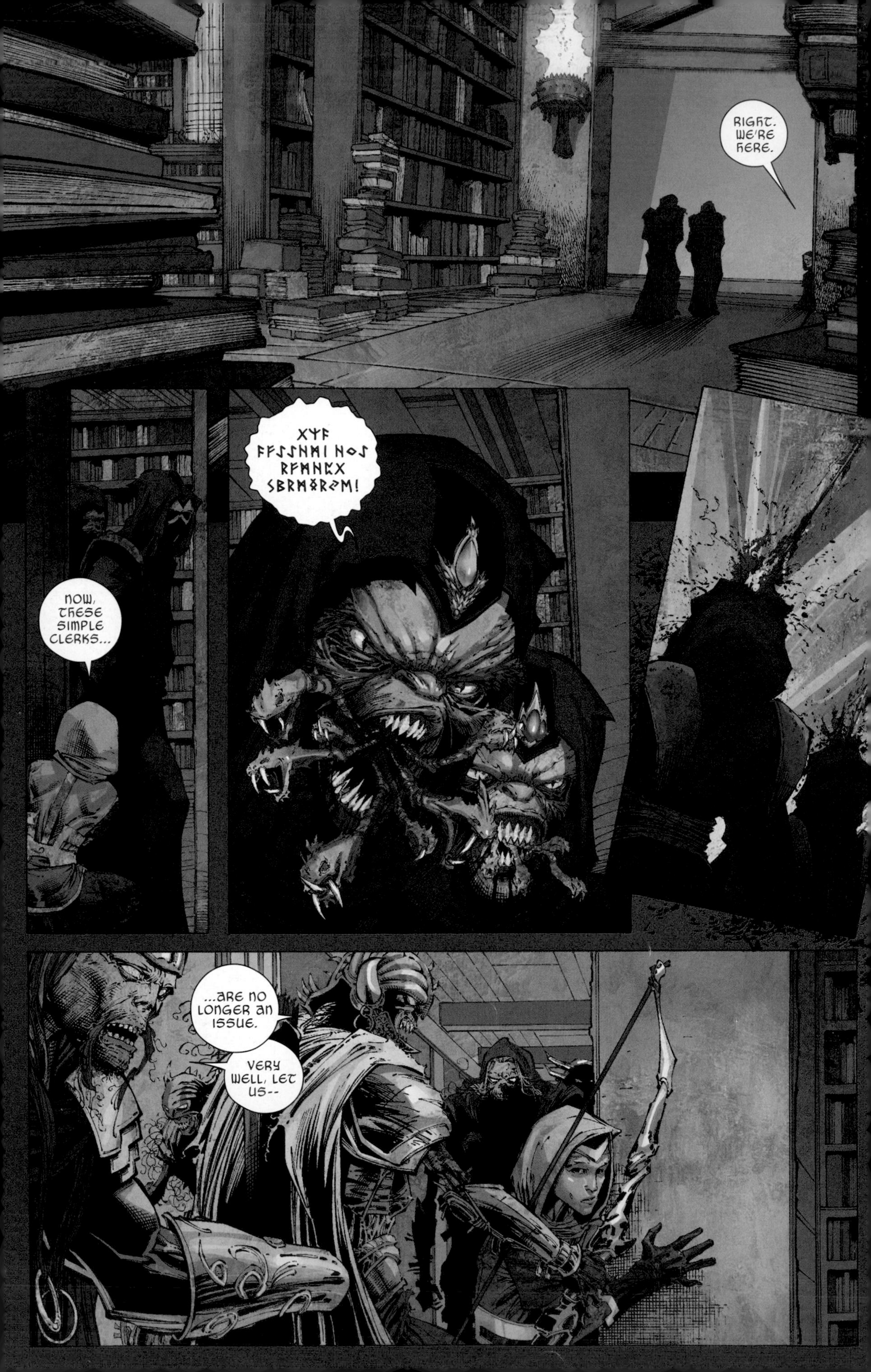
RIGHT. WE'RE HERE.
NOW, THESE SIMPLE CLERKS...
...ARE NO LONGER AN ISSUE.
VERY WELL, LET US--

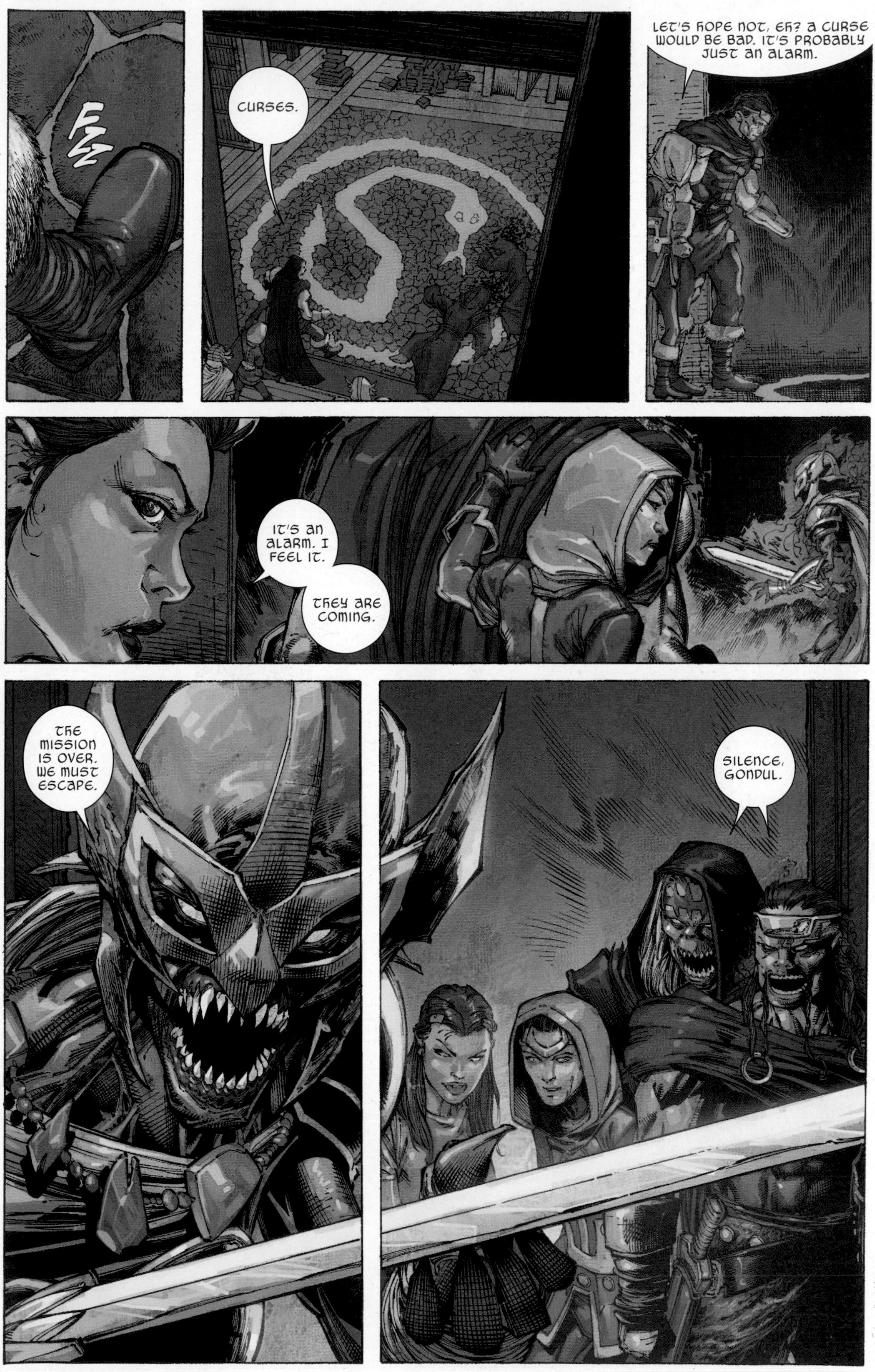
FZZ
CURSES.
LET'S HOPE NOT, EH? A CURSE WOULD BE BAD. IT'S PROBABLY JUST AN ALARM.
IT'S AN ALARM. I FEEL IT.
THEY ARE COMING.
THE MISSION IS OVER. WE MUST ESCAPE.
SILENCE, GONDUL.

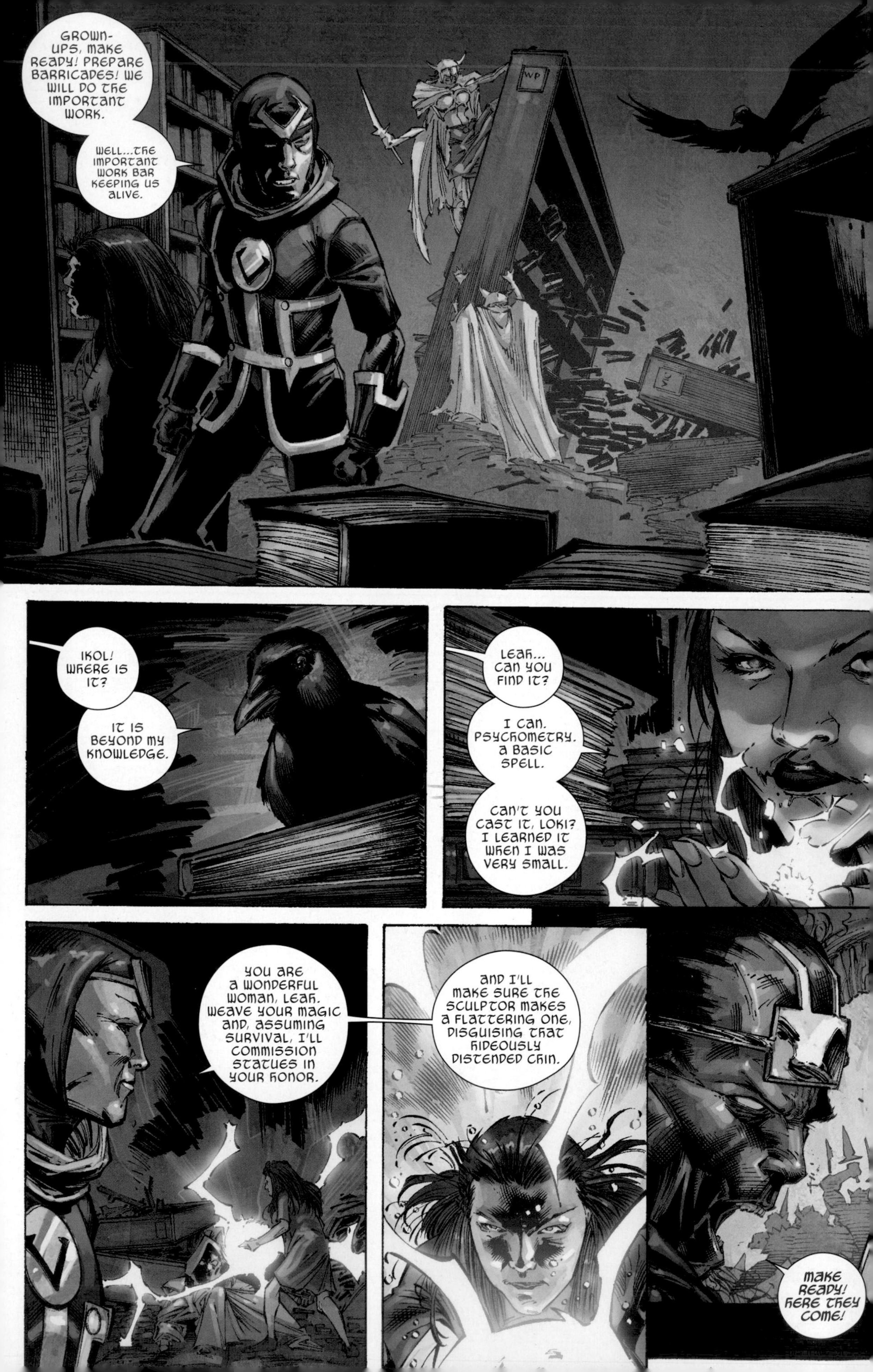
GROWN-UPS, MAKE READY! PREPARE BARRICADES! WE WILL DO THE IMPORTANT WORK.
WELL...THE IMPORTANT WORK BAR KEEPING US ALIVE.
IKOL! WHERE IS IT?
IT IS BEYOND MY KNOWLEDGE.
LEAH... CAN YOU FIND IT?
I CAN. PSYCHOMETRY. A BASIC SPELL.
CAN'T YOU CAST IT, LOKI? I LEARNED IT WHEN I WAS VERY SMALL.
YOU ARE A WONDERFUL WOMAN, LEAH. WEAVE YOUR MAGIC AND, ASSUMING SURVIVAL, I'LL COMMISSION STATUES IN YOUR HONOR.
AND I'LL MAKE SURE THE SCULPTOR MAKES A FLATTERING ONE, DISGUISING THAT HIDEOUSLY DISTENDED CHIN.
MAKE READY! HERE THEY COME!

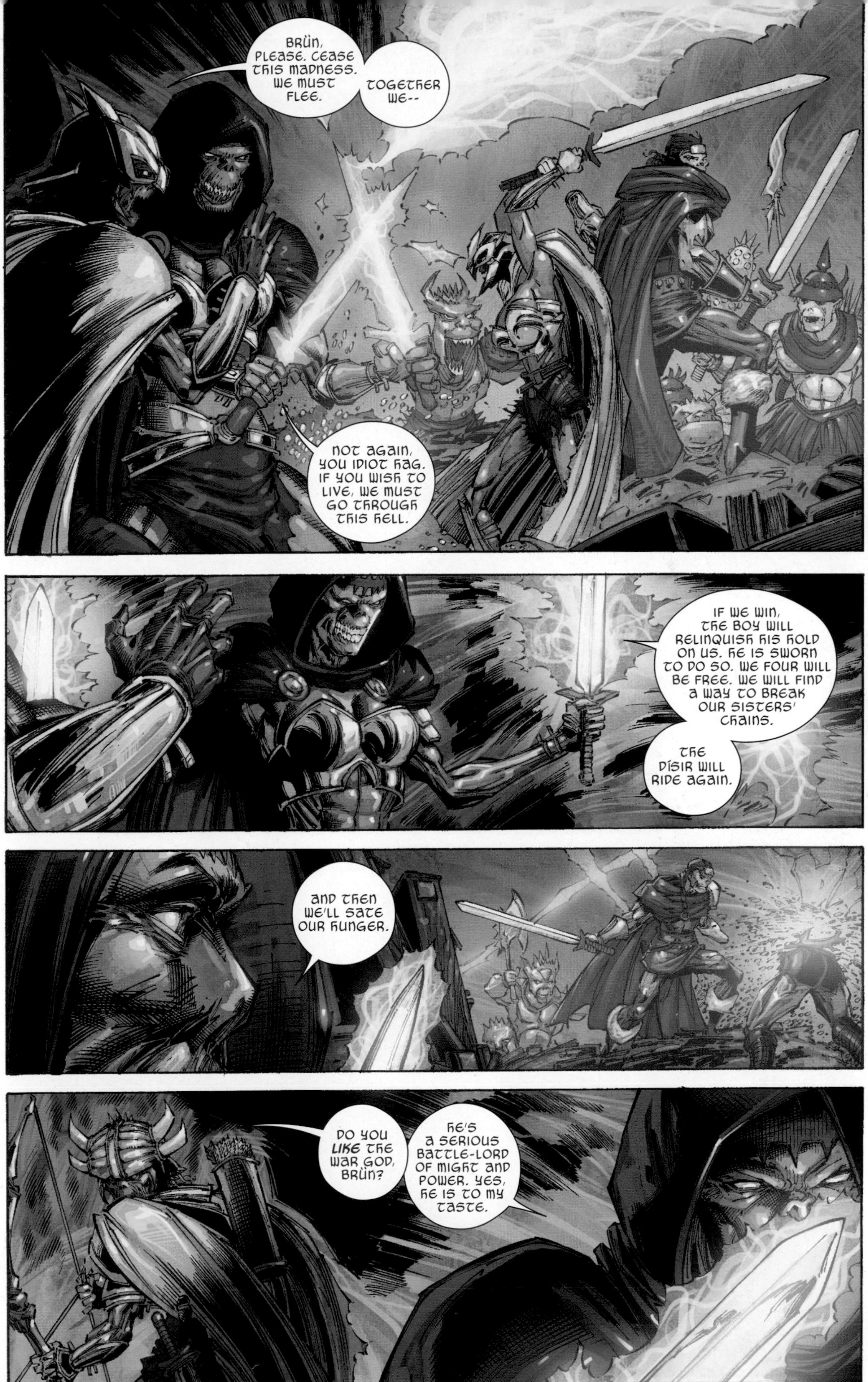
BRÜN, PLEASE. CEASE THIS MADNESS. WE MUST FLEE.
TOGETHER WE--
NOT AGAIN, YOU IDIOT HAG. IF YOU WISH TO LIVE, WE MUST GO THROUGH THIS HELL.
IF WE WIN, THE BOY WILL RELINQUISH HIS HOLD ON US. HE IS SWORN TO DO SO. WE FOUR WILL BE FREE. WE WILL FIND A WAY TO BREAK OUR SISTERS' CHAINS.
THE DÍSIR WILL RIDE AGAIN.
AND THEN WE'LL SATE OUR HUNGER.
DO YOU LIKE THE WAR GOD, BRÜN?
HE'S A SERIOUS BATTLE-LORD OF MIGHT AND POWER. YES, HE IS TO MY TASTE.

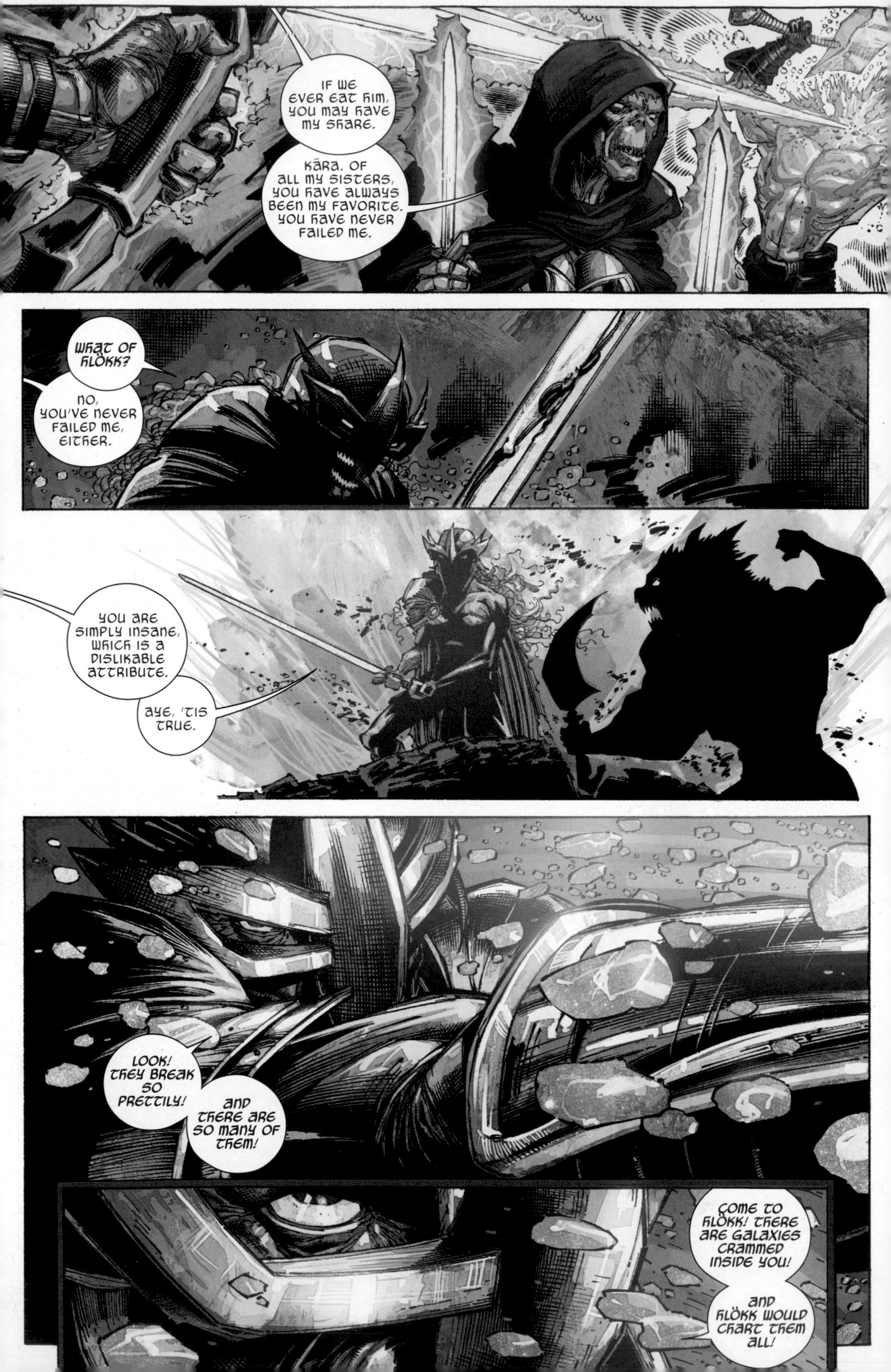
IF WE EVER EAT HIM, YOU MAY HAVE MY SHARE.
KÄRA. OF ALL MY SISTERS, YOU HAVE ALWAYS BEEN MY FAVORITE. YOU HAVE NEVER FAILED ME.
WHAT OF HLÖKK?
NO, YOU'VE NEVER FAILED ME, EITHER.
YOU ARE SIMPLY INSANE, WHICH IS A DISLIKABLE ATTRIBUTE.
AYE, 'TIS TRUE.
LOOK! THEY BREAK SO PRETTILY!
AND THERE ARE SO MANY OF THEM!
COME TO HLÖKK! THERE ARE GALAXIES CRAMMED INSIDE YOU!
AND HLÖKK WOULD CHART THEM ALL!

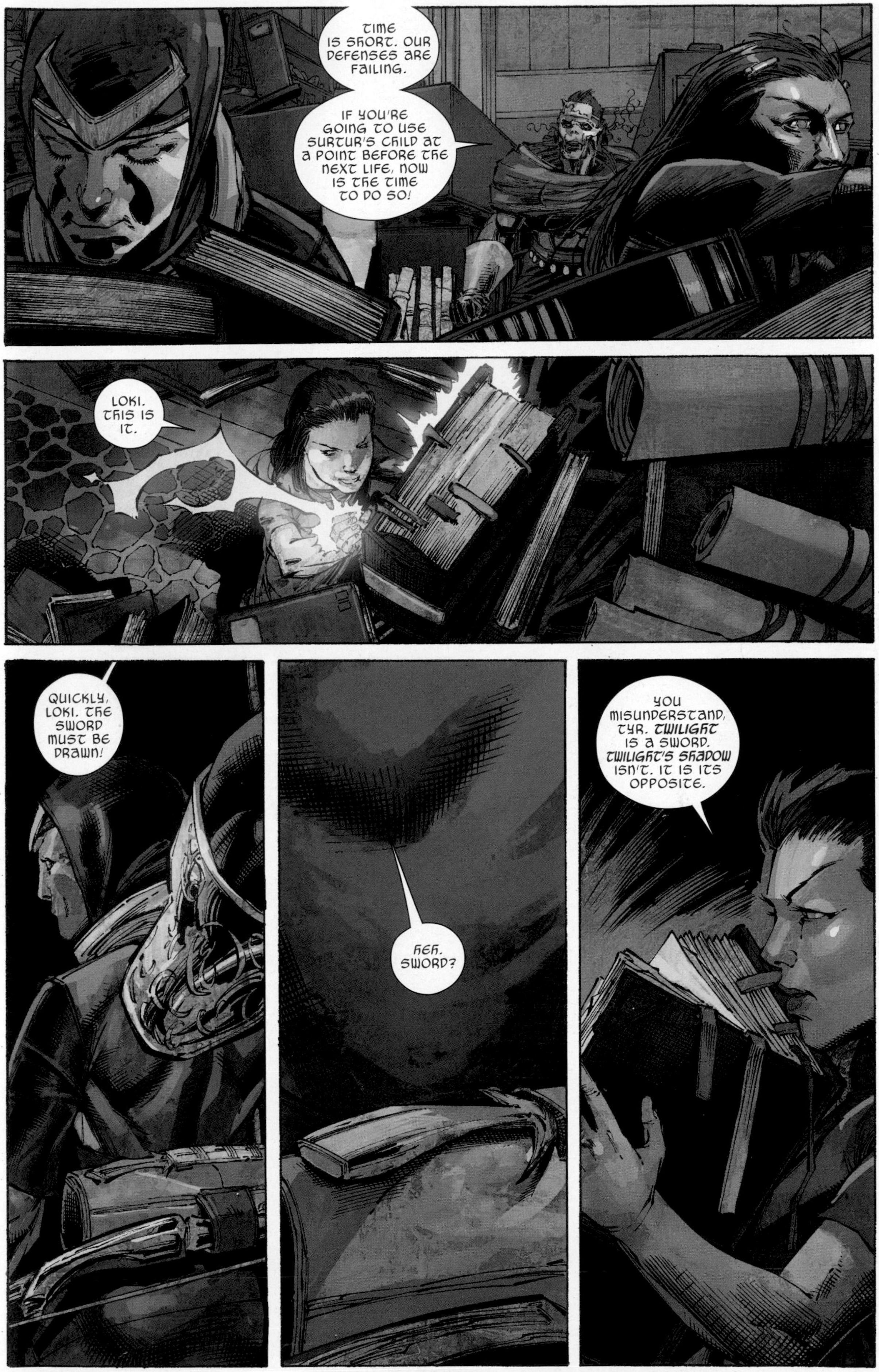
TIME IS SHORT. OUR DEFENSES ARE FAILING.
IF YOU'RE GOING TO USE SURTUR'S CHILD AT A POINT BEFORE THE NEXT LIFE, NOW IS THE TIME TO DO SO!
LOKI. THIS IS IT.
QUICKLY, LOKI. THE SWORD MUST BE DRAWN!
HEH. SWORD?
YOU MISUNDERSTAND, TYR. *TWILIGHT* IS A SWORD. *TWILIGHT'S SHADOW* ISN'T. IT IS ITS OPPOSITE.

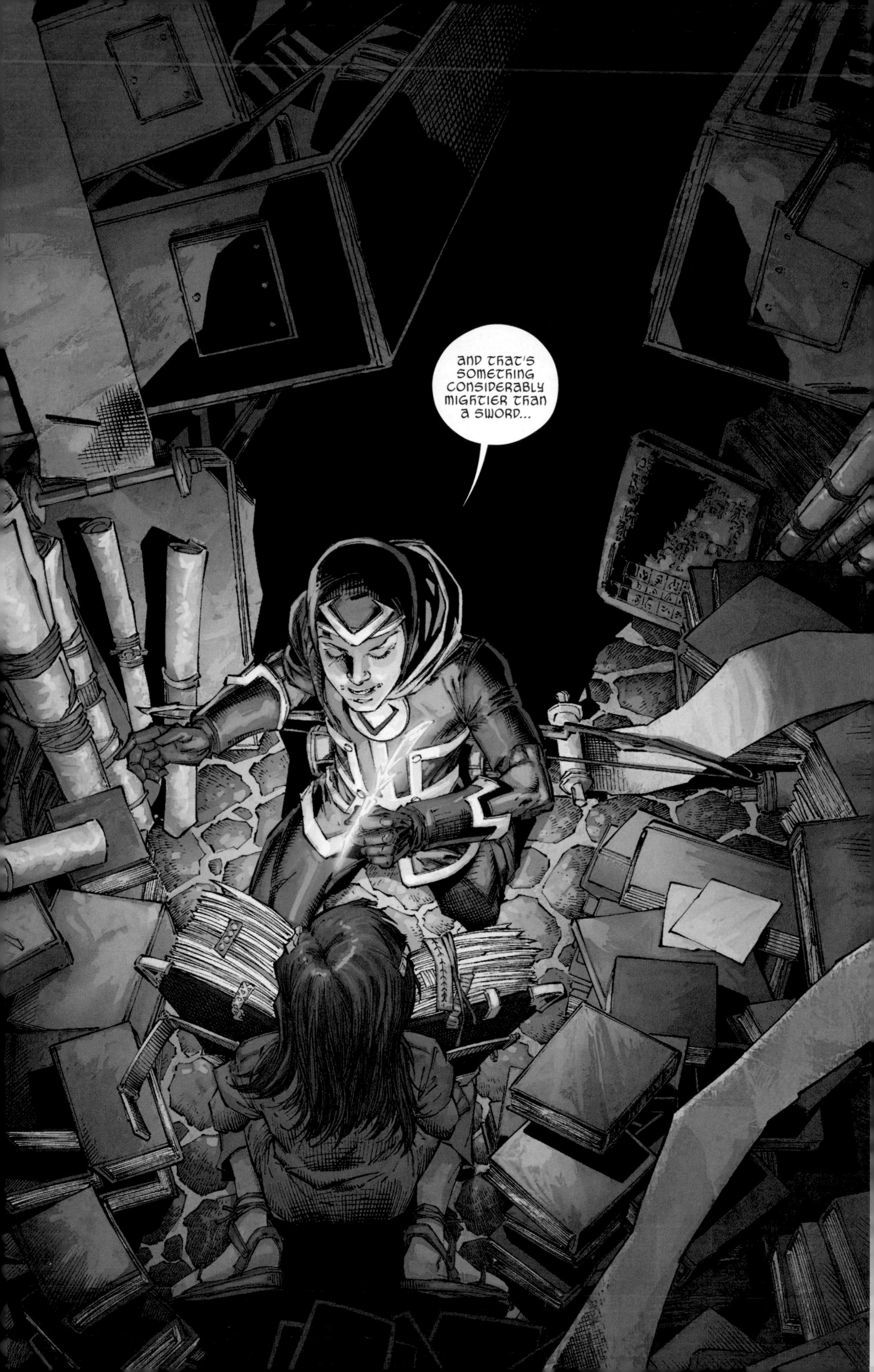
AND THAT'S SOMETHING CONSIDERABLY MIGHTIER THAN A SWORD...

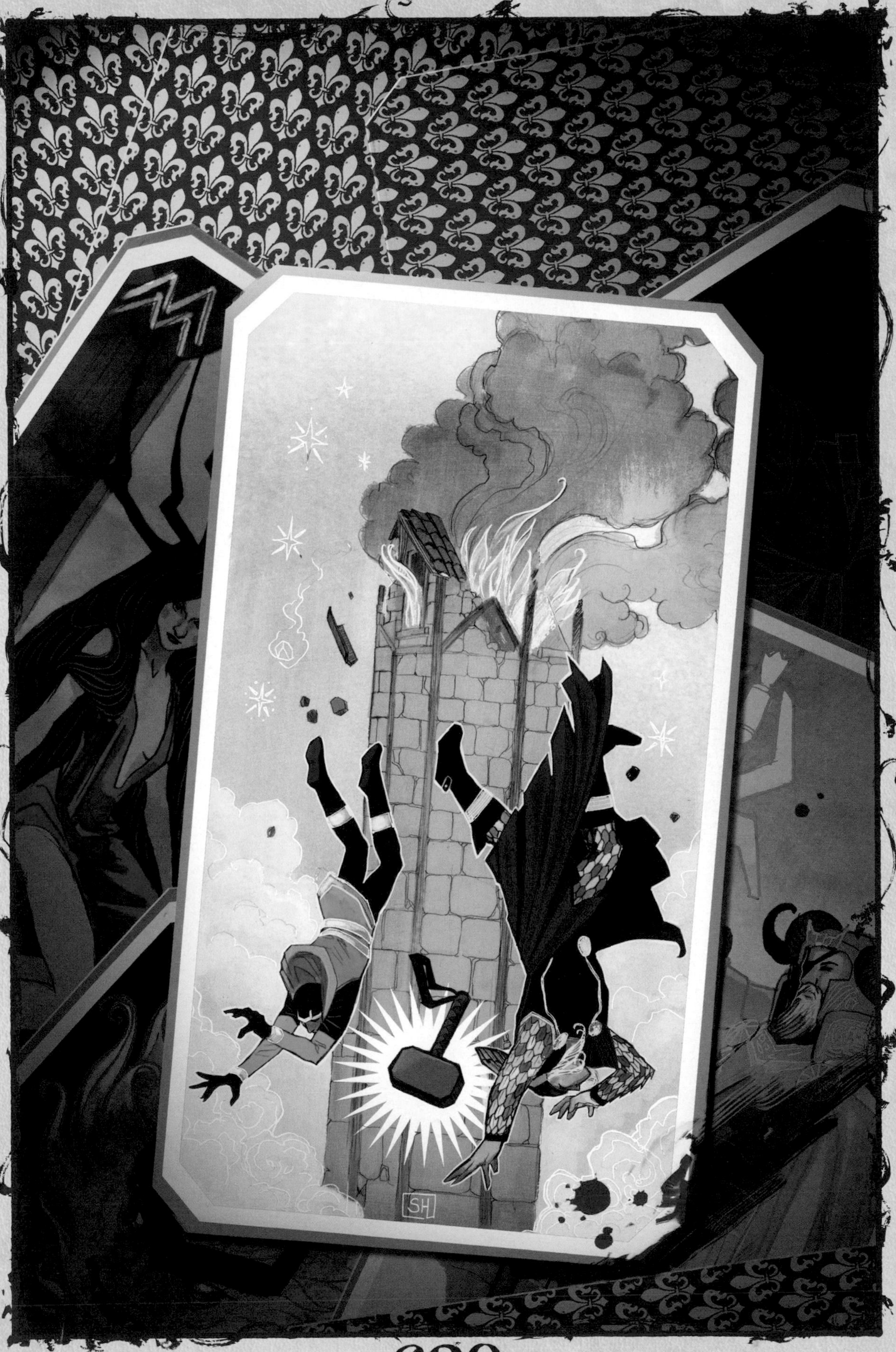
SH

629

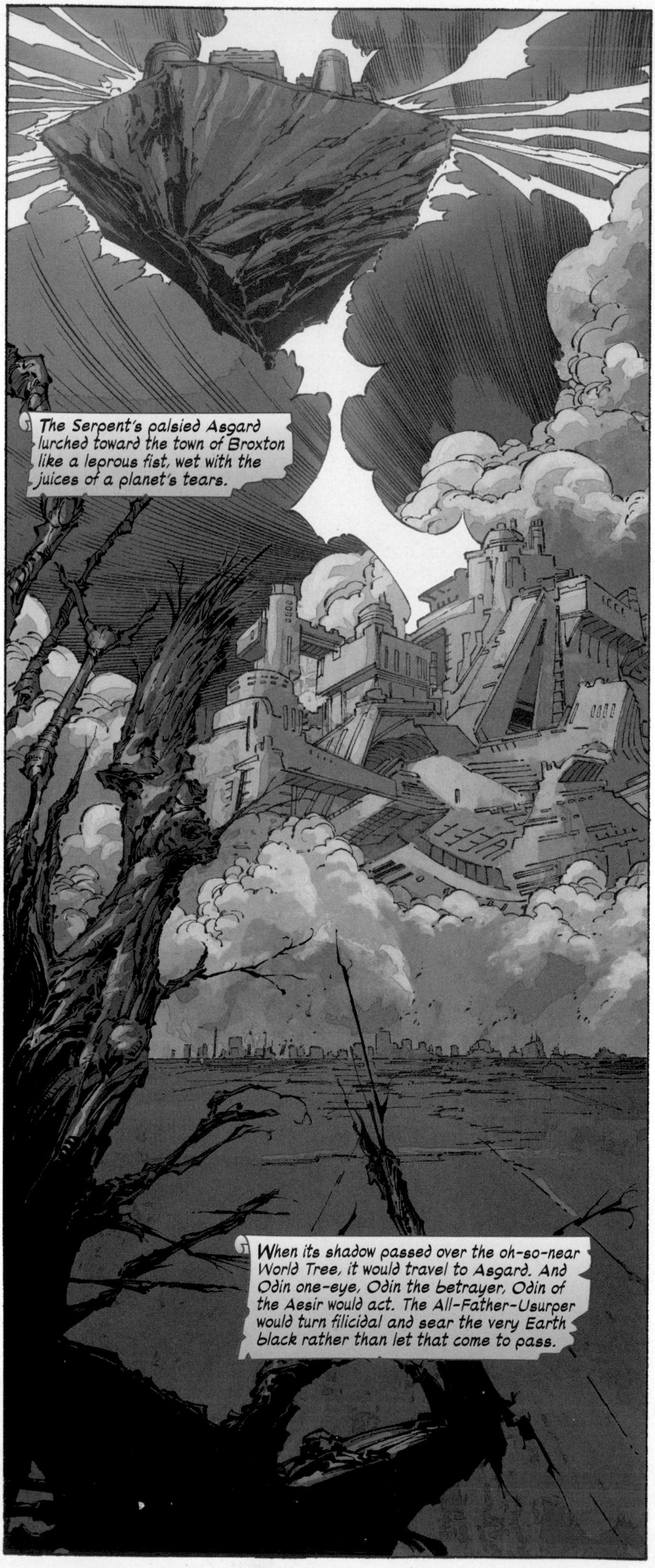
The Serpent's palsied Asgard lurched toward the town of Broxton like a leprous fist, wet with the juices of a planet's tears.
When its shadow passed over the oh-so-near World Tree, it would travel to Asgard. And Odin one-eye, Odin the betrayer, Odin of the Aesir would act. The All-Father-Usurper would turn filicidal and sear the very Earth black rather than let that come to pass.

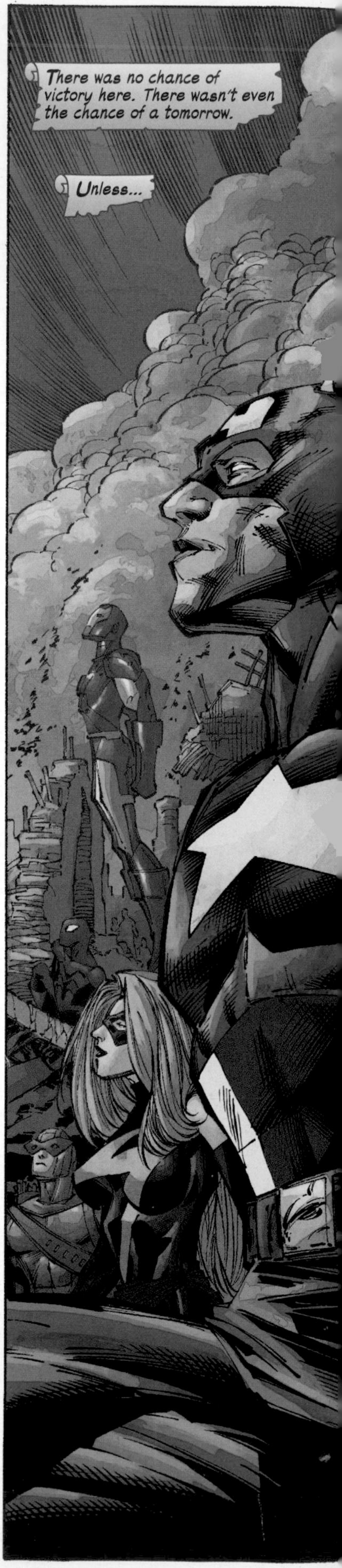
There was no chance of victory here. There wasn't even the chance of a tomorrow.
Unless...

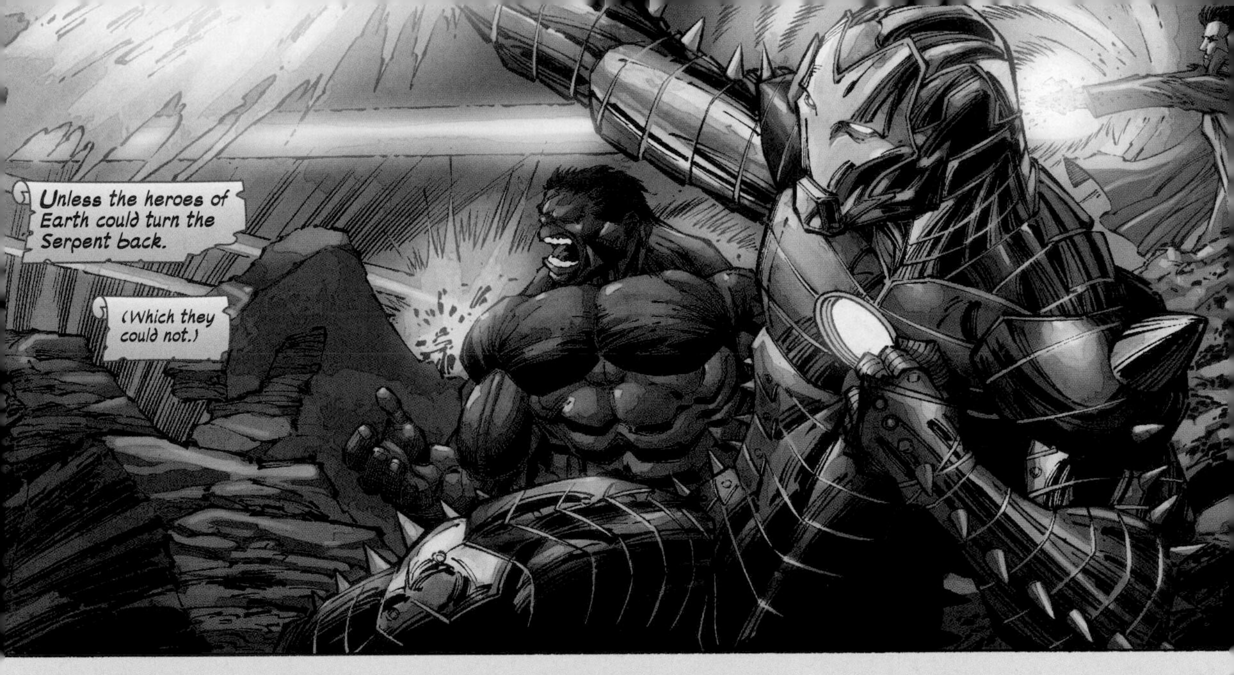
Unless the heroes of Earth could turn the Serpent back.
(Which they could not.)
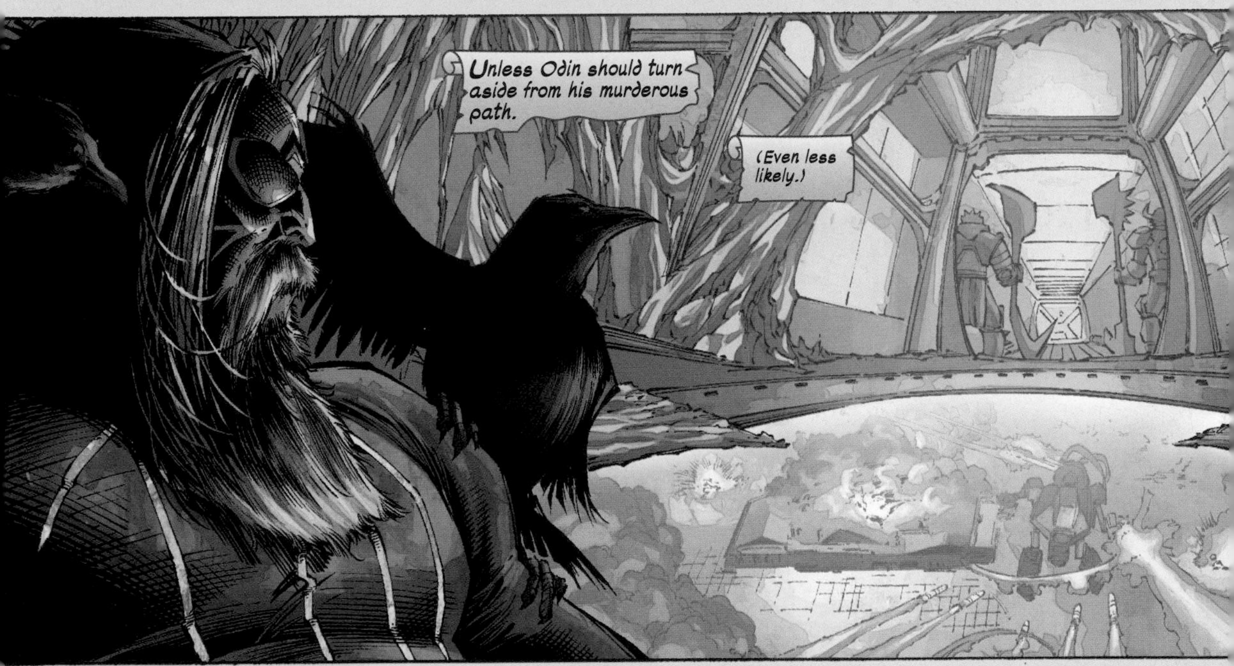
Unless Odin should turn aside from his murderous path.
(Even less likely.)
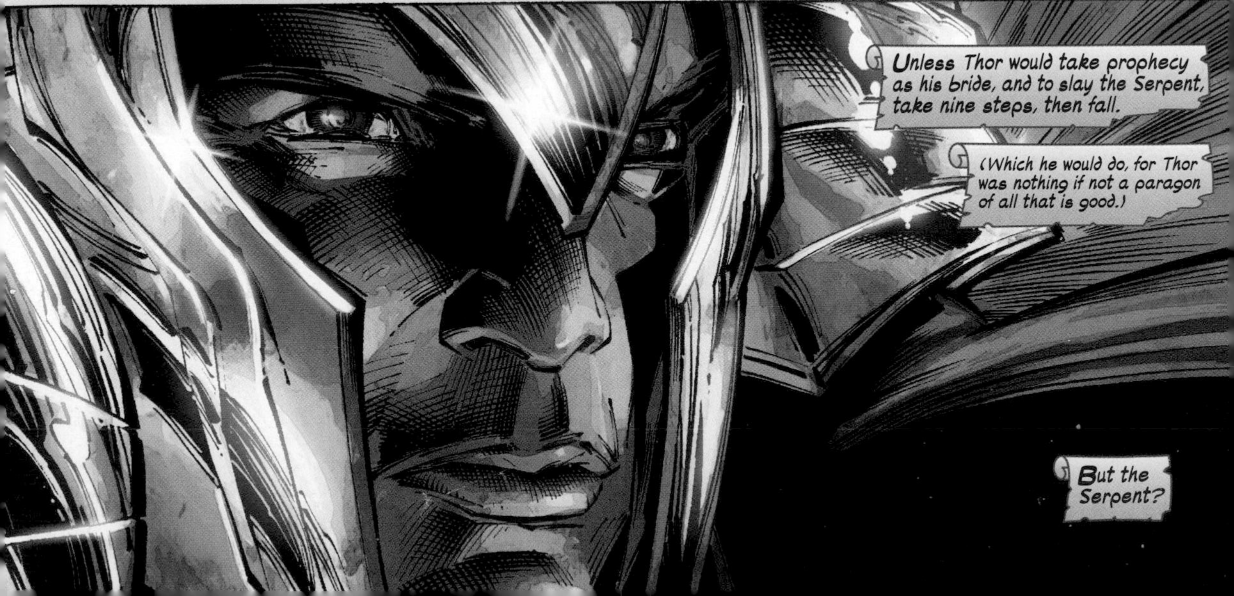
Unless Thor would take prophecy as his bride, and to slay the Serpent, take nine steps, then fall.
(Which he would do, for Thor was nothing if not a paragon of all that is good.)
But the Serpent?

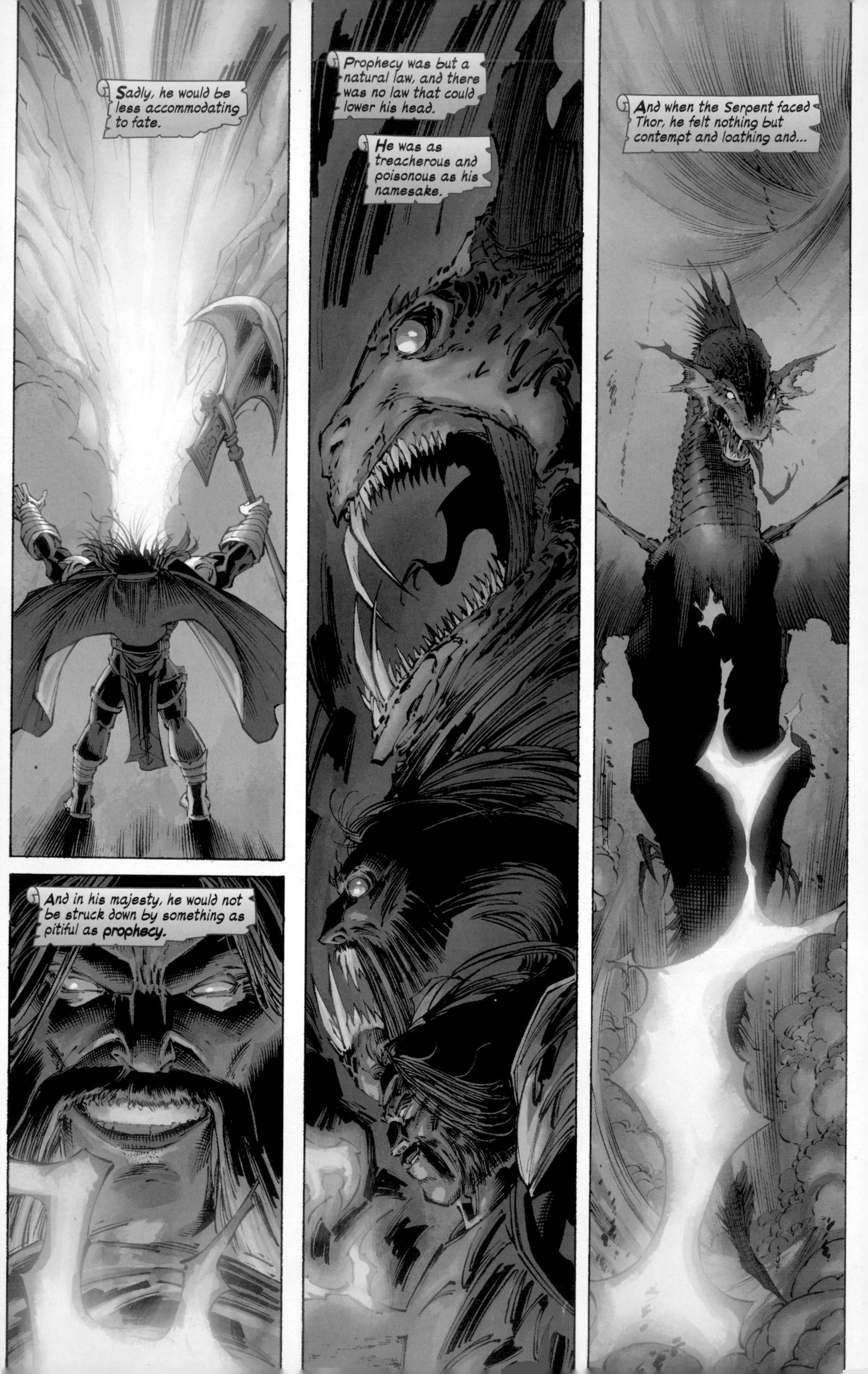
Sadly, he would be less accommodating to fate.
And in his majesty, he would not be struck down by something as pitiful as **prophecy**.
Prophecy was but a natural law, and there was no law that could lower his head.
He was as treacherous and poisonous as his namesake.
And when the Serpent faced Thor, he felt nothing but contempt and loathing and...

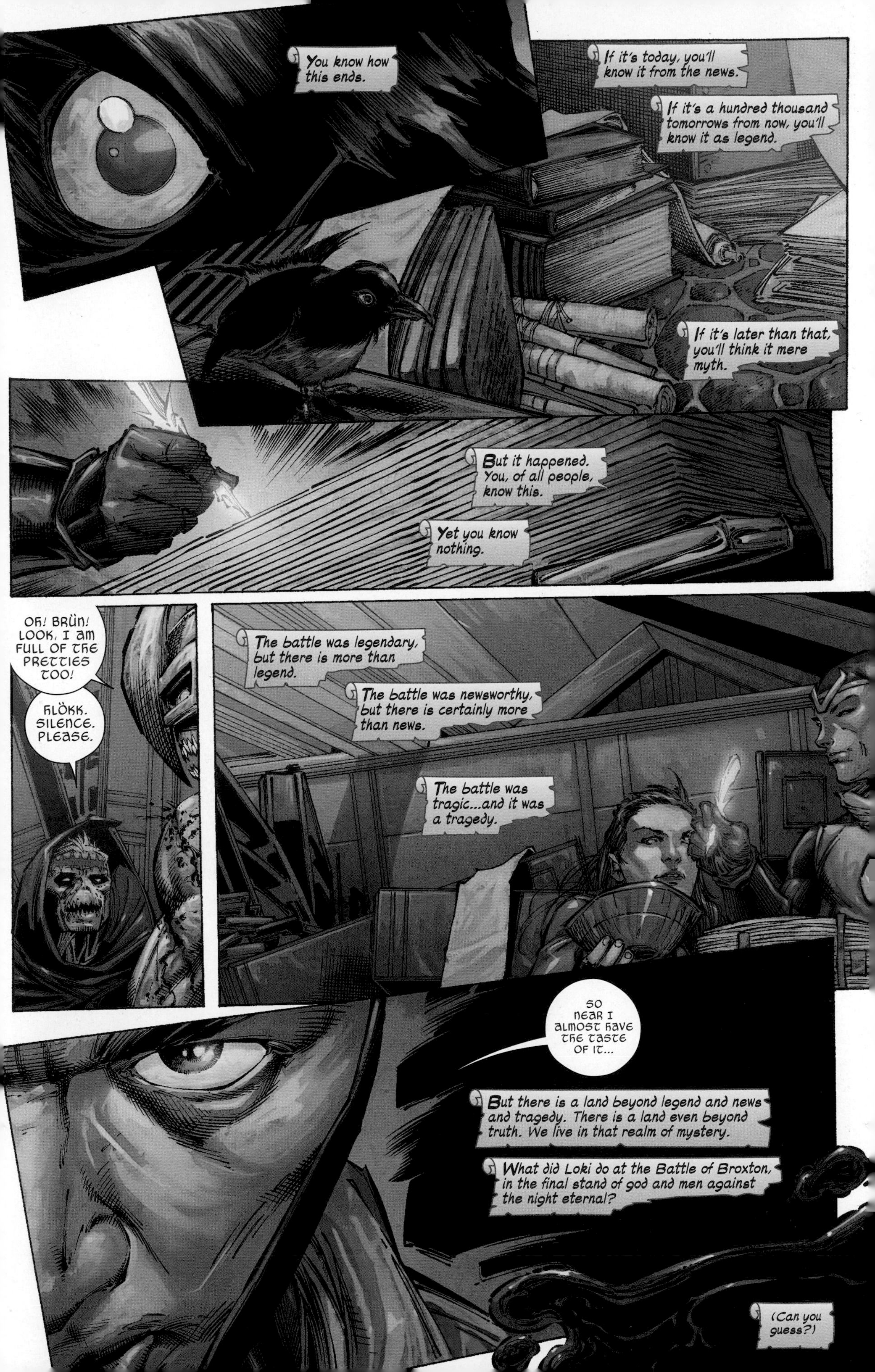
You know how this ends.
If it's today, you'll know it from the news.
If it's a hundred thousand tomorrows from now, you'll know it as legend.
If it's later than that, you'll think it mere myth.
But it happened. You, of all people, know this.
Yet you know nothing.
OH! BRÜN! LOOK, I AM FULL OF THE PRETTIES TOO!
FLÖKK. SILENCE. PLEASE.
The battle was legendary, but there is more than legend.
The battle was newsworthy, but there is certainly more than news.
The battle was tragic...and it was a tragedy.
SO NEAR I ALMOST HAVE THE TASTE OF IT...
But there is a land beyond legend and news and tragedy. There is a land even beyond truth. We live in that realm of mystery.
What did Loki do at the Battle of Broxton, in the final stand of god and men against the night eternal?
(Can you guess?)

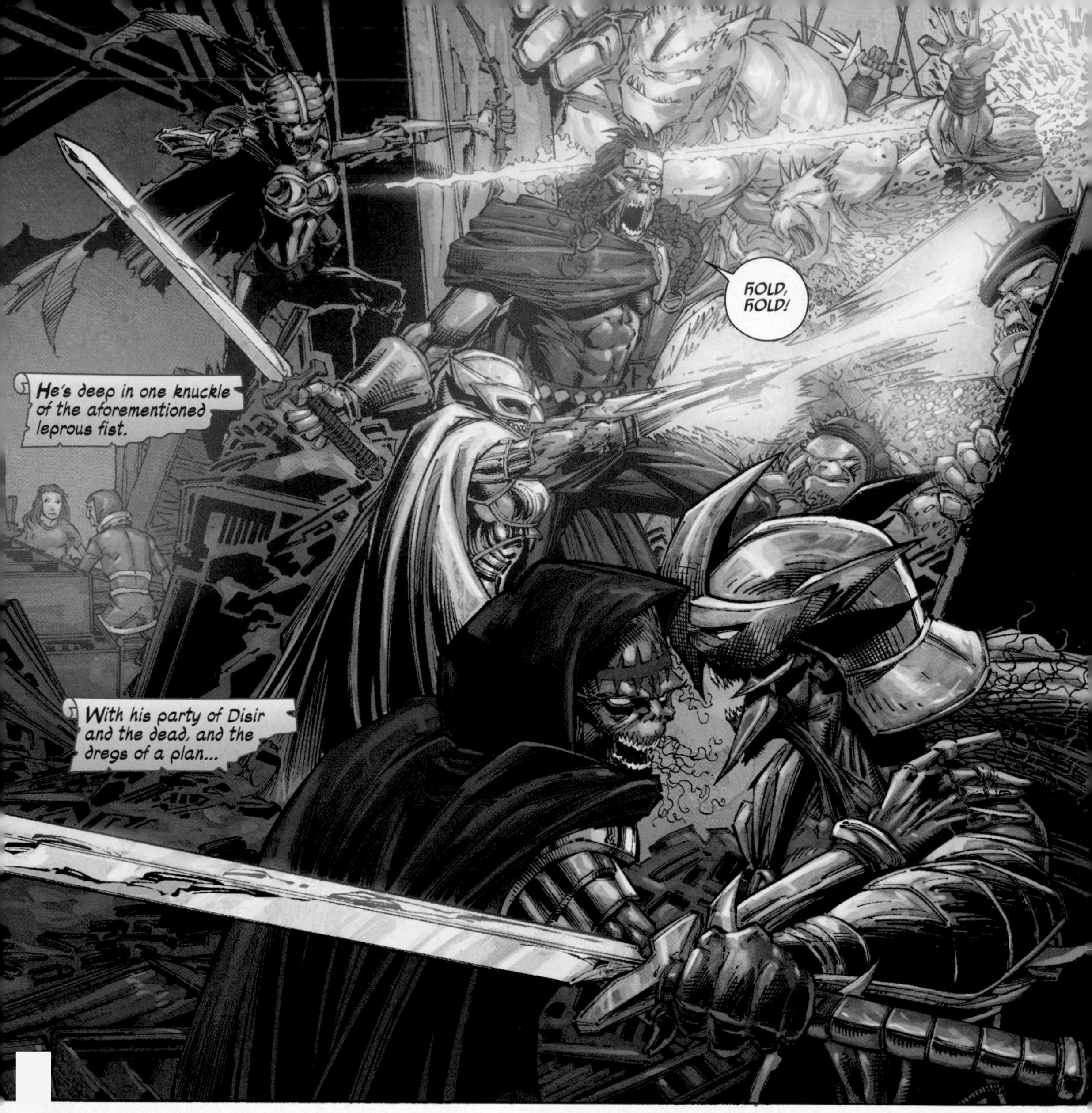
He's deep in one knuckle of the aforementioned leprous fist.
HOLD, HOLD!
With his party of Disir and the dead, and the dregs of a plan...

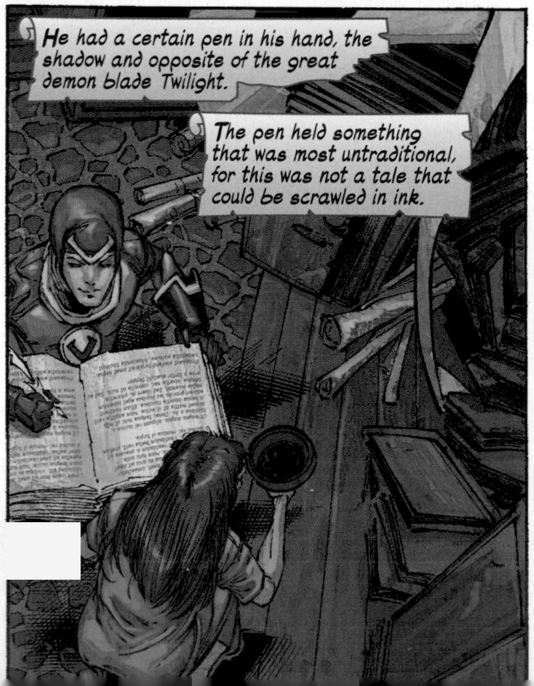
He had a certain pen in his hand, the shadow and opposite of the great demon blade Twilight.
The pen held something that was most untraditional, for this was not a tale that could be scrawled in ink.

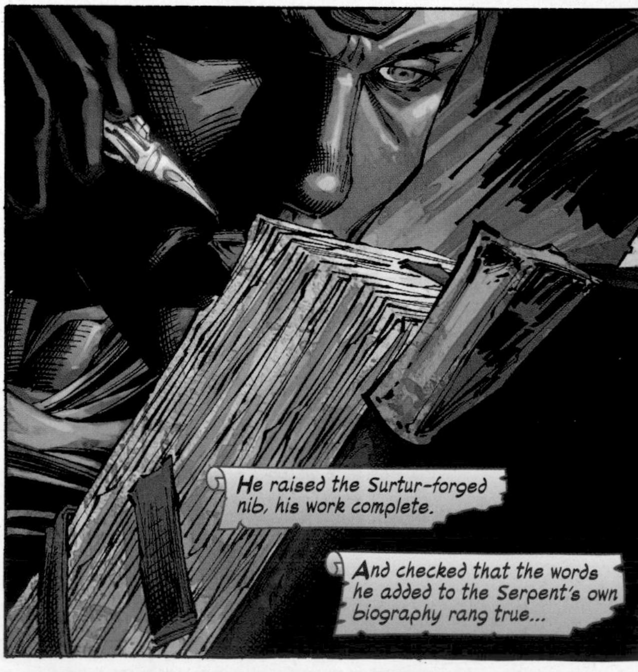
He raised the Surtur-forged nib, his work complete.
And checked that the words he added to the Serpent's own biography rang true...

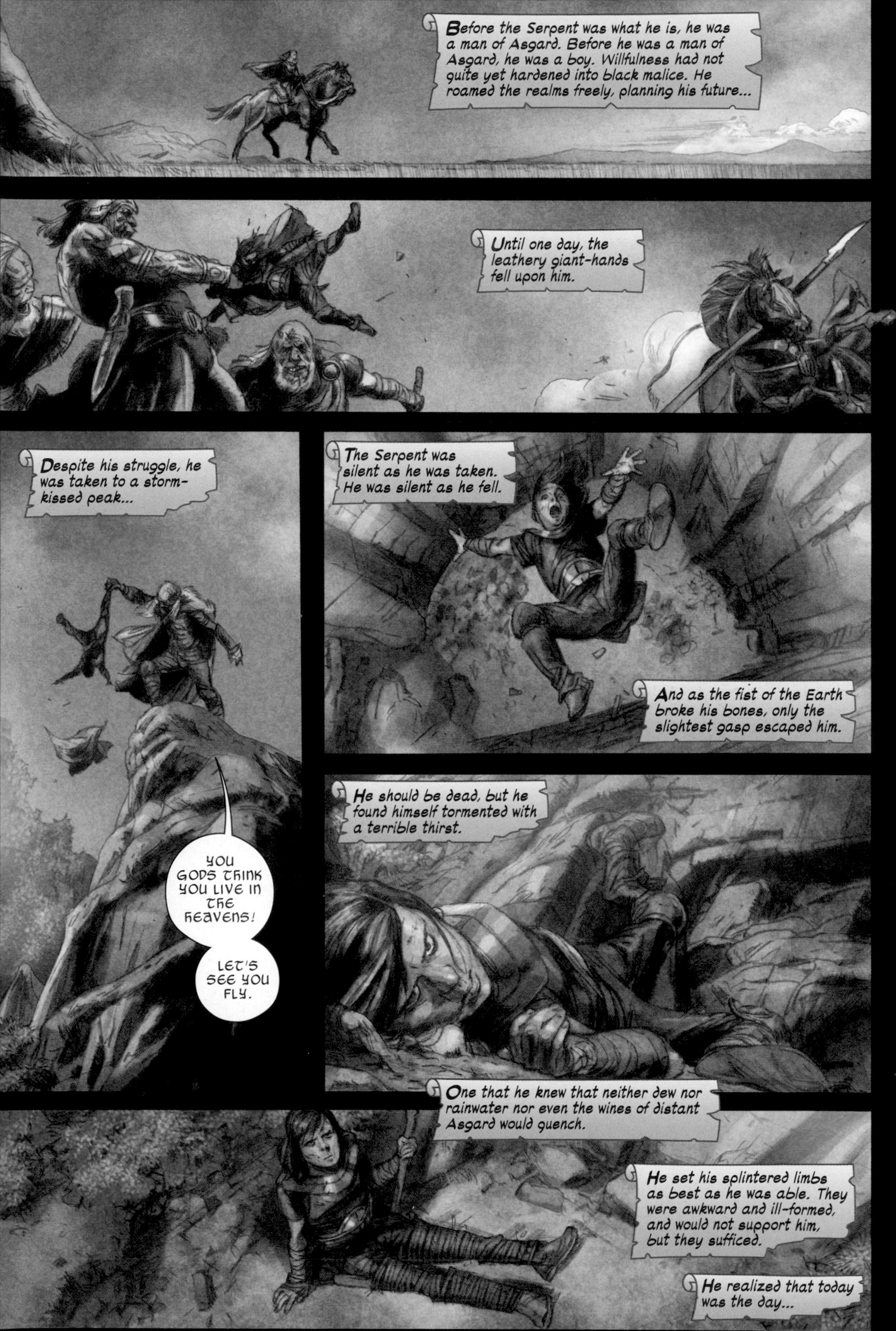

Before the Serpent was what he is, he was a man of Asgard. Before he was a man of Asgard, he was a boy. Willfulness had not quite yet hardened into black malice. He roamed the realms freely, planning his future...
Until one day, the leathery giant-hands fell upon him.
Despite his struggle, he was taken to a storm-kissed peak...
YOU GODS THINK YOU LIVE IN THE HEAVENS!
LET'S SEE YOU FLY.
The Serpent was silent as he was taken. He was silent as he fell.
And as the fist of the Earth broke his bones, only the slightest gasp escaped him.
He should be dead, but he found himself tormented with a terrible thirst.
One that he knew that neither dew nor rainwater nor even the wines of distant Asgard would quench.
He set his splintered limbs as best as he was able. They were awkward and ill-formed, and would not support him, but they sufficed.
He realized that today was the day...

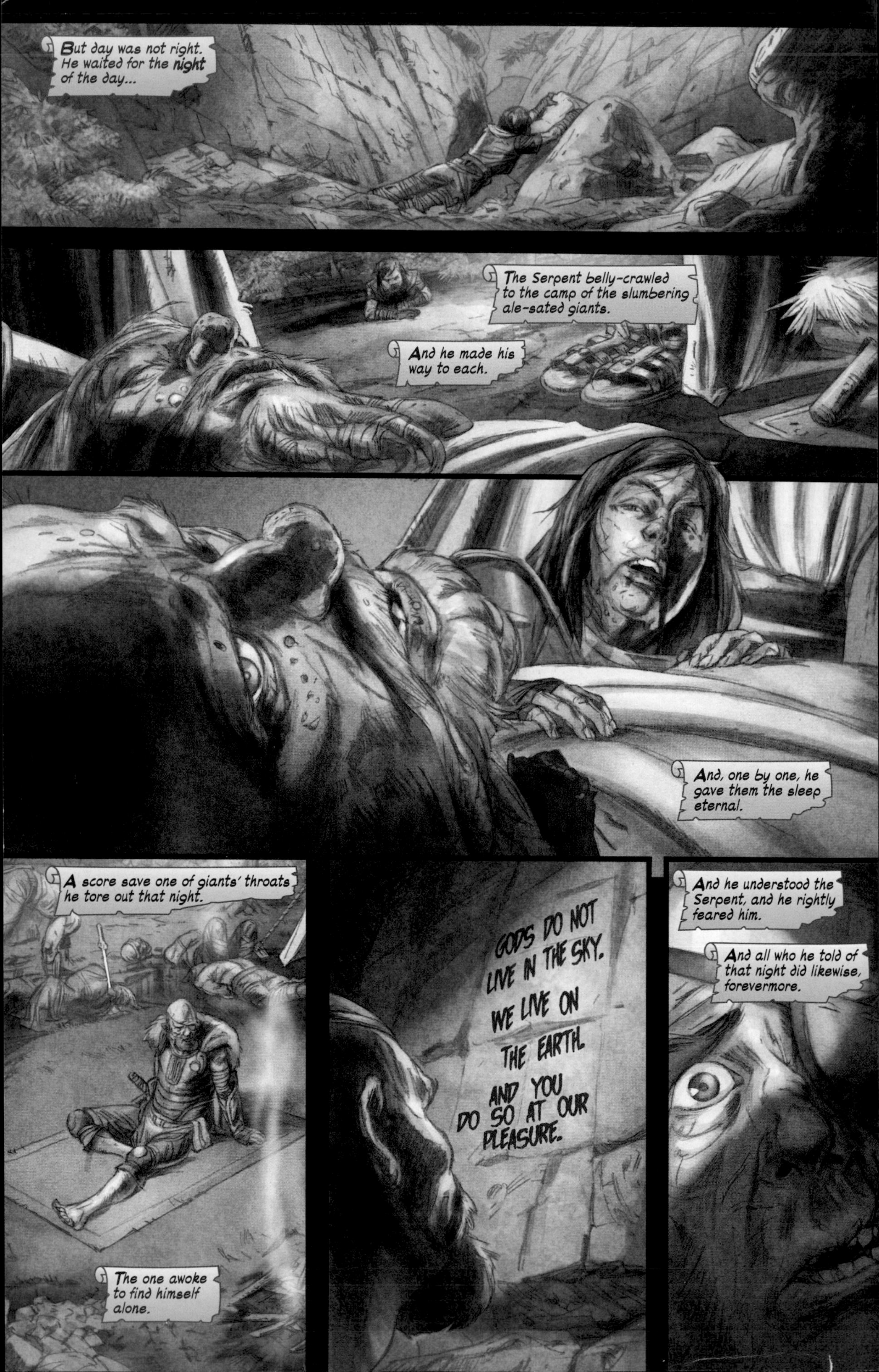
But day was not right. He waited for the night of the day...
The Serpent belly-crawled to the camp of the slumbering ale-sated giants.
And he made his way to each.
And, one by one, he gave them the sleep eternal.
A score save one of giants' throats he tore out that night.
The one awoke to find himself alone.
GODS DO NOT LIVE IN THE SKY. WE LIVE ON THE EARTH. AND YOU DO SO AT OUR PLEASURE.
And he understood the Serpent, and he rightly feared him.
And all who he told of that night did likewise, forevermore.

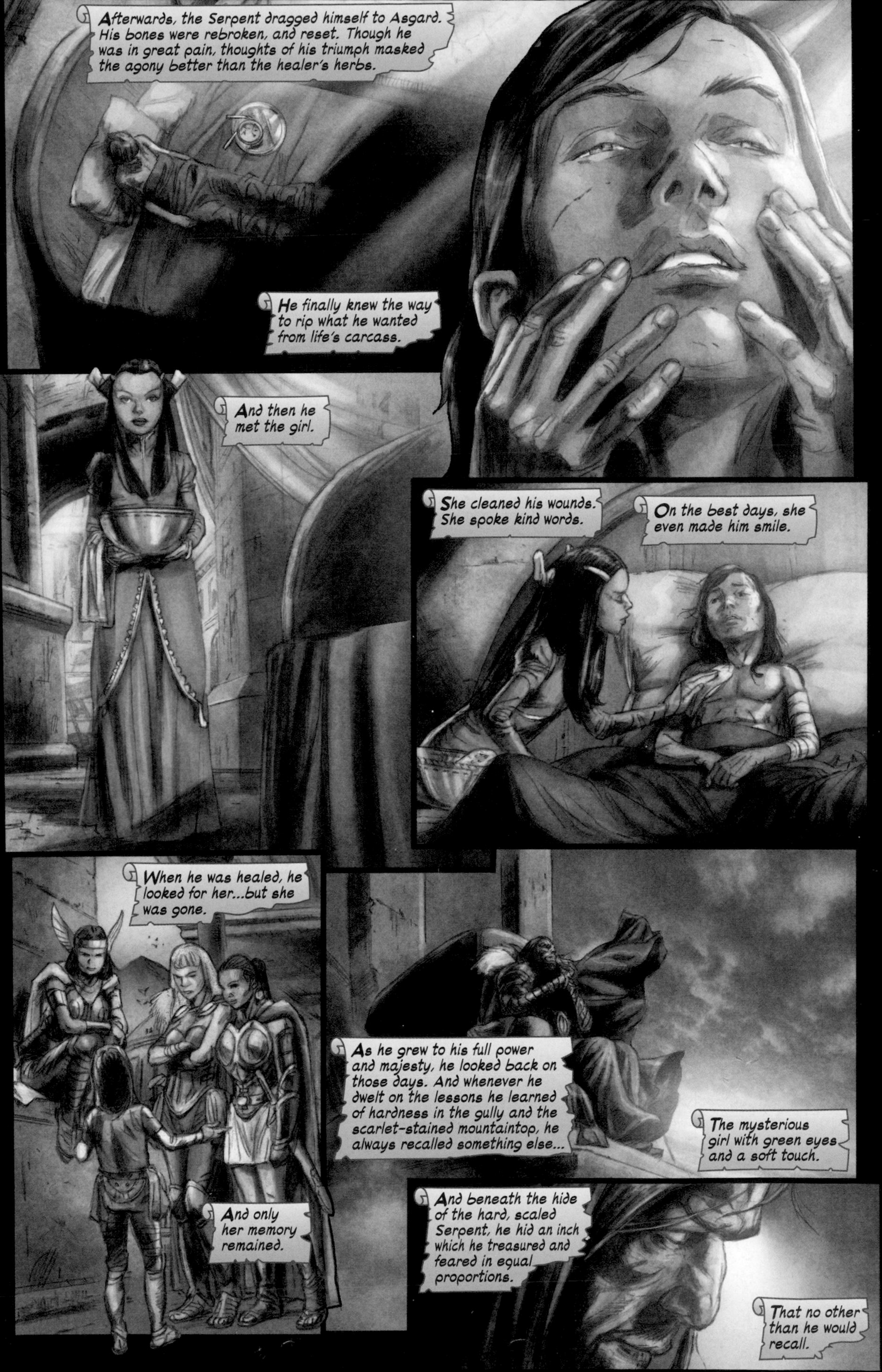
Afterwards, the Serpent dragged himself to Asgard. His bones were rebroken, and reset. Though he was in great pain, thoughts of his triumph masked the agony better than the healer's herbs.
He finally knew the way to rip what he wanted from life's carcass.
And then he met the girl.
She cleaned his wounds. She spoke kind words.
On the best days, she even made him smile.
When he was healed, he looked for her...but she was gone.
And only her memory remained.
As he grew to his full power and majesty, he looked back on those days. And whenever he dwelt on the lessons he learned of hardness in the gully and the scarlet-stained mountaintop, he always recalled something else...
The mysterious girl with green eyes and a soft touch.
And beneath the hide of the hard, scaled Serpent, he hid an inch which he treasured and feared in equal proportions.
That no other than he would recall.

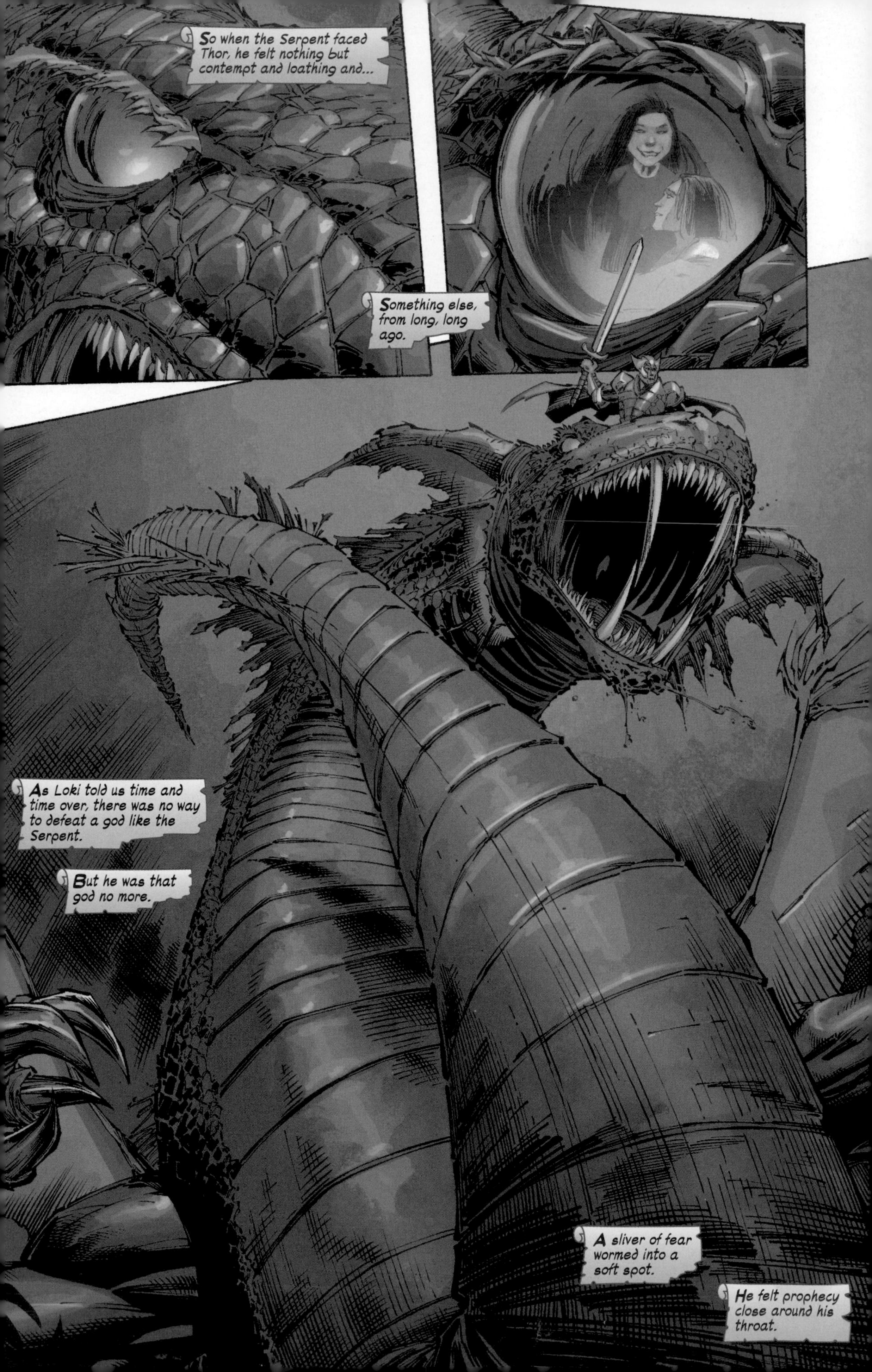
So when the Serpent faced Thor, he felt nothing but contempt and loathing and...
Something else, from long, long ago.
As Loki told us time and time over, there was no way to defeat a god like the Serpent.
But he was that god no more.
A sliver of fear wormed into a soft spot.
He felt prophecy close around his throat.

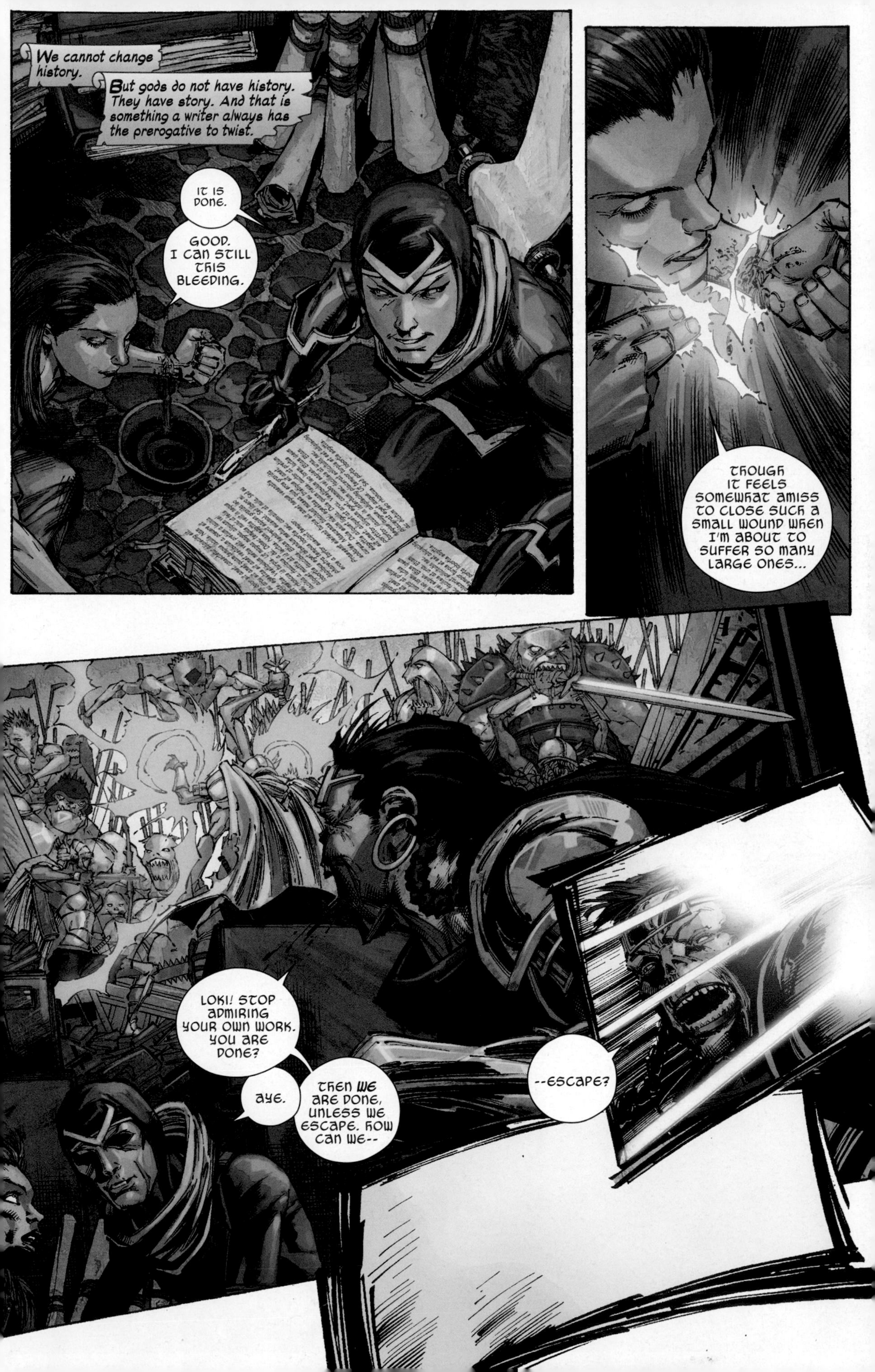
We cannot change history.
But gods do not have history. They have story. And that is something a writer always has the prerogative to twist.
IT IS DONE.
GOOD. I CAN STILL THIS BLEEDING.
THOUGH IT FEELS SOMEWHAT AMISS TO CLOSE SUCH A SMALL WOUND WHEN I'M ABOUT TO SUFFER SO MANY LARGE ONES...
LOKI! STOP ADMIRING YOUR OWN WORK. YOU ARE DONE?
AYE.
THEN WE ARE DONE, UNLESS WE ESCAPE. HOW CAN WE--
--ESCAPE?

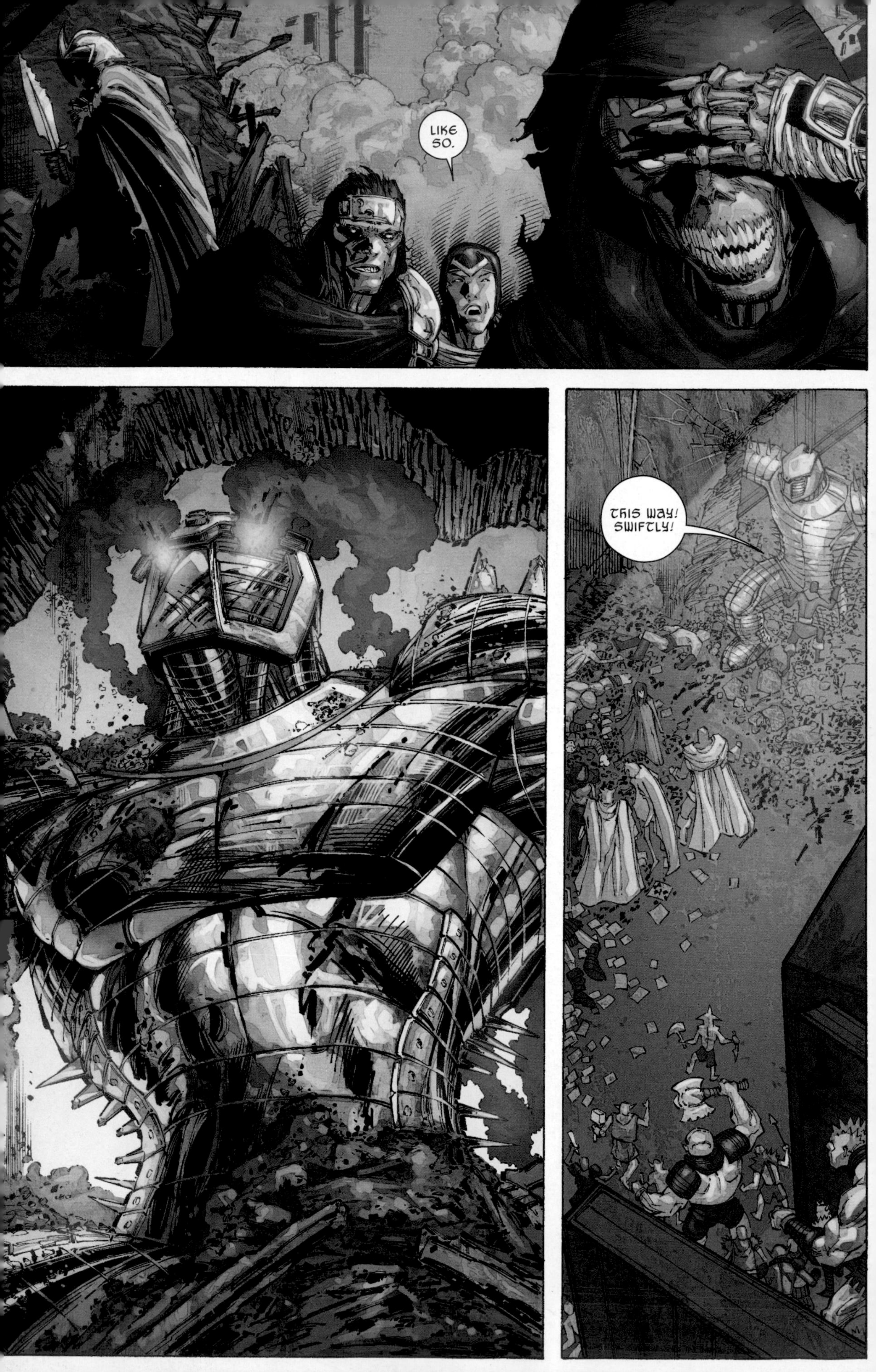
LIKE SO.
THIS WAY! SWIFTLY!

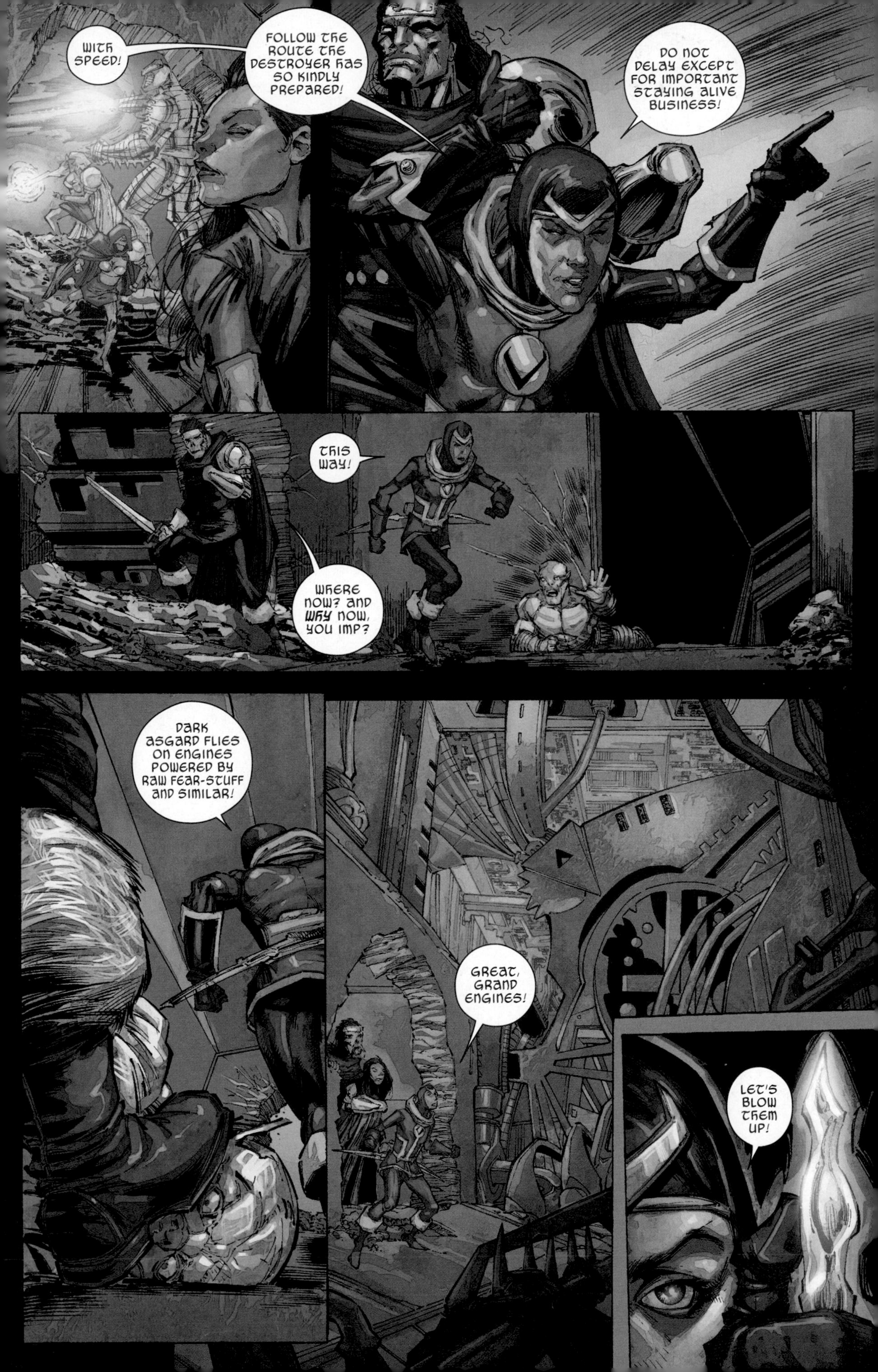
WITH SPEED!
FOLLOW THE ROUTE THE DESTROYER HAS SO KINDLY PREPARED!
DO NOT DELAY EXCEPT FOR IMPORTANT STAYING ALIVE BUSINESS!
THIS WAY!
WHERE NOW? AND WHY NOW, YOU IMP?
DARK ASGARD FLIES ON ENGINES POWERED BY RAW FEAR-STUFF AND SIMILAR!
GREAT, GRAND ENGINES!
LET'S BLOW THEM UP!

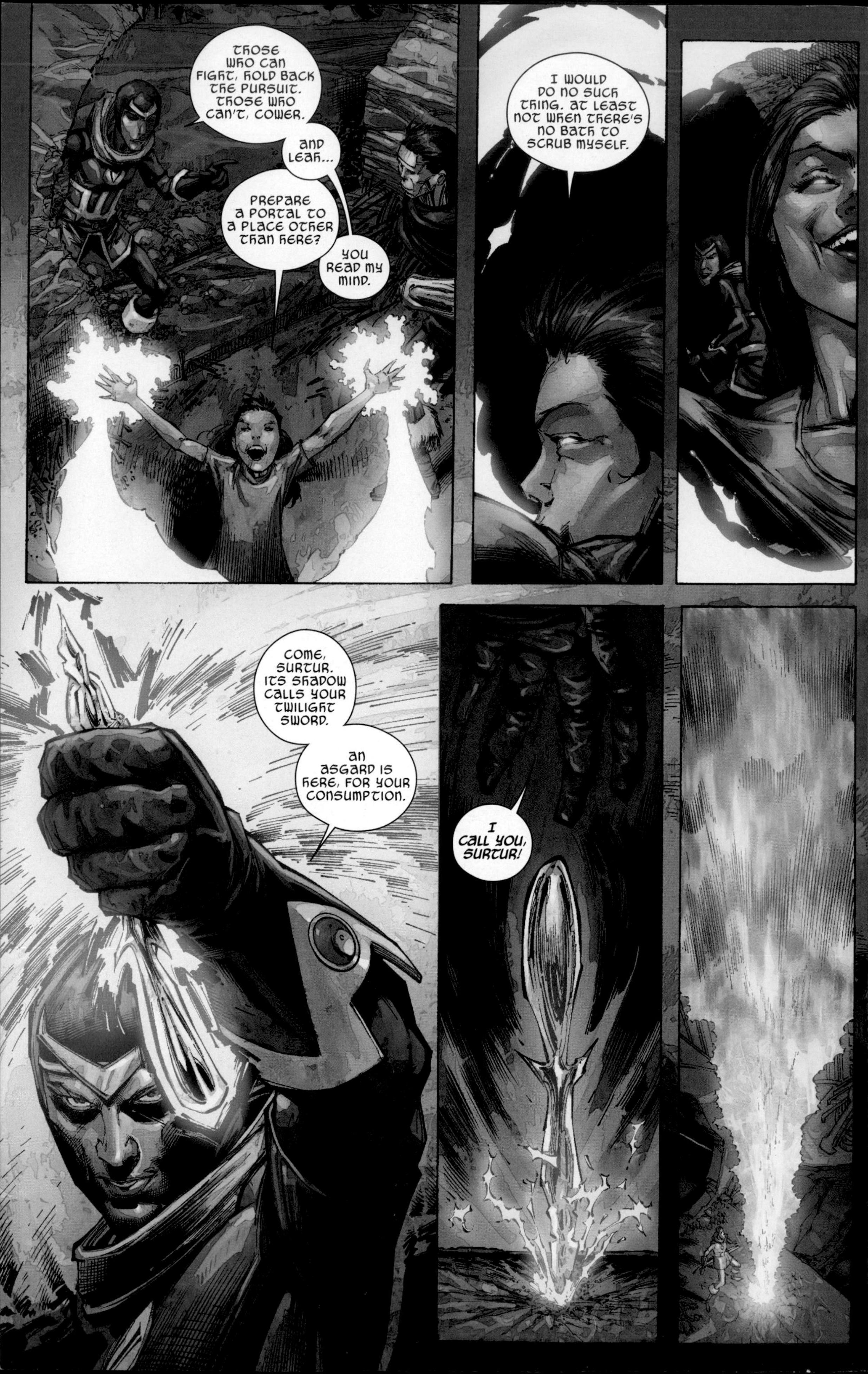
THOSE WHO CAN FIGHT, HOLD BACK THE PURSUIT. THOSE WHO CAN'T, COWER.
AND LEAH...
PREPARE A PORTAL TO A PLACE OTHER THAN HERE?
YOU READ MY MIND.
I WOULD DO NO SUCH THING. AT LEAST NOT WHEN THERE'S NO BATH TO SCRUB MYSELF.
COME, SURTUR. ITS SHADOW CALLS YOUR TWILIGHT SWORD.
AN ASGARD IS HERE, FOR YOUR CONSUMPTION.
I CALL YOU, SURTUR!

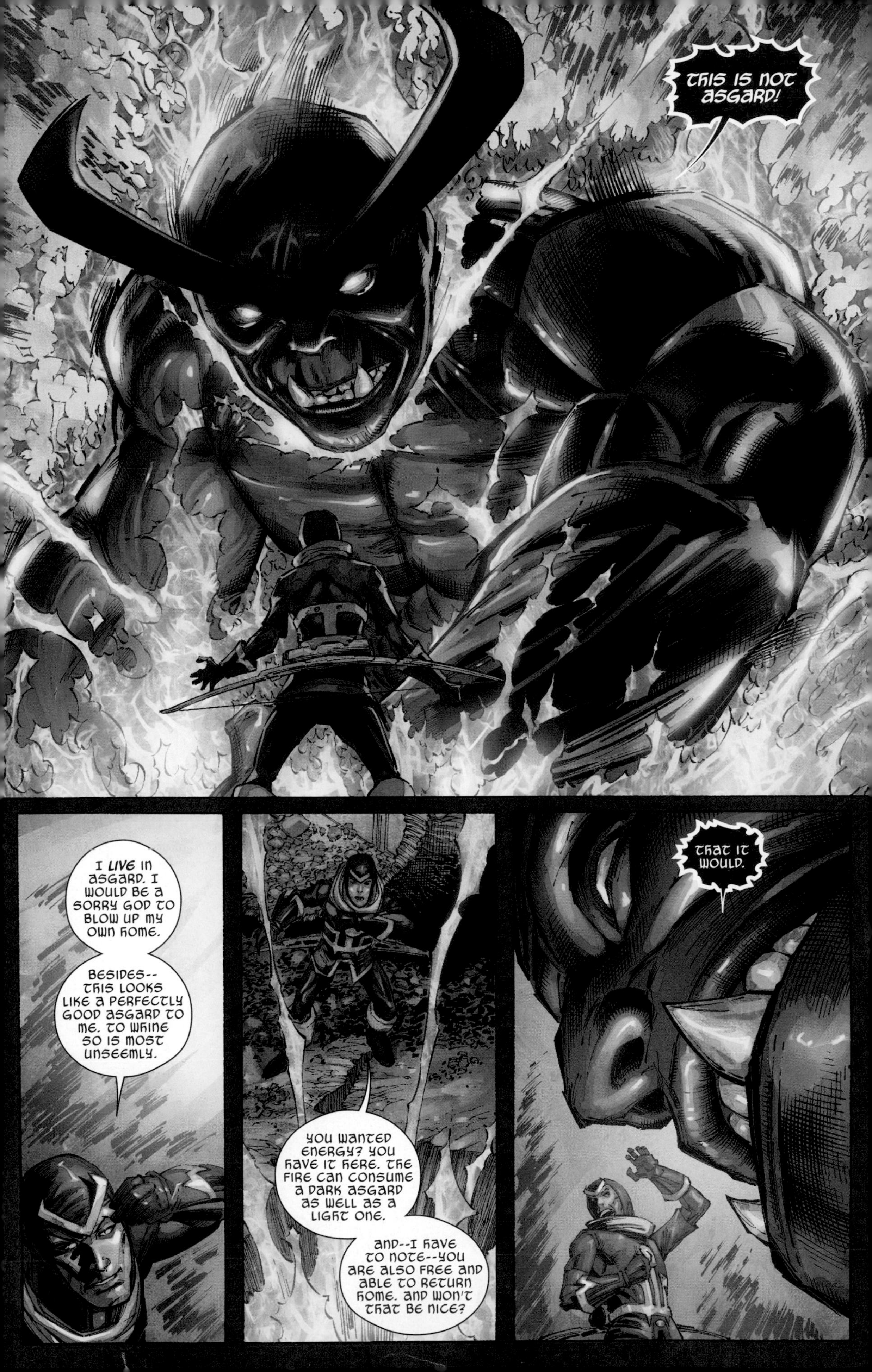
THIS IS NOT ASGARD!
I LIVE IN ASGARD. I WOULD BE A SORRY GOD TO BLOW UP MY OWN HOME.
BESIDES-- THIS LOOKS LIKE A PERFECTLY GOOD ASGARD TO ME. TO WHINE SO IS MOST UNSEEMLY.
YOU WANTED ENERGY? YOU HAVE IT HERE. THE FIRE CAN CONSUME A DARK ASGARD AS WELL AS A LIGHT ONE.
AND--I HAVE TO NOTE--YOU ARE ALSO FREE AND ABLE TO RETURN HOME. AND WON'T THAT BE NICE?
THAT IT WOULD.

A PLEASURE DOING BUSINESS WITH YOU.

FREE! FREE!

The lord-in-exile of Muspelheim turned and consumed the heart of the city... ...and a city is much like a bird...

...with no heart, it cannot hope to fly.

We are approaching the end of things.

Elsewhere, fate battles hope. And Loki realizes... .

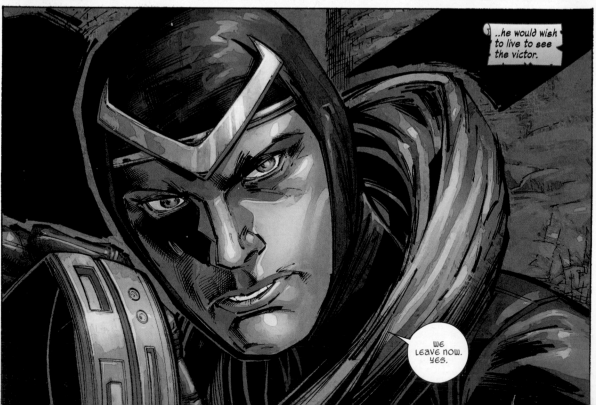

..he would wish to live to see the victor.

WE LEAVE NOW. YES.

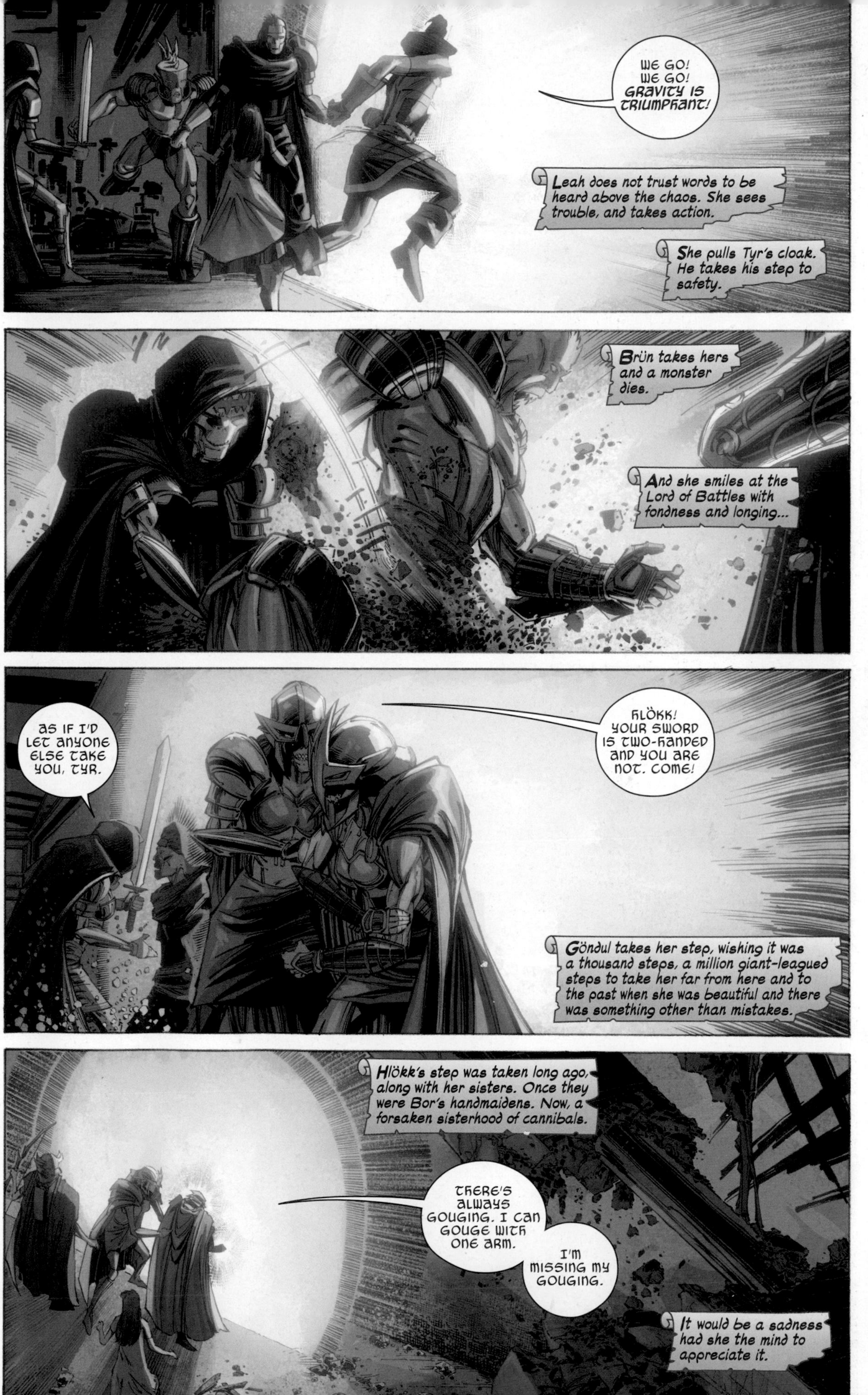
WE GO! WE GO! GRAVITY IS TRIUMPHANT!
Leah does not trust words to be heard above the chaos. She sees trouble, and takes action.
She pulls Tyr's cloak. He takes his step to safety.
Brün takes hers and a monster dies.
And she smiles at the Lord of Battles with fondness and longing...
AS IF I'D LET ANYONE ELSE TAKE YOU, TYR.
HLÖKK! YOUR SWORD IS TWO-HANDED AND YOU ARE NOT. COME!
Göndul takes her step, wishing it was a thousand steps, a million giant-leagued steps to take her far from here and to the past when she was beautiful and there was something other than mistakes.
Hlökk's step was taken long ago, along with her sisters. Once they were Bor's handmaidens. Now, a forsaken sisterhood of cannibals.
THERE'S ALWAYS GOUGING. I CAN GOUGE WITH ONE ARM.
I'M MISSING MY GOUGING.
It would be a sadness had she the mind to appreciate it.

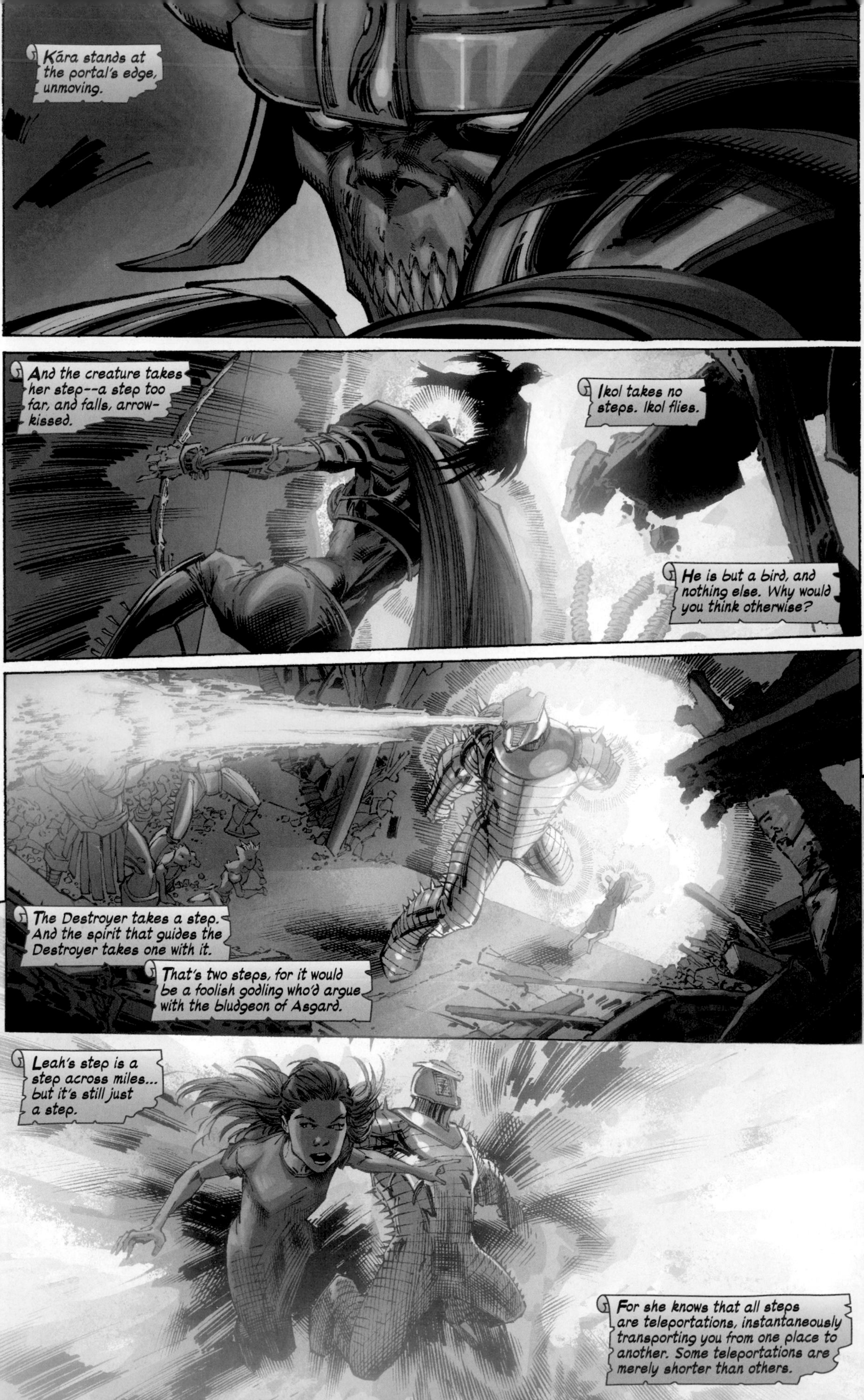

Kāra stands at the portal's edge, unmoving.
And the creature takes her step--a step too far, and falls, arrow-kissed.
Ikol takes no steps. Ikol flies.
He is but a bird, and nothing else. Why would you think otherwise?
The Destroyer takes a step. And the spirit that guides the Destroyer takes one with it.
That's two steps, for it would be a foolish godling who'd argue with the bludgeon of Asgard.
Leah's step is a step across miles... but it's still just a step.
For she knows that all steps are teleportations, instantaneously transporting you from one place to another. Some teleportations are merely shorter than others.

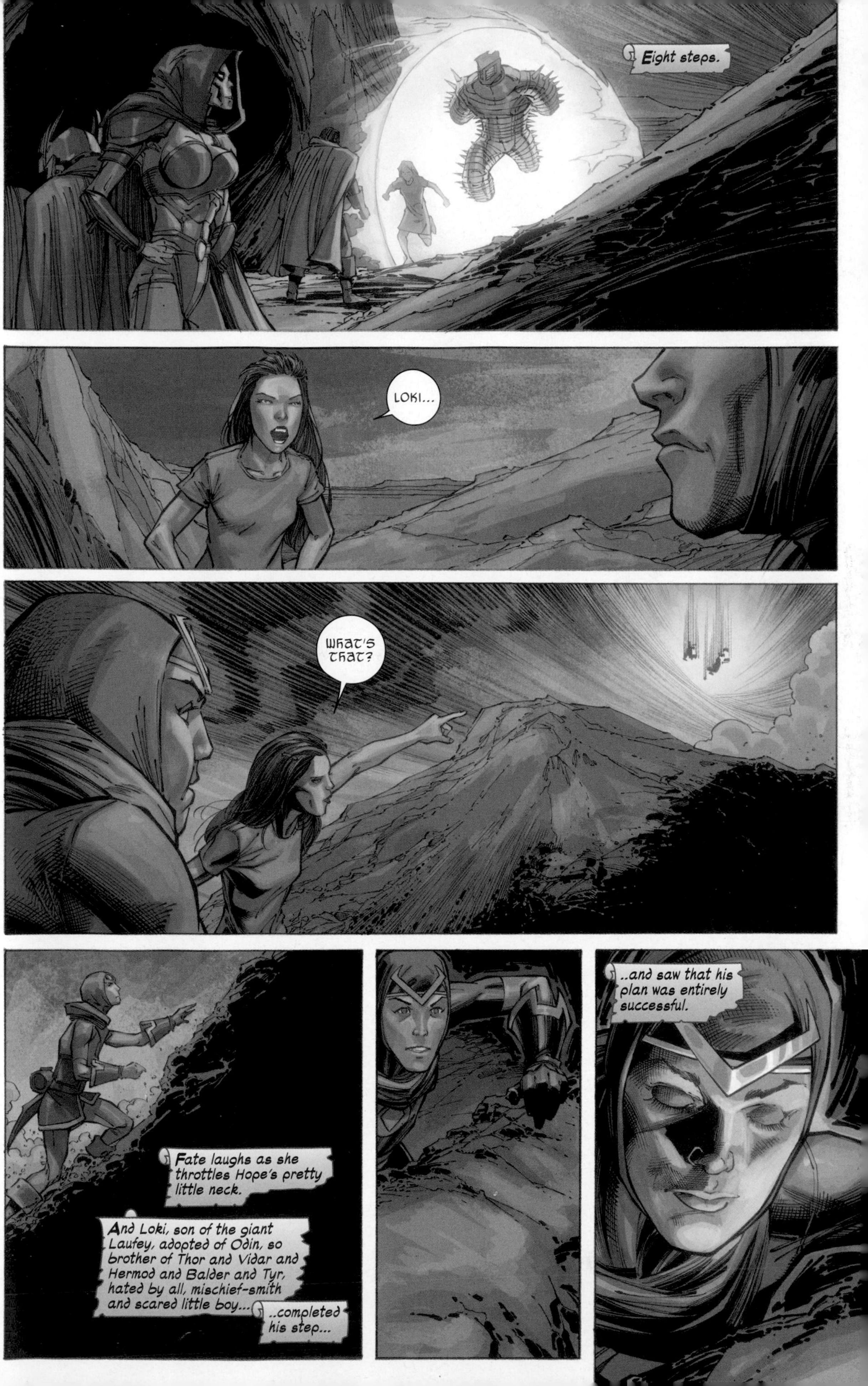
Eight steps.
LOKI...
WHAT'S THAT?
Fate laughs as she throttles Hope's pretty little neck.
And Loki, son of the giant Laufey, adopted of Odin, so brother of Thor and Vidar and Hermod and Balder and Tyr, hated by all, mischief-smith and scared little boy...
..completed his step...
..and saw that his plan was entirely successful.

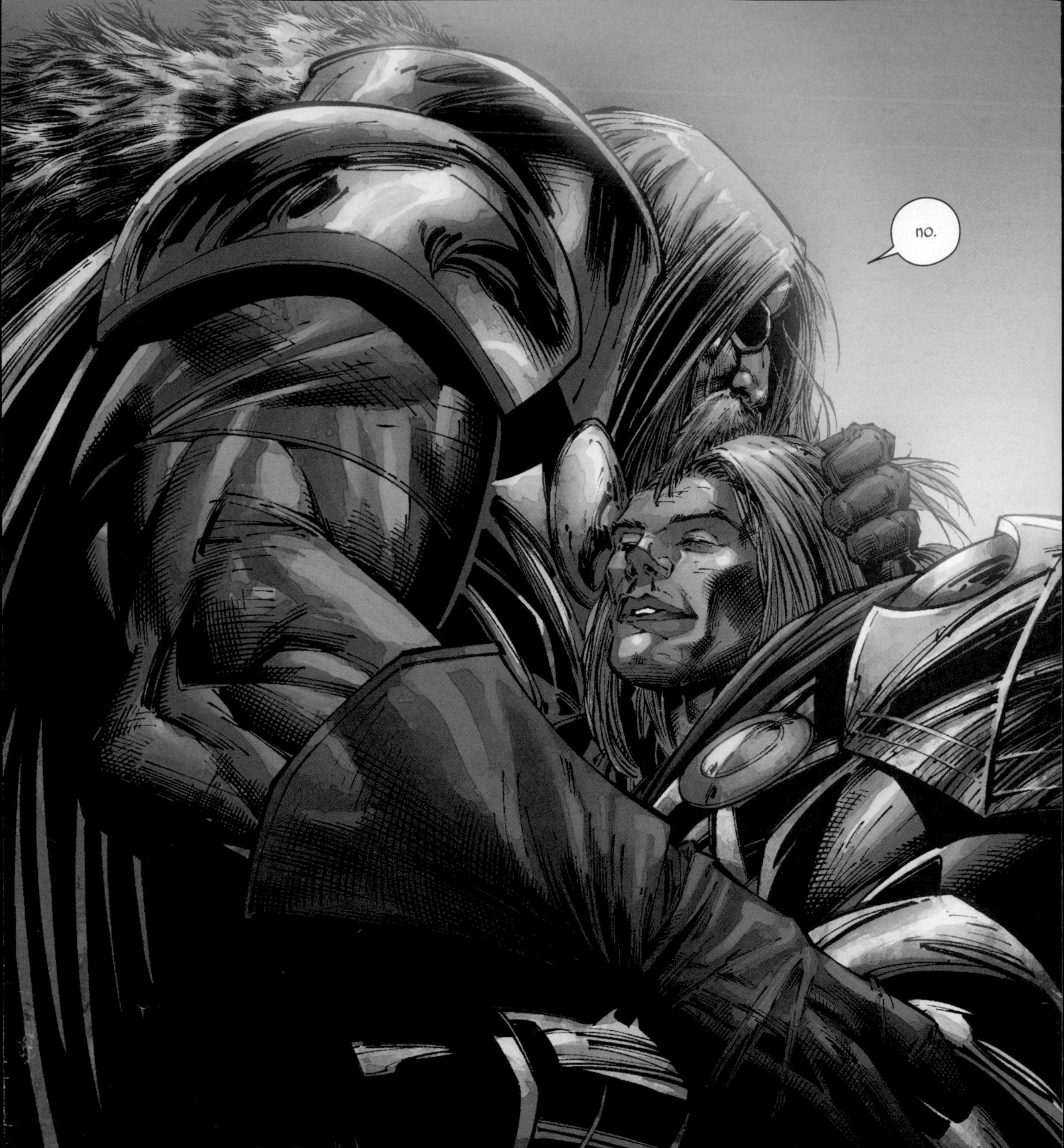
no.

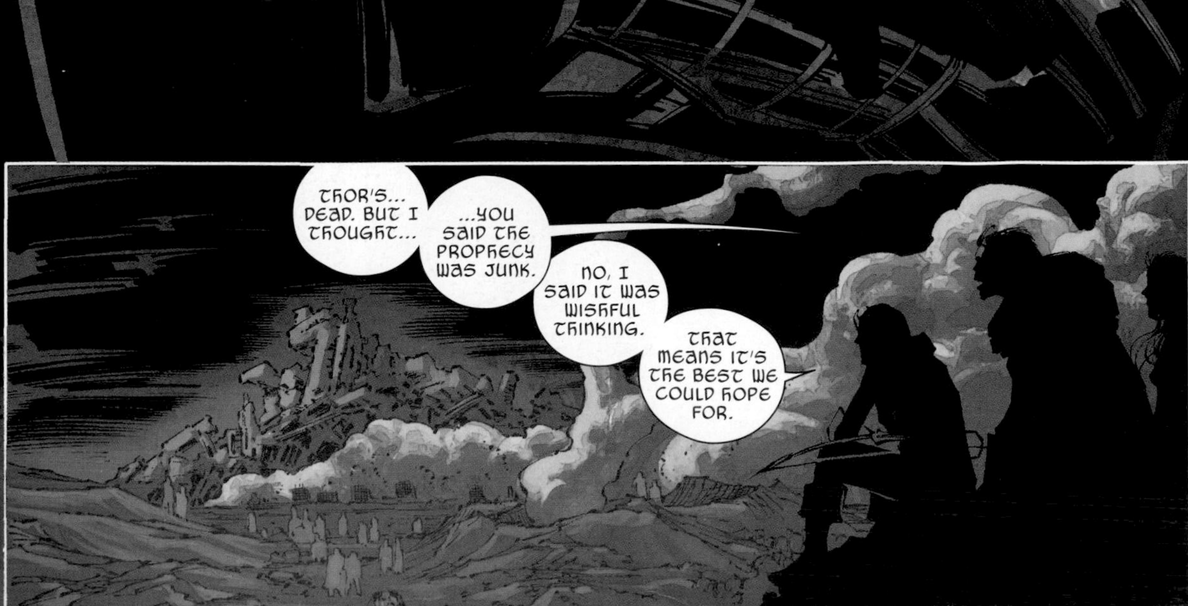
THOR'S... DEAD. BUT I THOUGHT...
...YOU SAID THE PROPHECY WAS JUNK.
NO, I SAID IT WAS WISHFUL THINKING.
THAT MEANS IT'S THE BEST WE COULD HOPE FOR.

EVERYTHING HAS ITS COST. THE SERPENT'S LIFE FOR THOR'S.

I KNEW IT ALL ALONG. WHAT DO YOU THINK THE WORLD TREE TOLD ME?

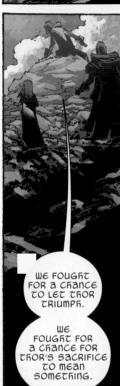

WE FOUGHT FOR A CHANCE TO LET THOR TRIUMPH.

WE FOUGHT FOR A CHANCE FOR THOR'S SACRIFICE TO MEAN SOMETHING.

AYE. SO I GUESS WE WON.

YOU FOUGHT FOR A CHANCE FOR YOUR BROTHER TO DIE.

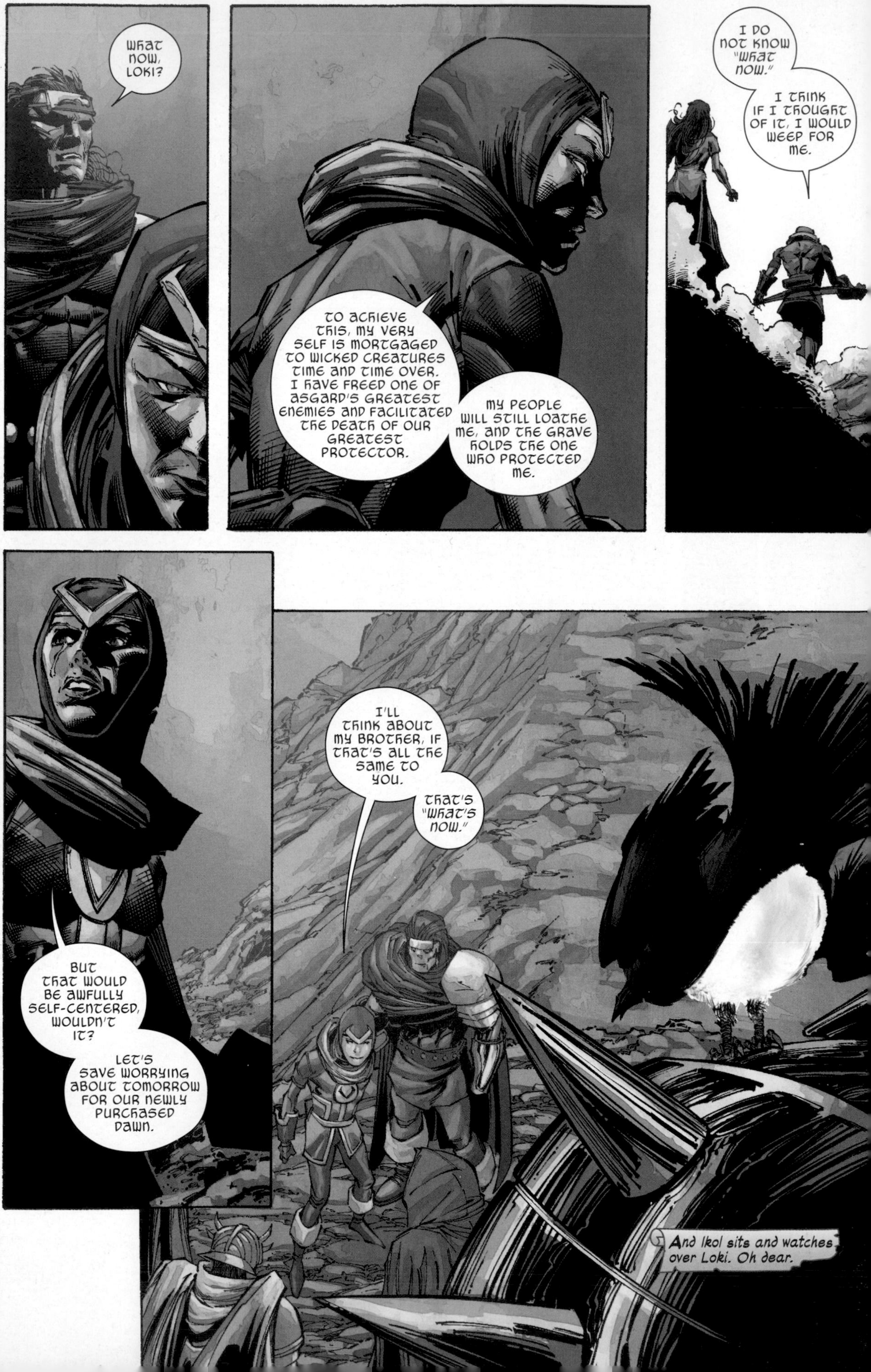
WHAT NOW, LOKI?
TO ACHIEVE THIS, MY VERY SELF IS MORTGAGED TO WICKED CREATURES TIME AND TIME OVER. I HAVE FREED ONE OF ASGARD'S GREATEST ENEMIES AND FACILITATED THE DEATH OF OUR GREATEST PROTECTOR.
MY PEOPLE WILL STILL LOATHE ME, AND THE GRAVE HOLDS THE ONE WHO PROTECTED ME.
I DO NOT KNOW "WHAT NOW."
I THINK IF I THOUGHT OF IT, I WOULD WEEP FOR ME.
BUT THAT WOULD BE AWFULLY SELF-CENTERED, WOULDN'T IT?
LET'S SAVE WORRYING ABOUT TOMORROW FOR OUR NEWLY PURCHASED DAWN.
I'LL THINK ABOUT MY BROTHER, IF THAT'S ALL THE SAME TO YOU.
THAT'S "WHAT'S NOW."
And Ikol sits and watches over Loki. Oh dear.

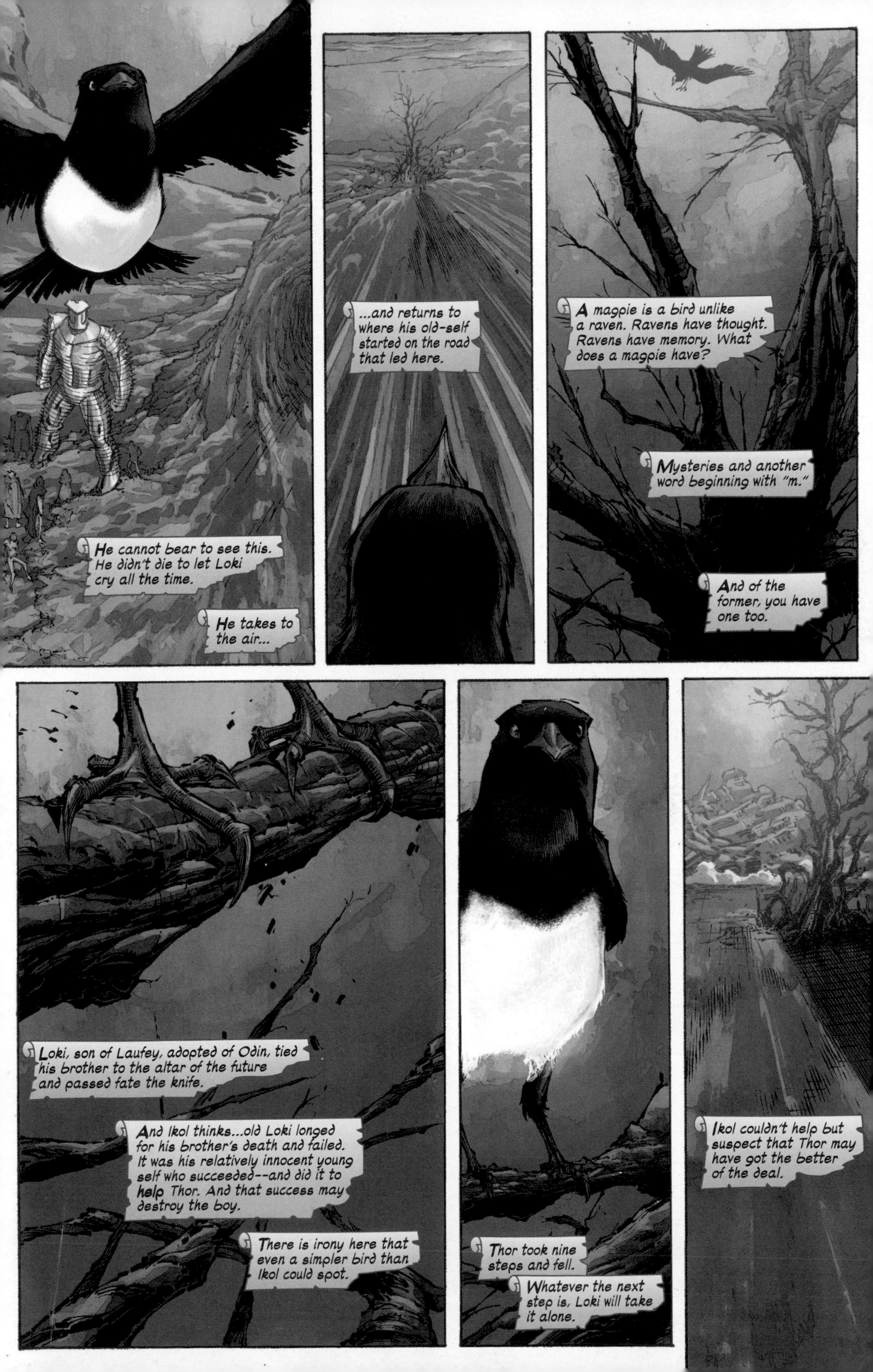
He cannot bear to see this. He didn't die to let Loki cry all the time.
He takes to the air...
...and returns to where his old-self started on the road that led here.
A magpie is a bird unlike a raven. Ravens have thought. Ravens have memory. What does a magpie have?
Mysteries and another word beginning with "m."
And of the former, you have one too.
Loki, son of Laufey, adopted of Odin, tied his brother to the altar of the future and passed fate the knife.
And Ikol thinks...old Loki longed for his brother's death and failed. It was his relatively innocent young self who succeeded--and did it to help Thor. And that success may destroy the boy.
There is irony here that even a simpler bird than Ikol could spot.
Thor took nine steps and fell.
Whatever the next step is, Loki will take it alone.
Ikol couldn't help but suspect that Thor may have got the better of the deal.

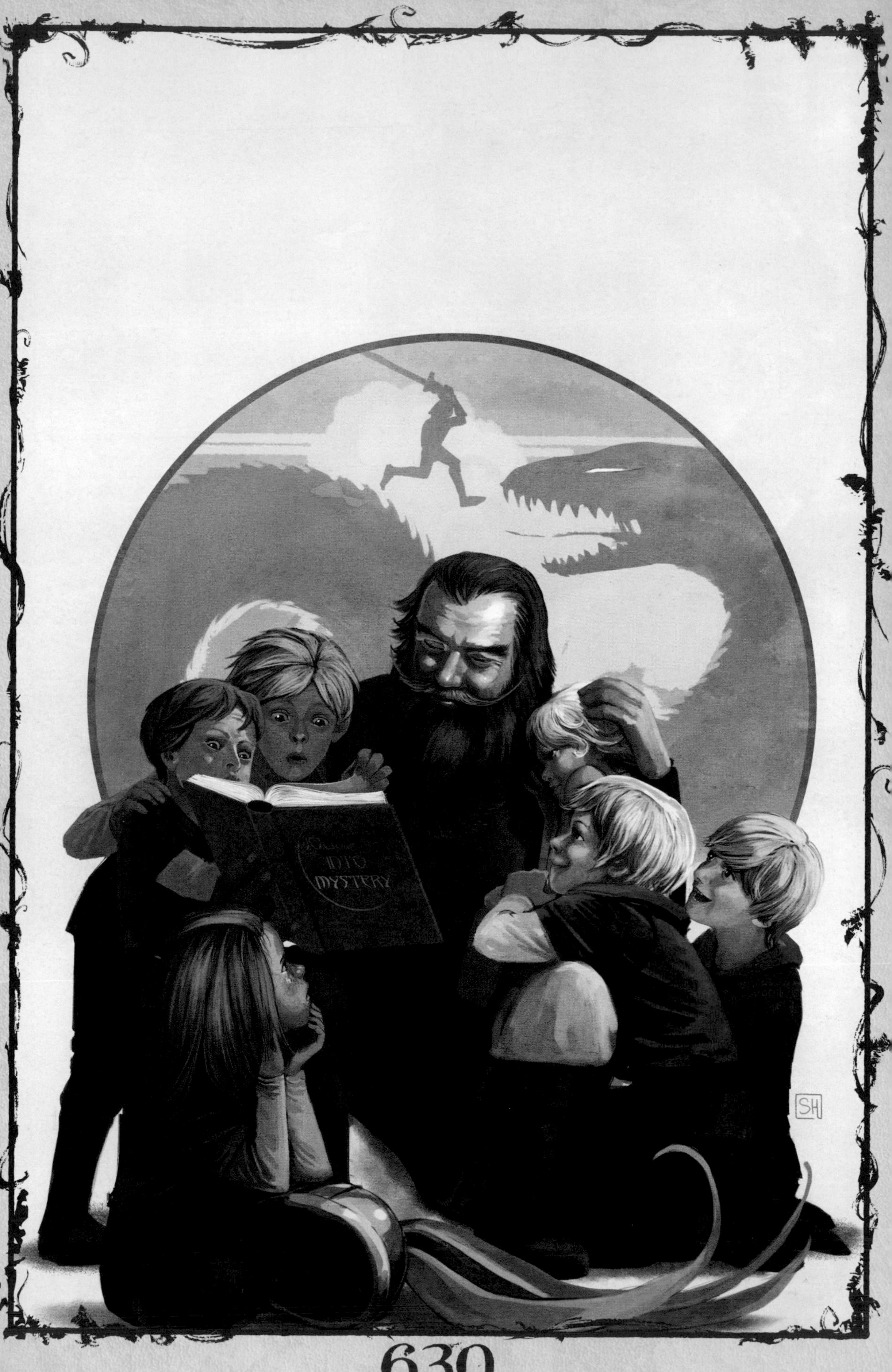
INTO
MYSTERY
SH

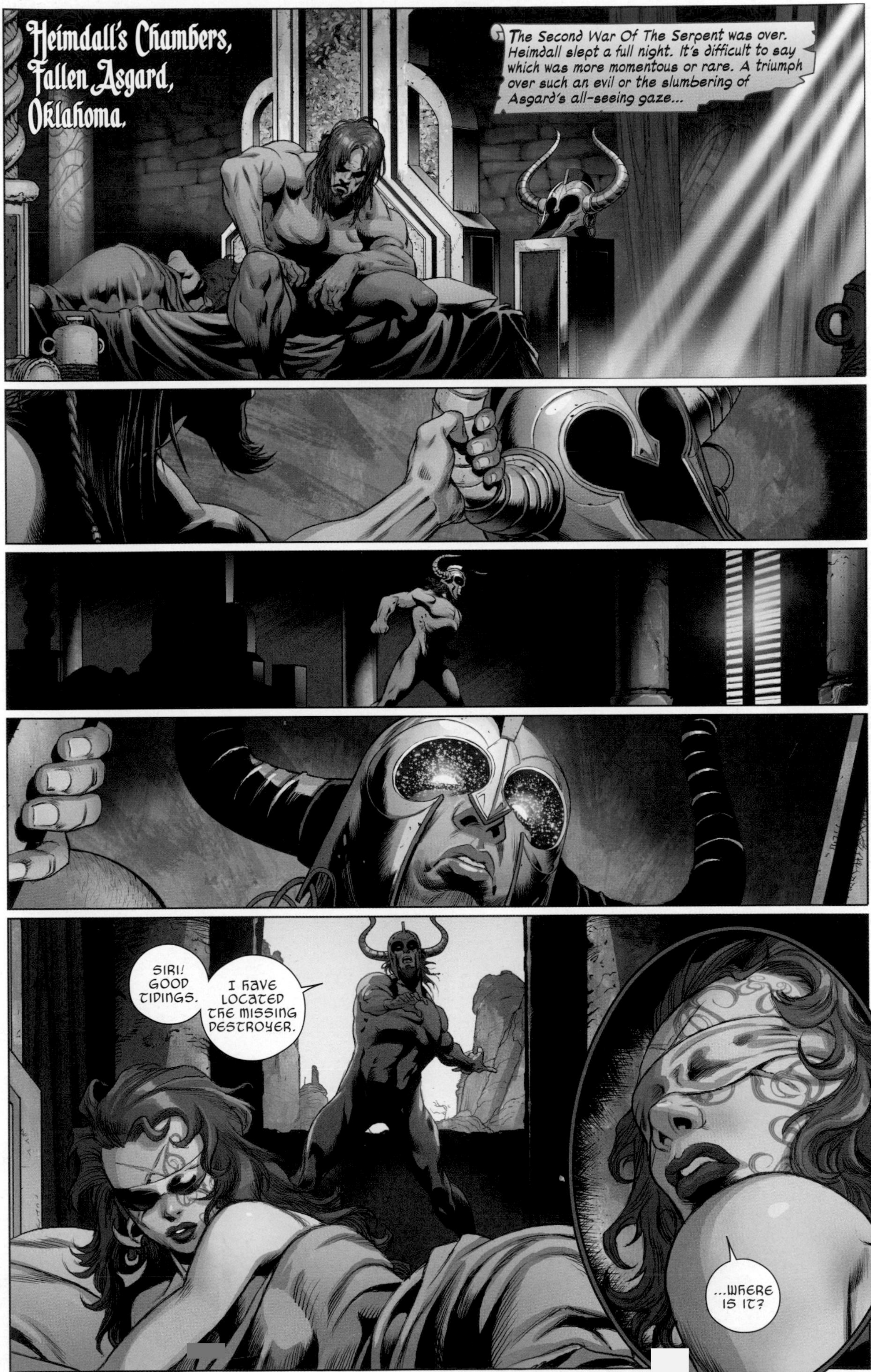

Heimdall's Chambers, Fallen Asgard, Oklahoma.
The Second War Of The Serpent was over. Heimdall slept a full night. It's difficult to say which was more momentous or rare. A triumph over such an evil or the slumbering of Asgard's all-seeing gaze...
SIRI! GOOD TIDINGS.
I HAVE LOCATED THE MISSING DESTROYER.
...WHERE IS IT?

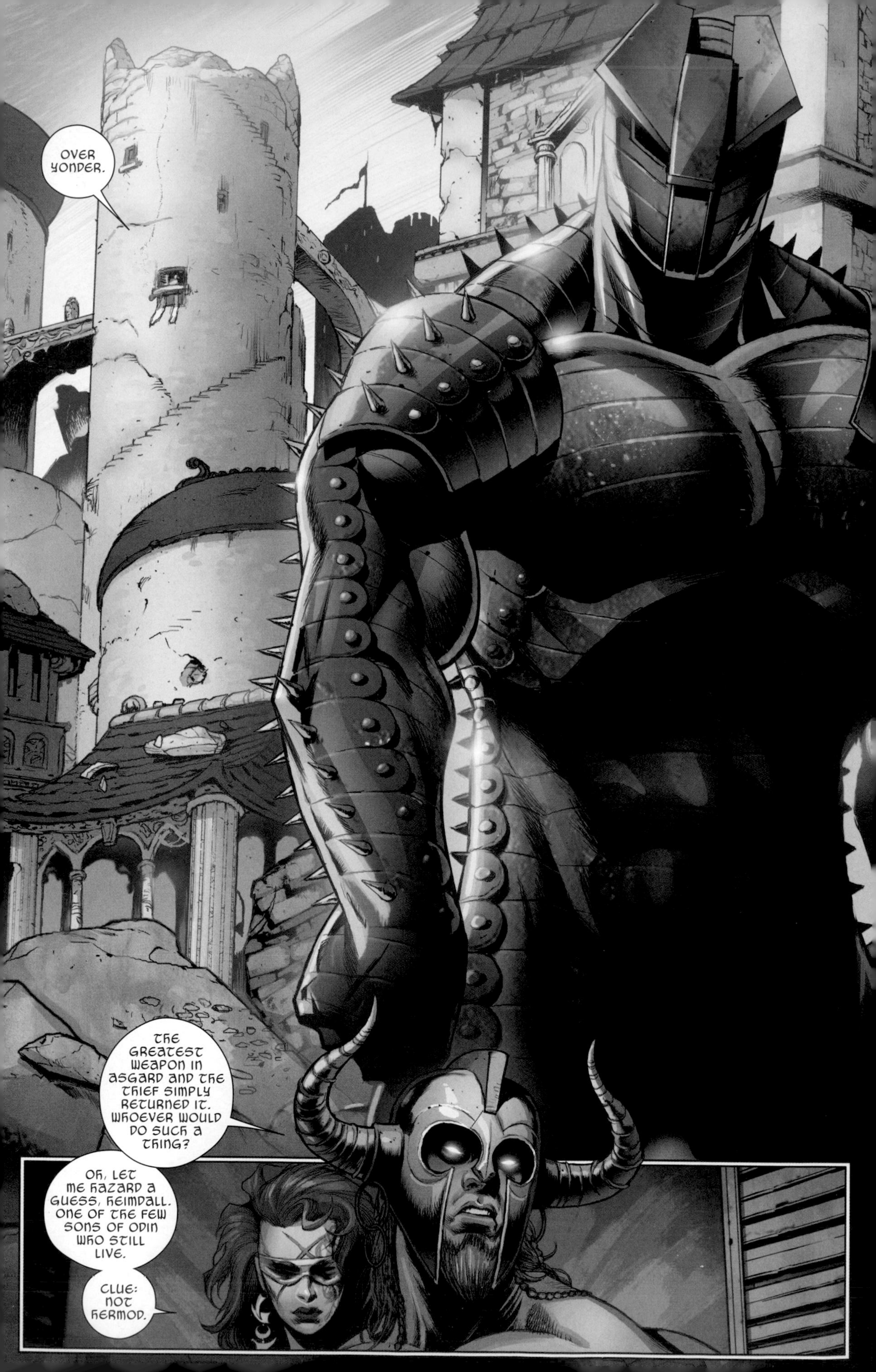
OVER YONDER.
THE GREATEST WEAPON IN ASGARD AND THE THIEF SIMPLY RETURNED IT. WHOEVER WOULD DO SUCH A THING?
OH, LET ME HAZARD A GUESS, HEIMDALL. ONE OF THE FEW SONS OF ODIN WHO STILL LIVE.
CLUE: NOT HERMOD.

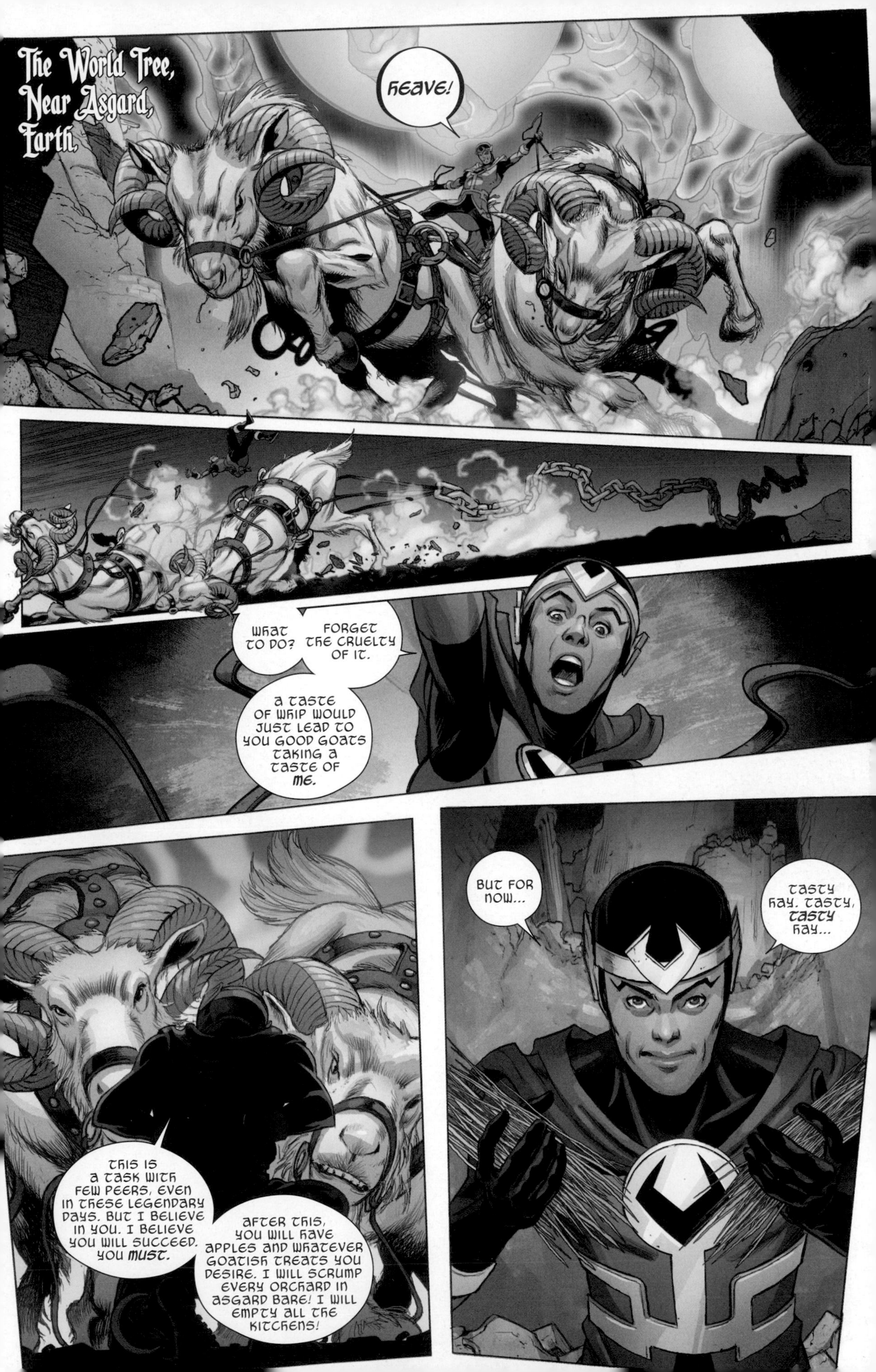
The World Tree, Near Asgard, Earth.
HEAVE!
WHAT TO DO?
FORGET THE CRUELTY OF IT.
A TASTE OF WHIP WOULD JUST LEAD TO YOU GOOD GOATS TAKING A TASTE OF ME.
THIS IS A TASK WITH FEW PEERS, EVEN IN THESE LEGENDARY DAYS. BUT I BELIEVE IN YOU. I BELIEVE YOU WILL SUCCEED. YOU MUST.
AFTER THIS, YOU WILL HAVE APPLES AND WHATEVER GOATISH TREATS YOU DESIRE. I WILL SCRUMP EVERY ORCHARD IN ASGARD BARE! I WILL EMPTY ALL THE KITCHENS!
BUT FOR NOW...
TASTY HAY. TASTY, TASTY HAY...

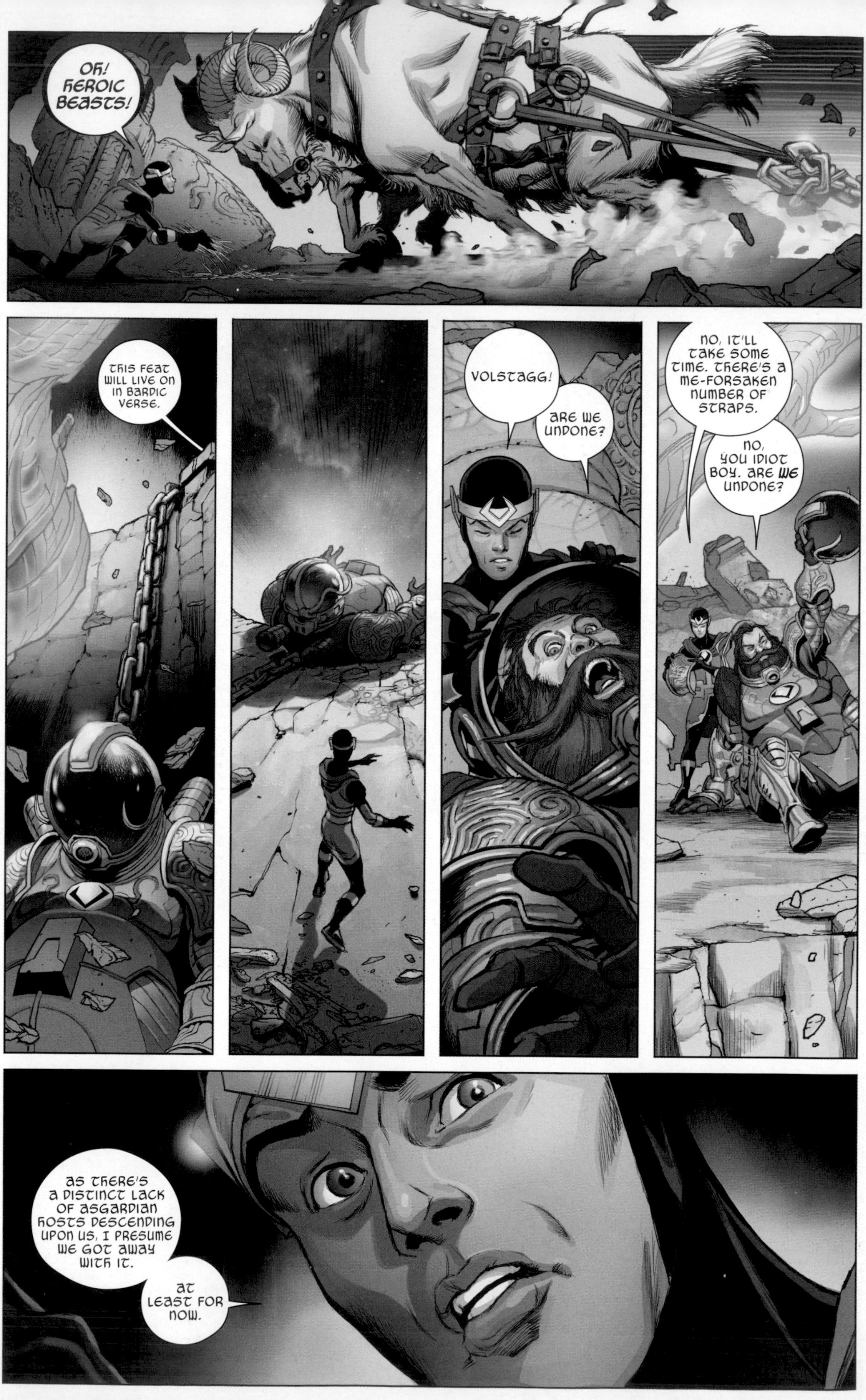
OH! HEROIC BEASTS!
THIS FEAT WILL LIVE ON IN BARDIC VERSE.
VOLSTAGG!
ARE WE UNDONE?
NO, IT'LL TAKE SOME TIME. THERE'S A ME-FORSAKEN NUMBER OF STRAPS.
NO, YOU IDIOT BOY. ARE WE UNDONE?
AS THERE'S A DISTINCT LACK OF ASGARDIAN HOSTS DESCENDING UPON US, I PRESUME WE GOT AWAY WITH IT.
AT LEAST FOR NOW.

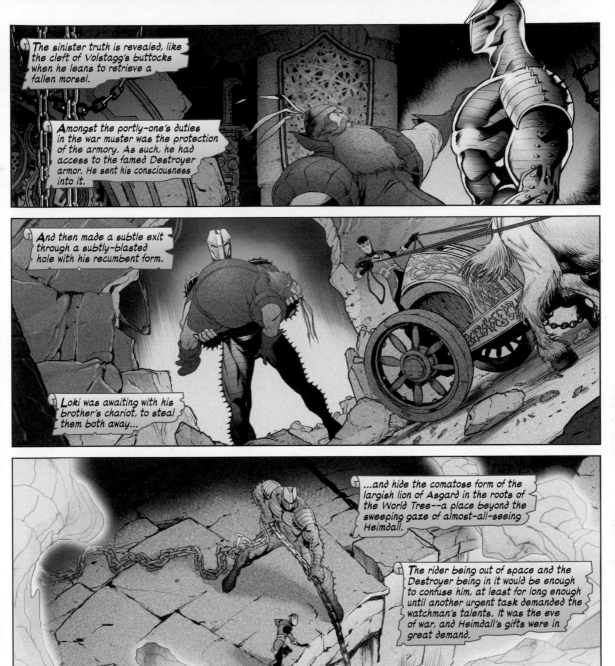

The sinister truth is revealed, like the cleft of Volstagg's buttocks when he leans to retrieve a fallen morsel.

Amongst the portly-one's duties in the war muster was the protection of the armory. As such, he had access to the famed Destroyer armor. He sent his consciousness into it.

And then made a subtle exit through a subtly-blasted hole with his recumbent form.

Loki was awaiting with his brother's chariot, to steal them both away...

...and hide the comatose form of the largish lion of Asgard in the roots of the World Tree--a place beyond the sweeping gaze of almost-all-seeing Heimdall.

The rider being out of space and the Destroyer being in it would be enough to confuse him, at least for long enough until another urgent task demanded the watchman's talents. It was the eve of war, and Heimdall's gifts were in great demand.

So, with one whom no one would suspect piloting it, the Destroyer marched into the heart of the Serpent's domain to smite monsters and masonry alike. With all the consequences to the narrative that regular readers will be all too aware.

NO ONE MUST KNOW OF THIS.

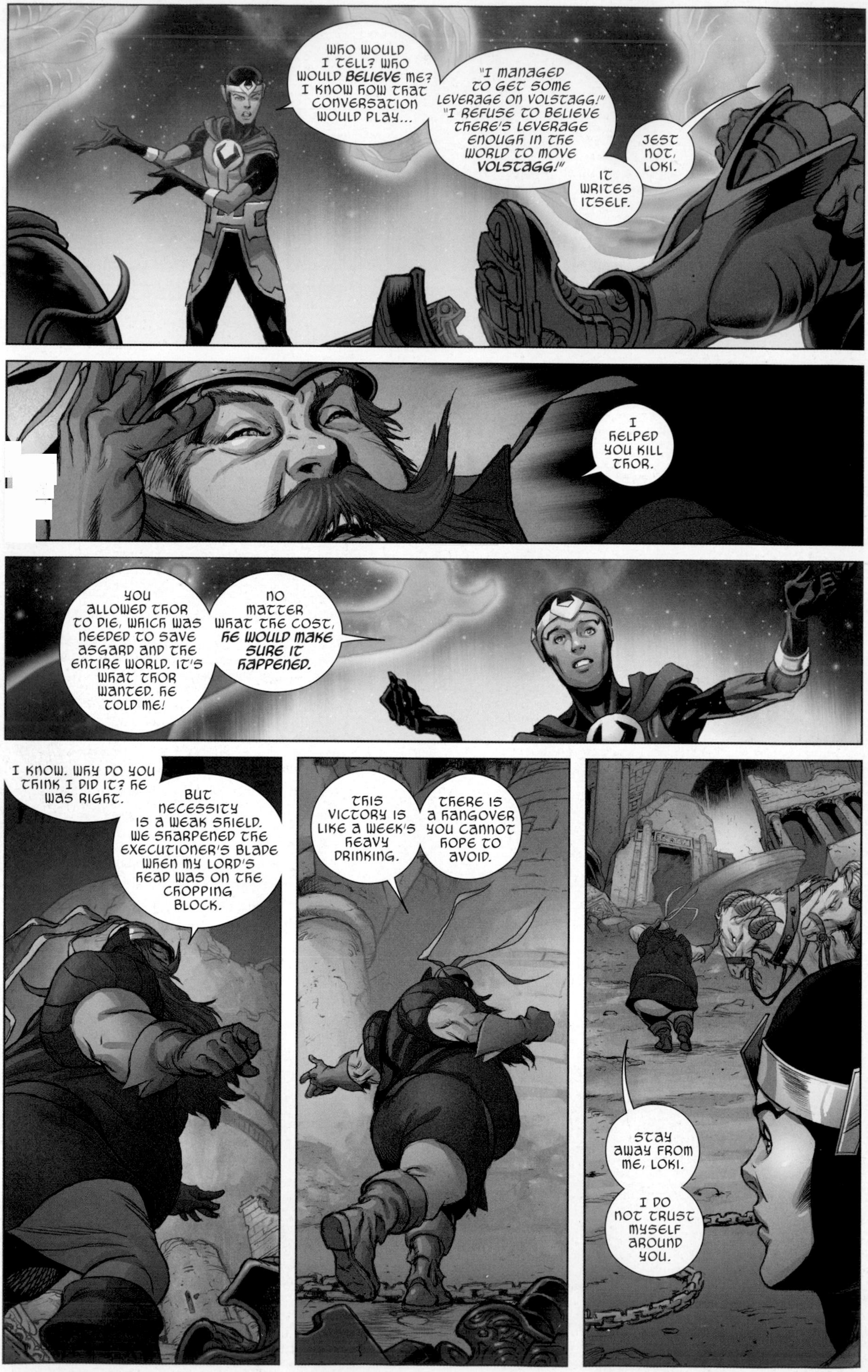
WHO WOULD I TELL? WHO WOULD BELIEVE ME? I KNOW HOW THAT CONVERSATION WOULD PLAY...
"I MANAGED TO GET SOME LEVERAGE ON VOLSTAGG!" "I REFUSE TO BELIEVE THERE'S LEVERAGE ENOUGH IN THE WORLD TO MOVE VOLSTAGG!"
IT WRITES ITSELF.
JEST NOT, LOKI.
I HELPED YOU KILL THOR.
YOU ALLOWED THOR TO DIE, WHICH WAS NEEDED TO SAVE ASGARD AND THE ENTIRE WORLD. IT'S WHAT THOR WANTED. HE TOLD ME!
NO MATTER WHAT THE COST, HE WOULD MAKE SURE IT HAPPENED.
I KNOW. WHY DO YOU THINK I DID IT? HE WAS RIGHT.
BUT NECESSITY IS A WEAK SHIELD. WE SHARPENED THE EXECUTIONER'S BLADE WHEN MY LORD'S HEAD WAS ON THE CHOPPING BLOCK.
THIS VICTORY IS LIKE A WEEK'S HEAVY DRINKING.
THERE IS A HANGOVER YOU CANNOT HOPE TO AVOID.
STAY AWAY FROM ME, LOKI.
I DO NOT TRUST MYSELF AROUND YOU.

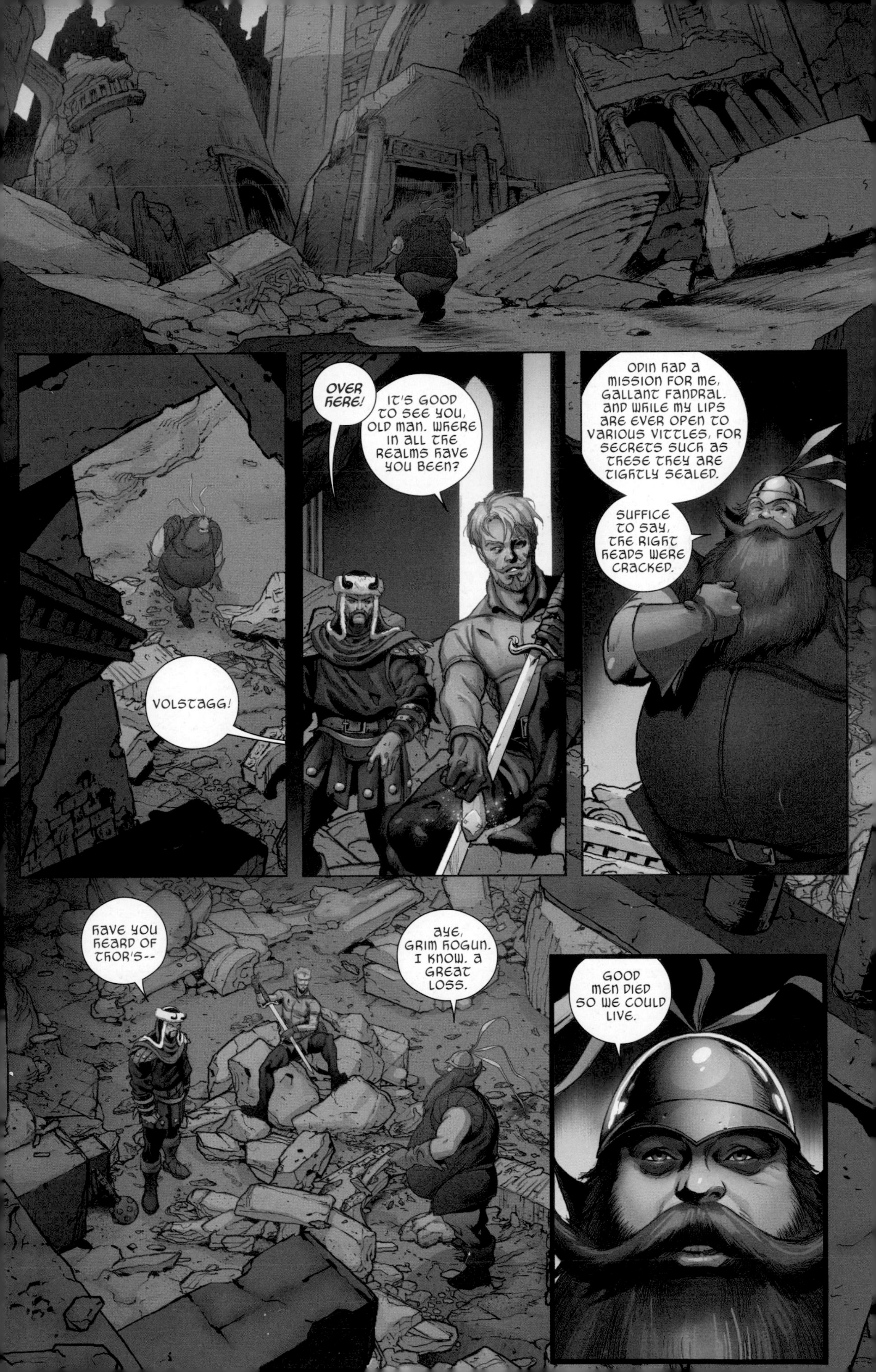
VOLSTAGG!
OVER HERE!
IT'S GOOD TO SEE YOU, OLD MAN. WHERE IN ALL THE REALMS HAVE YOU BEEN?
ODIN HAD A MISSION FOR ME, GALLANT FANDRAL. AND WHILE MY LIPS ARE EVER OPEN TO VARIOUS VITTLES, FOR SECRETS SUCH AS THESE THEY ARE TIGHTLY SEALED.
SUFFICE TO SAY, THE RIGHT HEADS WERE CRACKED.
HAVE YOU HEARD OF THOR'S--
AYE, GRIM HOGUN. I KNOW. A GREAT LOSS.
GOOD MEN DIED SO WE COULD LIVE.

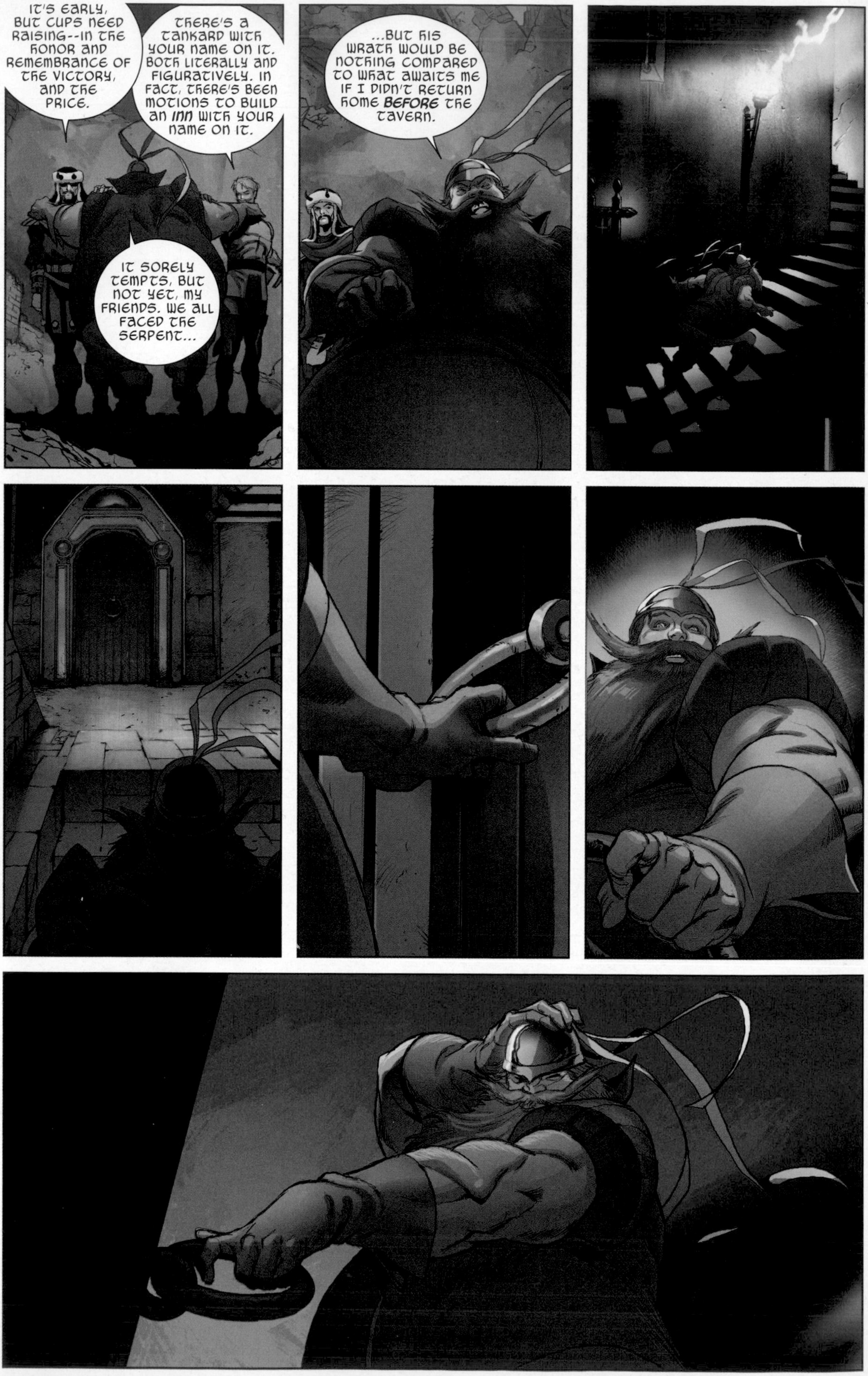
IT'S EARLY, BUT CUPS NEED RAISING--IN THE HONOR AND REMEMBRANCE OF THE VICTORY, AND THE PRICE.
THERE'S A TANKARD WITH YOUR NAME ON IT. BOTH LITERALLY AND FIGURATIVELY. IN FACT, THERE'S BEEN MOTIONS TO BUILD AN INN WITH YOUR NAME ON IT.
IT SORELY TEMPTS, BUT NOT YET, MY FRIENDS. WE ALL FACED THE SERPENT...
...BUT HIS WRATH WOULD BE NOTHING COMPARED TO WHAT AWAITS ME IF I DIDN'T RETURN HOME BEFORE THE TAVERN.

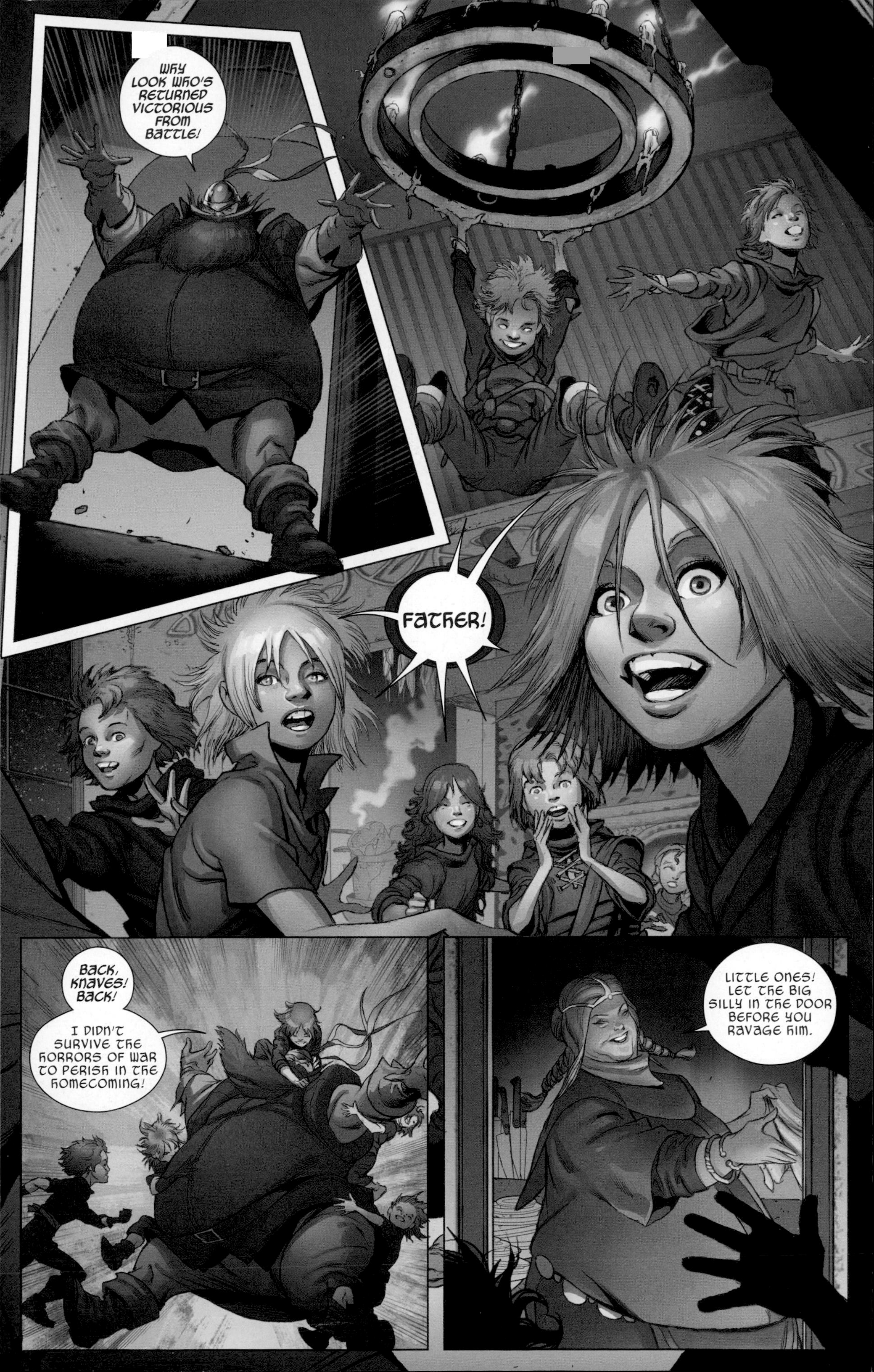
WHY LOOK WHO'S RETURNED VICTORIOUS FROM BATTLE!
FATHER!
BACK, KNAVES! BACK!
I DIDN'T SURVIVE THE HORRORS OF WAR TO PERISH IN THE HOMECOMING!
LITTLE ONES! LET THE BIG SILLY IN THE DOOR BEFORE YOU RAVAGE HIM.

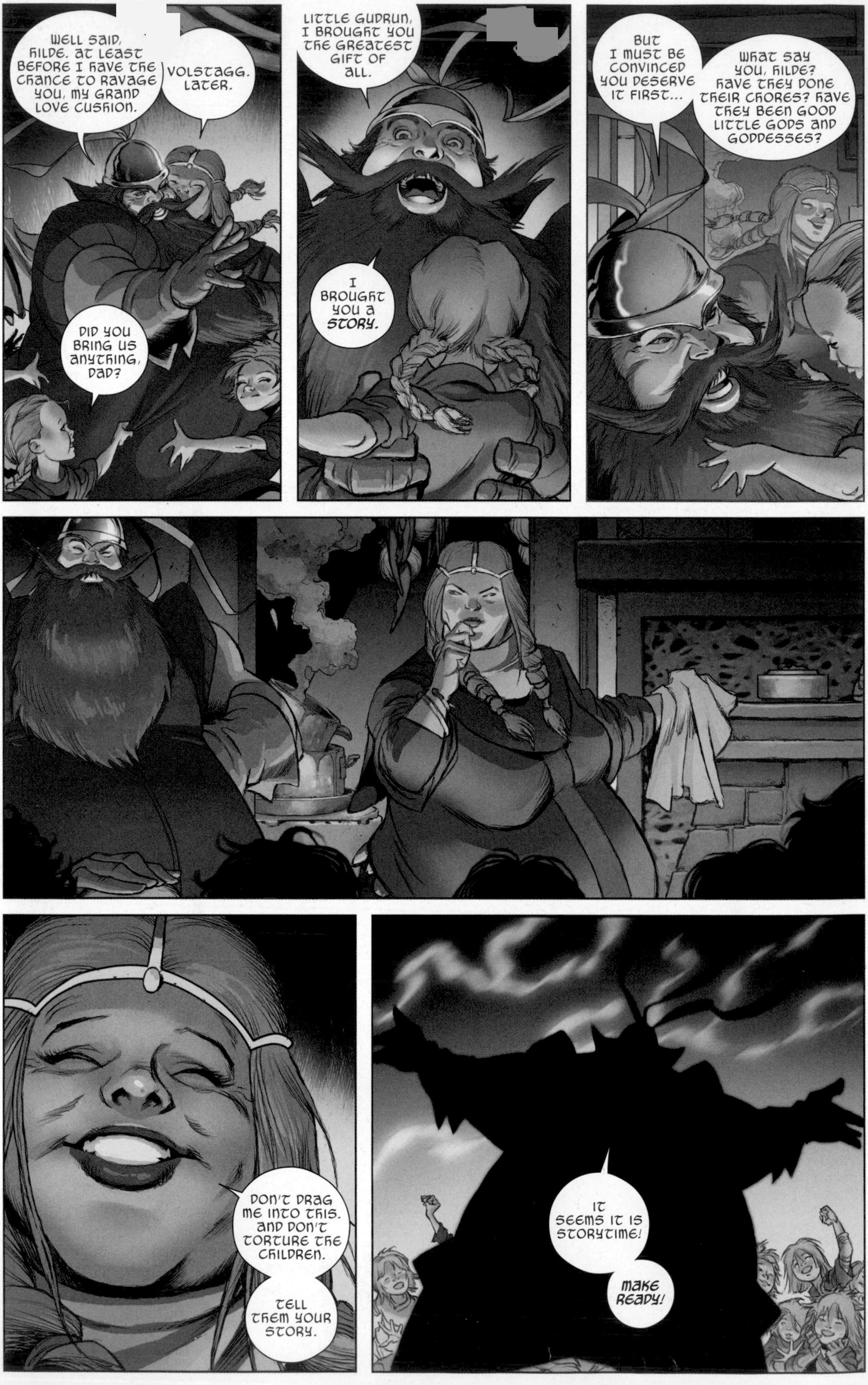
WELL SAID, HILDE. AT LEAST BEFORE I HAVE THE CHANCE TO RAVAGE YOU, MY GRAND LOVE CUSHION.
VOLSTAGG. LATER.
DID YOU BRING US ANYTHING, DAD?
LITTLE GUDRUN, I BROUGHT YOU THE GREATEST GIFT OF ALL.
I BROUGHT YOU A STORY.
BUT I MUST BE CONVINCED YOU DESERVE IT FIRST...
WHAT SAY YOU, HILDE? HAVE THEY DONE THEIR CHORES? HAVE THEY BEEN GOOD LITTLE GODS AND GODDESSES?
DON'T DRAG ME INTO THIS. AND DON'T TORTURE THE CHILDREN.
TELL THEM YOUR STORY.
IT SEEMS IT IS STORYTIME!
MAKE READY!

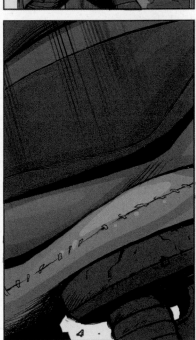

VERY WELL! I WILL TELL YOU THE TALE OF...

HOW VOLSTAGG DEFEATED THE SERPENT! TWICE!

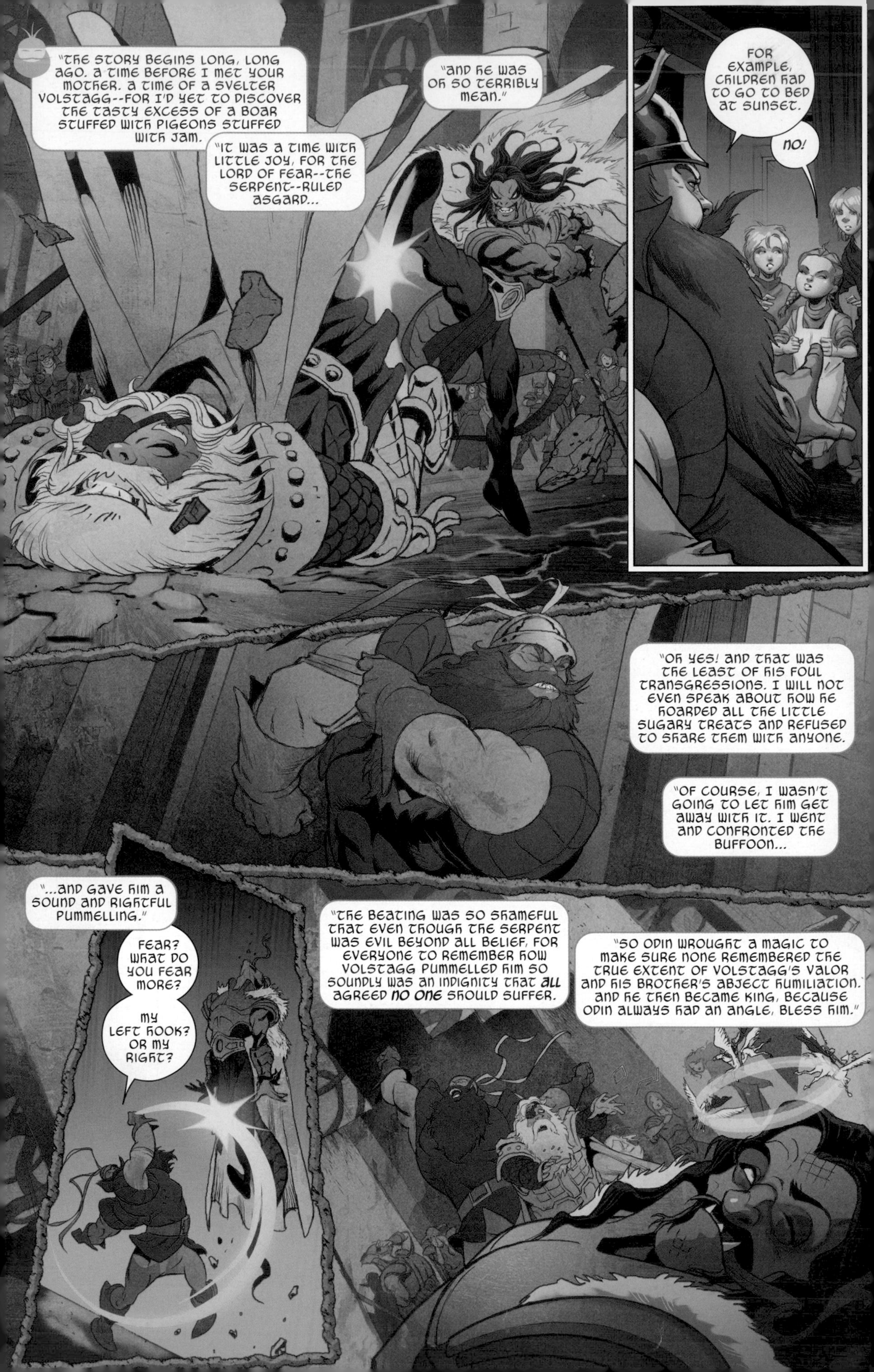
"THE STORY BEGINS LONG, LONG AGO. A TIME BEFORE I MET YOUR MOTHER. A TIME OF A SVELTER VOLSTAGG--FOR I'D YET TO DISCOVER THE TASTY EXCESS OF A BOAR STUFFED WITH PIGEONS STUFFED WITH JAM.
"IT WAS A TIME WITH LITTLE JOY, FOR THE LORD OF FEAR--THE SERPENT--RULED ASGARD...
"AND HE WAS OH SO TERRIBLY MEAN."
FOR EXAMPLE, CHILDREN HAD TO GO TO BED AT SUNSET.
NO!
"OH YES! AND THAT WAS THE LEAST OF HIS FOUL TRANSGRESSIONS. I WILL NOT EVEN SPEAK ABOUT HOW HE HOARDED ALL THE LITTLE SUGARY TREATS AND REFUSED TO SHARE THEM WITH ANYONE.
"OF COURSE, I WASN'T GOING TO LET HIM GET AWAY WITH IT. I WENT AND CONFRONTED THE BUFFOON...
"...AND GAVE HIM A SOUND AND RIGHTFUL PUMMELLING."
FEAR? WHAT DO YOU FEAR MORE?
MY LEFT HOOK? OR MY RIGHT?
"THE BEATING WAS SO SHAMEFUL THAT EVEN THOUGH THE SERPENT WAS EVIL BEYOND ALL BELIEF, FOR EVERYONE TO REMEMBER HOW VOLSTAGG PUMMELLED HIM SO SOUNDLY WAS AN INDIGNITY THAT ALL AGREED NO ONE SHOULD SUFFER.
"SO ODIN WROUGHT A MAGIC TO MAKE SURE NONE REMEMBERED THE TRUE EXTENT OF VOLSTAGG'S VALOR AND HIS BROTHER'S ABJECT HUMILIATION. AND HE THEN BECAME KING, BECAUSE ODIN ALWAYS HAD AN ANGLE, BLESS HIM."

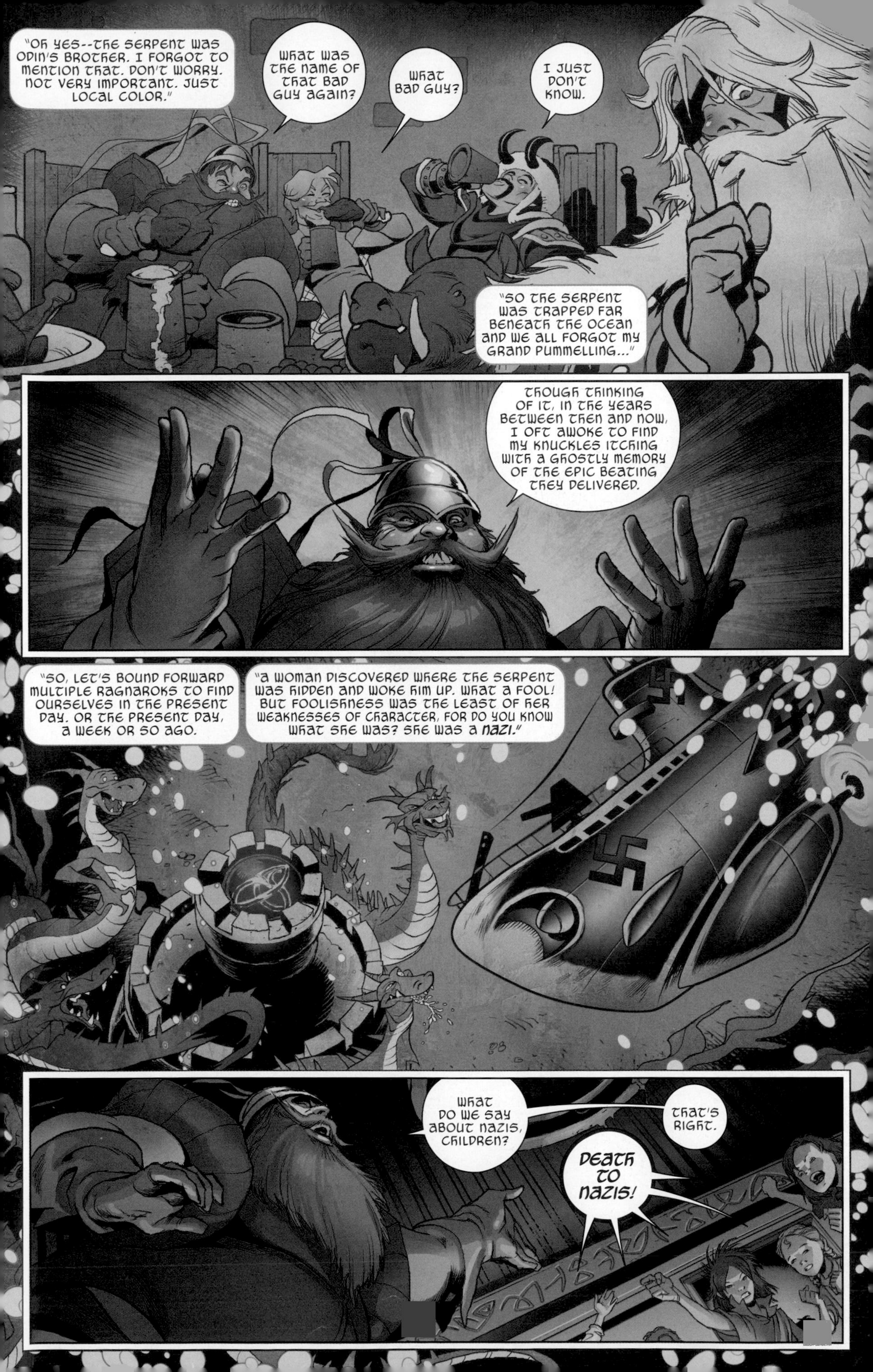
"OH YES--THE SERPENT WAS ODIN'S BROTHER. I FORGOT TO MENTION THAT. DON'T WORRY. NOT VERY IMPORTANT. JUST LOCAL COLOR."
WHAT WAS THE NAME OF THAT BAD GUY AGAIN?
WHAT BAD GUY?
I JUST DON'T KNOW.
"SO THE SERPENT WAS TRAPPED FAR BENEATH THE OCEAN AND WE ALL FORGOT MY GRAND PUMMELLING..."
THOUGH THINKING OF IT, IN THE YEARS BETWEEN THEN AND NOW, I OFT AWOKE TO FIND MY KNUCKLES ITCHING WITH A GHOSTLY MEMORY OF THE EPIC BEATING THEY DELIVERED.
"SO, LET'S BOUND FORWARD MULTIPLE RAGNAROKS TO FIND OURSELVES IN THE PRESENT DAY. OR THE PRESENT DAY, A WEEK OR SO AGO.
"A WOMAN DISCOVERED WHERE THE SERPENT WAS HIDDEN AND WOKE HIM UP. WHAT A FOOL! BUT FOOLISHNESS WAS THE LEAST OF HER WEAKNESSES OF CHARACTER, FOR DO YOU KNOW WHAT SHE WAS? SHE WAS A *NAZI.*"
WHAT DO WE SAY ABOUT NAZIS, CHILDREN?
DEATH TO NAZIS!
THAT'S RIGHT.

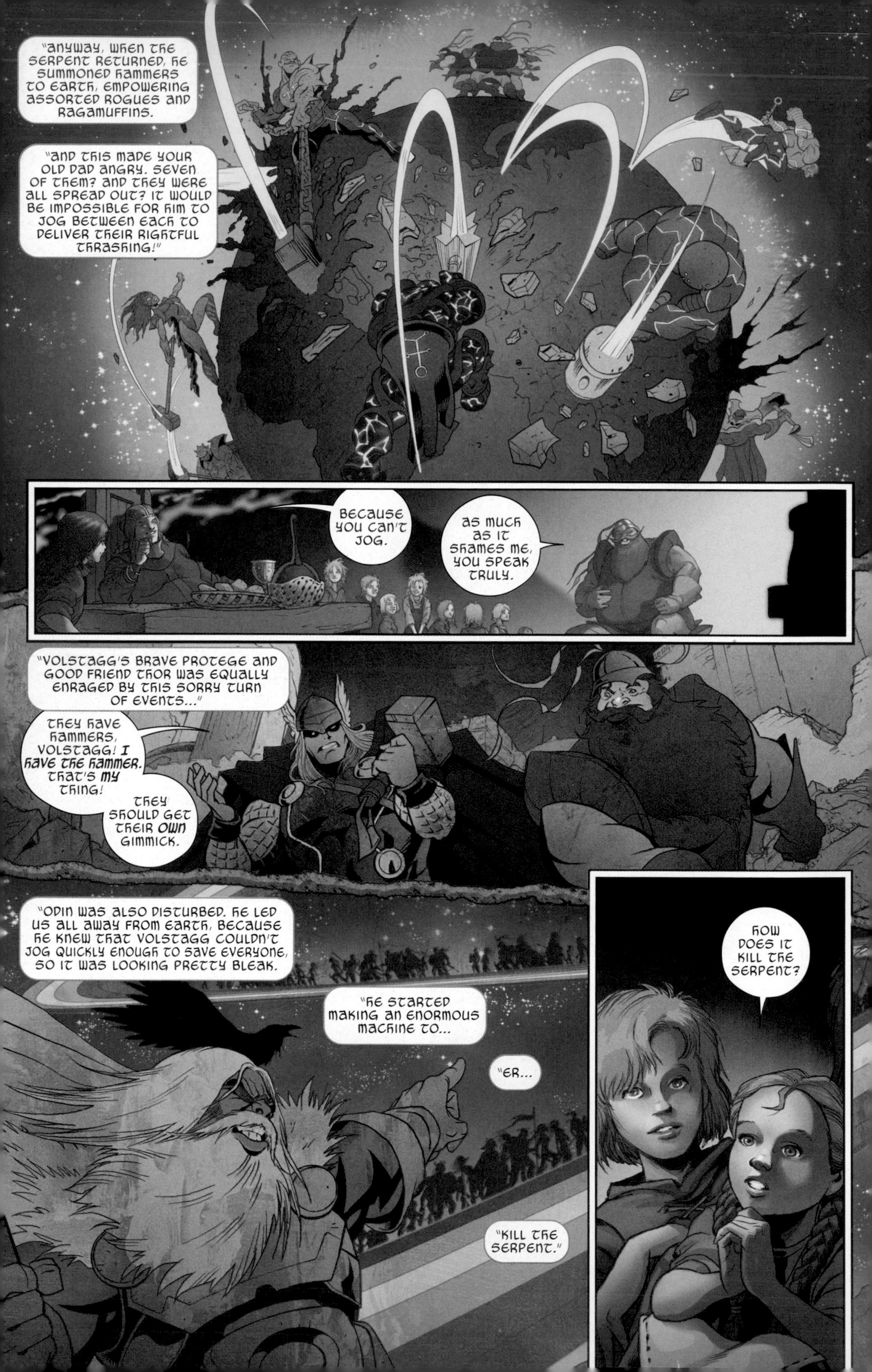
"ANYWAY, WHEN THE SERPENT RETURNED, HE SUMMONED HAMMERS TO EARTH, EMPOWERING ASSORTED ROGUES AND RAGAMUFFINS.
"AND THIS MADE YOUR OLD DAD ANGRY. SEVEN OF THEM? AND THEY WERE ALL SPREAD OUT? IT WOULD BE IMPOSSIBLE FOR HIM TO JOG BETWEEN EACH TO DELIVER THEIR RIGHTFUL THRASHING!"
BECAUSE YOU CAN'T JOG.
AS MUCH AS IT SHAMES ME, YOU SPEAK TRULY.
"VOLSTAGG'S BRAVE PROTEGE AND GOOD FRIEND THOR WAS EQUALLY ENRAGED BY THIS SORRY TURN OF EVENTS..."
THEY HAVE HAMMERS, VOLSTAGG! I HAVE THE HAMMER. THAT'S MY THING!
THEY SHOULD GET THEIR OWN GIMMICK.
"ODIN WAS ALSO DISTURBED. HE LED US ALL AWAY FROM EARTH, BECAUSE HE KNEW THAT VOLSTAGG COULDN'T JOG QUICKLY ENOUGH TO SAVE EVERYONE, SO IT WAS LOOKING PRETTY BLEAK.
"HE STARTED MAKING AN ENORMOUS MACHINE TO...
"ER...
"KILL THE SERPENT."
HOW DOES IT KILL THE SERPENT?

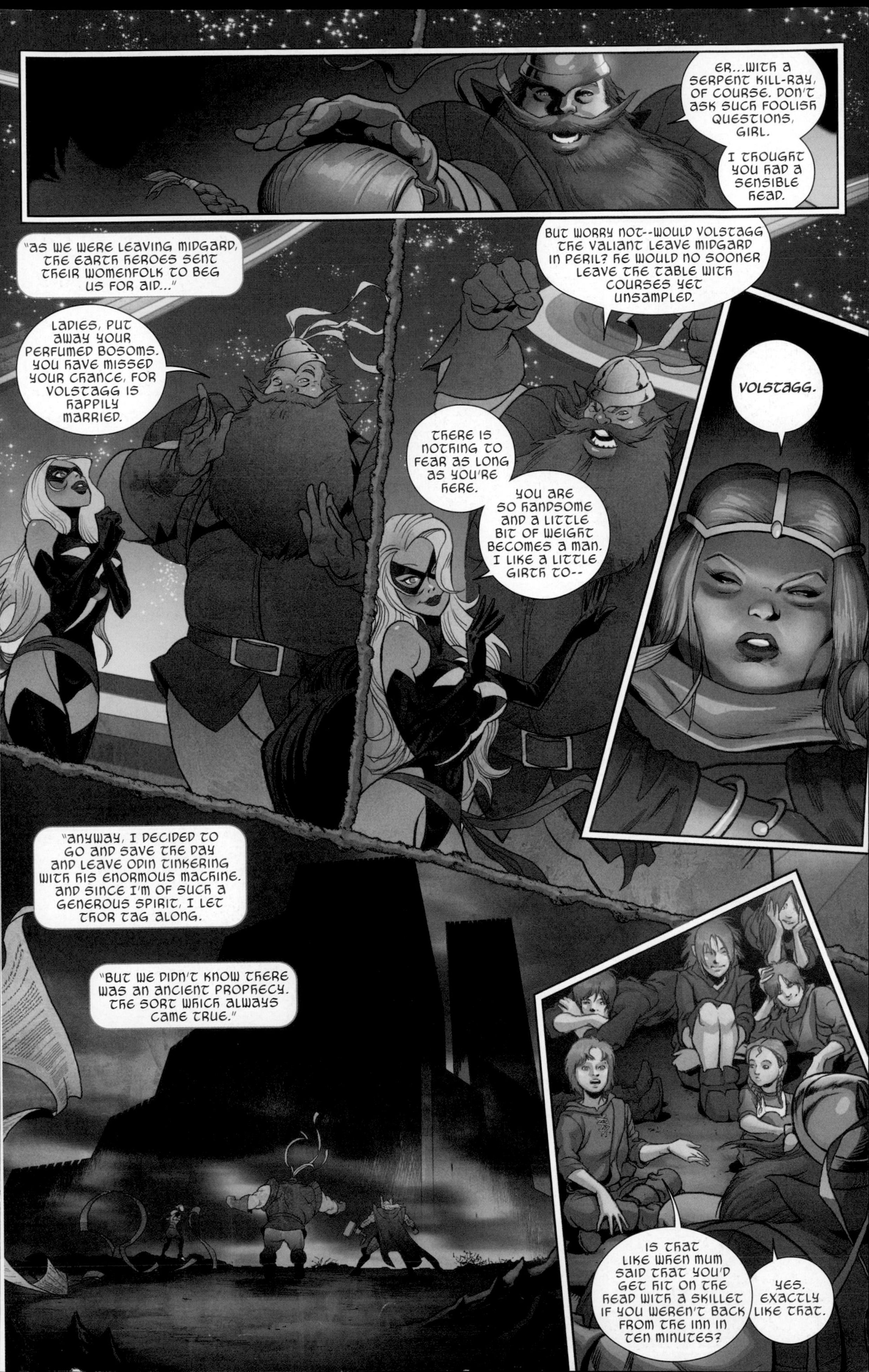
ER...WITH A SERPENT KILL-RAY, OF COURSE. DON'T ASK SUCH FOOLISH QUESTIONS, GIRL.
I THOUGHT YOU HAD A SENSIBLE HEAD.
"AS WE WERE LEAVING MIDGARD, THE EARTH HEROES SENT THEIR WOMENFOLK TO BEG US FOR AID..."
LADIES, PUT AWAY YOUR PERFUMED BOSOMS. YOU HAVE MISSED YOUR CHANCE, FOR VOLSTAGG IS HAPPILY MARRIED.
BUT WORRY NOT--WOULD VOLSTAGG THE VALIANT LEAVE MIDGARD IN PERIL? HE WOULD NO SOONER LEAVE THE TABLE WITH COURSES YET UNSAMPLED.
THERE IS NOTHING TO FEAR AS LONG AS YOU'RE HERE.
YOU ARE SO HANDSOME AND A LITTLE BIT OF WEIGHT BECOMES A MAN. I LIKE A LITTLE GIRTH TO--
VOLSTAGG.
"ANYWAY, I DECIDED TO GO AND SAVE THE DAY AND LEAVE ODIN TINKERING WITH HIS ENORMOUS MACHINE. AND SINCE I'M OF SUCH A GENEROUS SPIRIT, I LET THOR TAG ALONG.
"BUT WE DIDN'T KNOW THERE WAS AN ANCIENT PROPHECY. THE SORT WHICH ALWAYS CAME TRUE."
IS THAT LIKE WHEN MUM SAID THAT YOU'D GET HIT ON THE HEAD WITH A SKILLET IF YOU WEREN'T BACK FROM THE INN IN TEN MINUTES?
YES. EXACTLY LIKE THAT.

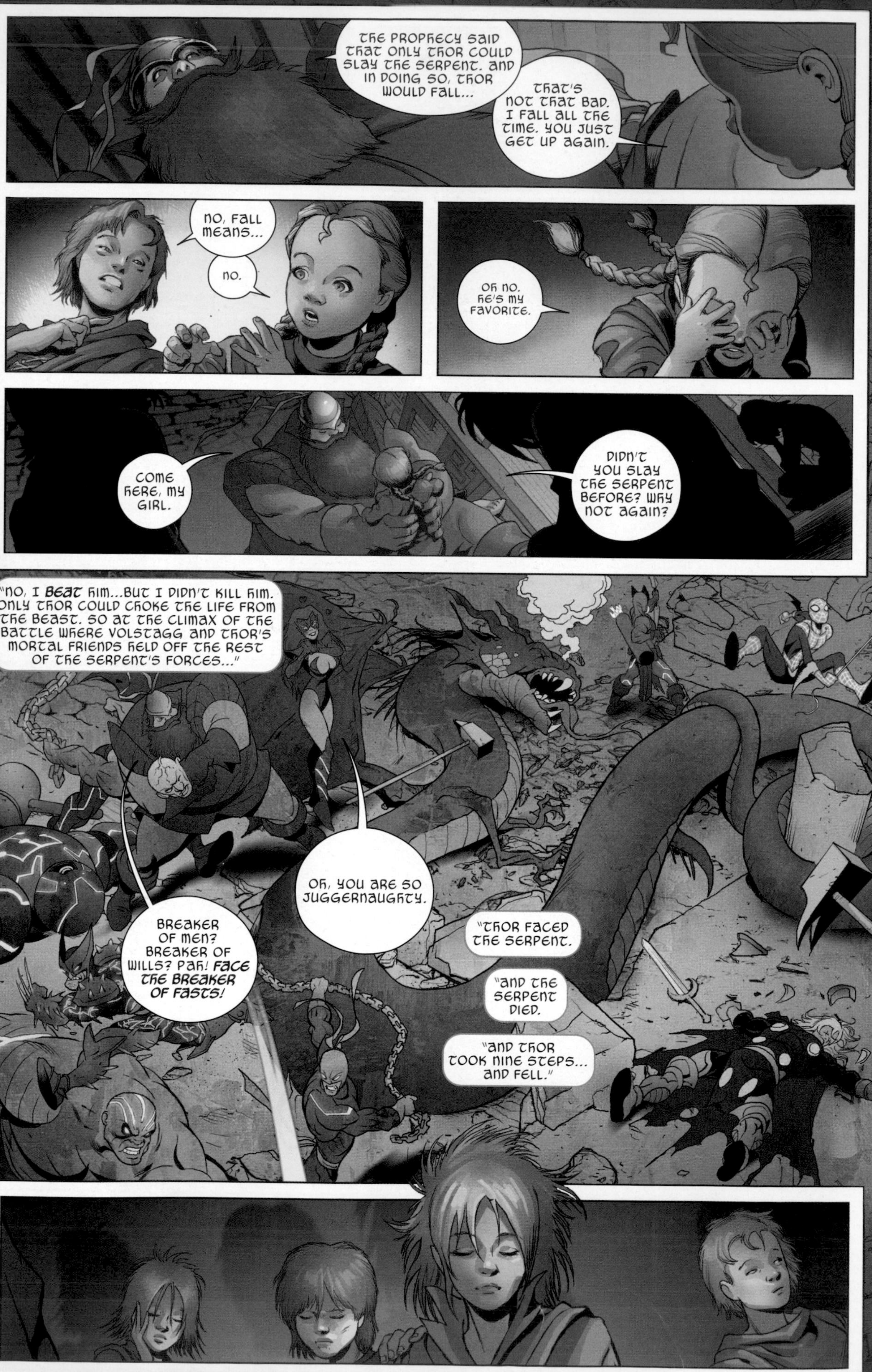
THE PROPHECY SAID THAT ONLY THOR COULD SLAY THE SERPENT. AND IN DOING SO, THOR WOULD FALL...
THAT'S NOT THAT BAD. I FALL ALL THE TIME. YOU JUST GET UP AGAIN.
NO, FALL MEANS...
NO.
OH NO. HE'S MY FAVORITE.
COME HERE, MY GIRL.
DIDN'T YOU SLAY THE SERPENT BEFORE? WHY NOT AGAIN?
"NO, I BEAT HIM...BUT I DIDN'T KILL HIM. ONLY THOR COULD CHOKE THE LIFE FROM THE BEAST. SO AT THE CLIMAX OF THE BATTLE WHERE VOLSTAGG AND THOR'S MORTAL FRIENDS HELD OFF THE REST OF THE SERPENT'S FORCES..."
BREAKER OF MEN? BREAKER OF WILLS? PAH! FACE THE BREAKER OF FASTS!
OH, YOU ARE SO JUGGERNAUGHTY.
"THOR FACED THE SERPENT.
"AND THE SERPENT DIED.
"AND THOR TOOK NINE STEPS... AND FELL."

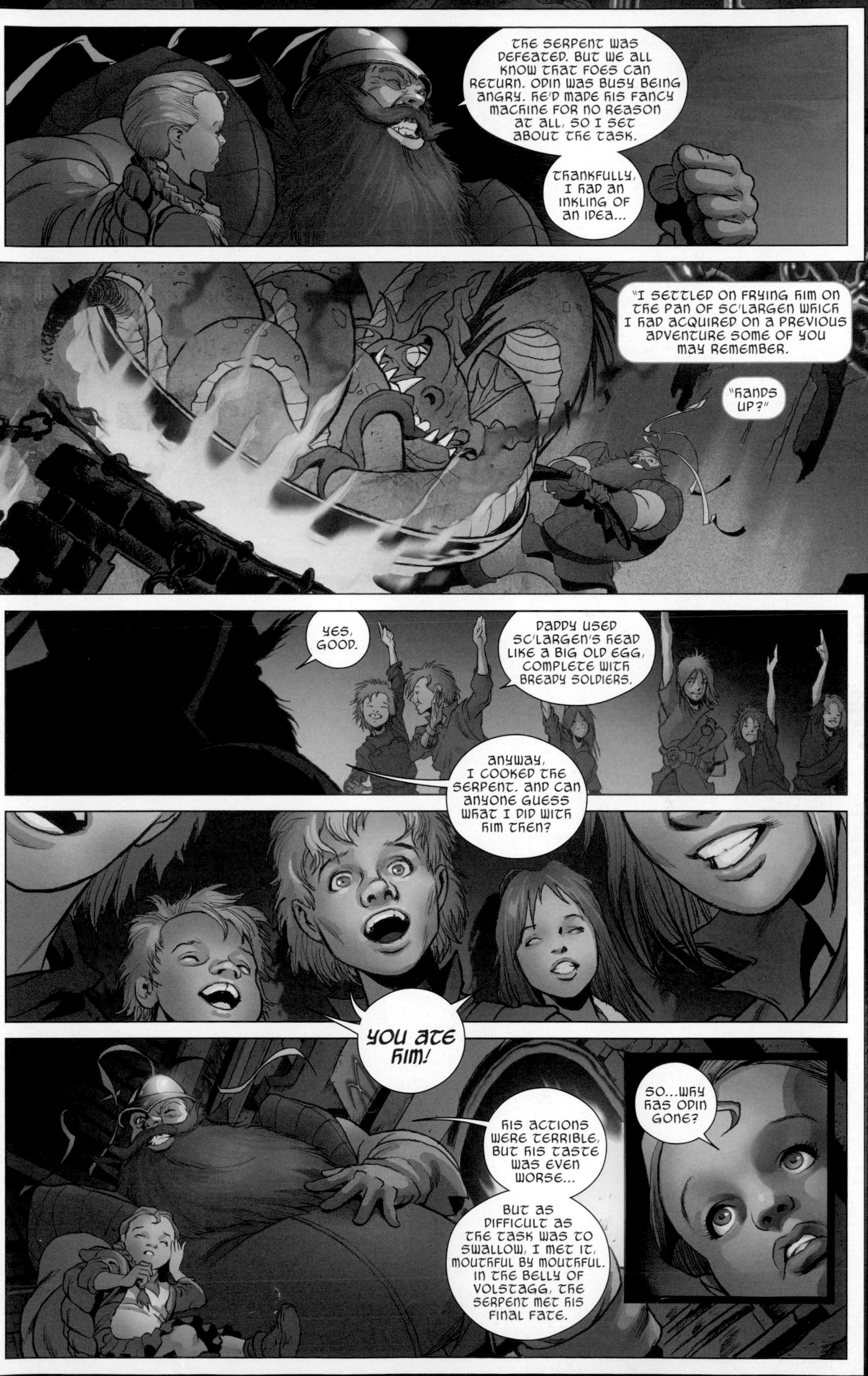
THE SERPENT WAS DEFEATED. BUT WE ALL KNOW THAT FOES CAN RETURN. ODIN WAS BUSY BEING ANGRY. HE'D MADE HIS FANCY MACHINE FOR NO REASON AT ALL, SO I SET ABOUT THE TASK.
THANKFULLY, I HAD AN INKLING OF AN IDEA...
"I SETTLED ON FRYING HIM ON THE PAN OF SC'LARGEN WHICH I HAD ACQUIRED ON A PREVIOUS ADVENTURE SOME OF YOU MAY REMEMBER.
"HANDS UP?"
YES, GOOD.
DADDY USED SC'LARGEN'S HEAD LIKE A BIG OLD EGG, COMPLETE WITH BREADY SOLDIERS.
ANYWAY, I COOKED THE SERPENT. AND CAN ANYONE GUESS WHAT I DID WITH HIM THEN?
YOU ATE HIM!
HIS ACTIONS WERE TERRIBLE, BUT HIS TASTE WAS EVEN WORSE...
BUT AS DIFFICULT AS THE TASK WAS TO SWALLOW, I MET IT, MOUTHFUL BY MOUTHFUL. IN THE BELLY OF VOLSTAGG, THE SERPENT MET HIS FINAL FATE.
SO...WHY HAS ODIN GONE?

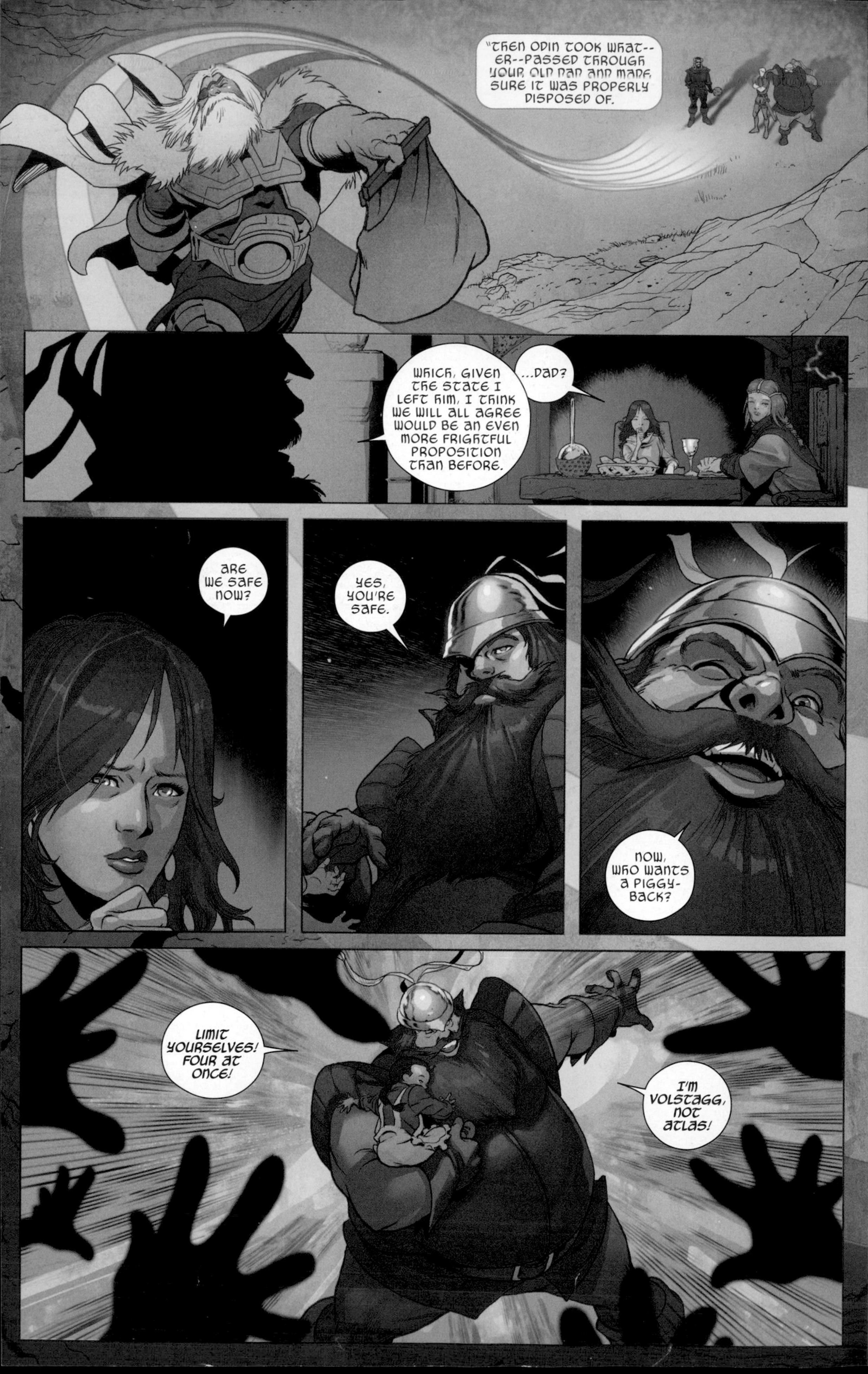
"THEN ODIN TOOK WHAT-- ER--PASSED THROUGH YOUR OLD DAD AND MADE SURE IT WAS PROPERLY DISPOSED OF.
WHICH, GIVEN THE STATE I LEFT HIM, I THINK WE WILL ALL AGREE WOULD BE AN EVEN MORE FRIGHTFUL PROPOSITION THAN BEFORE.
...DAD?
ARE WE SAFE NOW?
YES, YOU'RE SAFE.
NOW, WHO WANTS A PIGGY-BACK?
LIMIT YOURSELVES! FOUR AT ONCE!
I'M VOLSTAGG, NOT ATLAS!

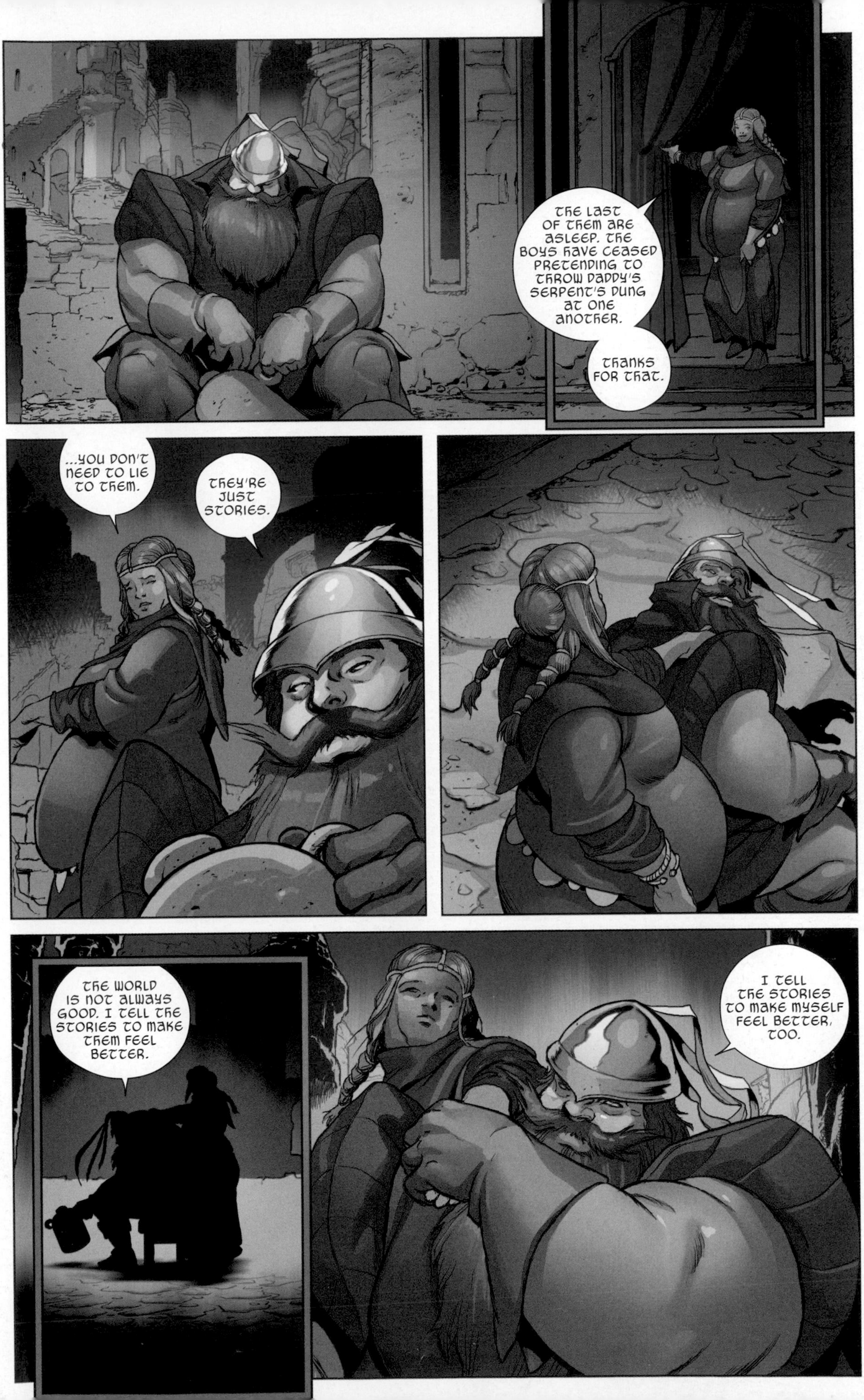
THE LAST OF THEM ARE ASLEEP. THE BOYS HAVE CEASED PRETENDING TO THROW DADDY'S SERPENT'S DUNG AT ONE ANOTHER.
THANKS FOR THAT.
...YOU DON'T NEED TO LIE TO THEM.
THEY'RE JUST STORIES.
THE WORLD IS NOT ALWAYS GOOD. I TELL THE STORIES TO MAKE THEM FEEL BETTER.
I TELL THE STORIES TO MAKE MYSELF FEEL BETTER, TOO.

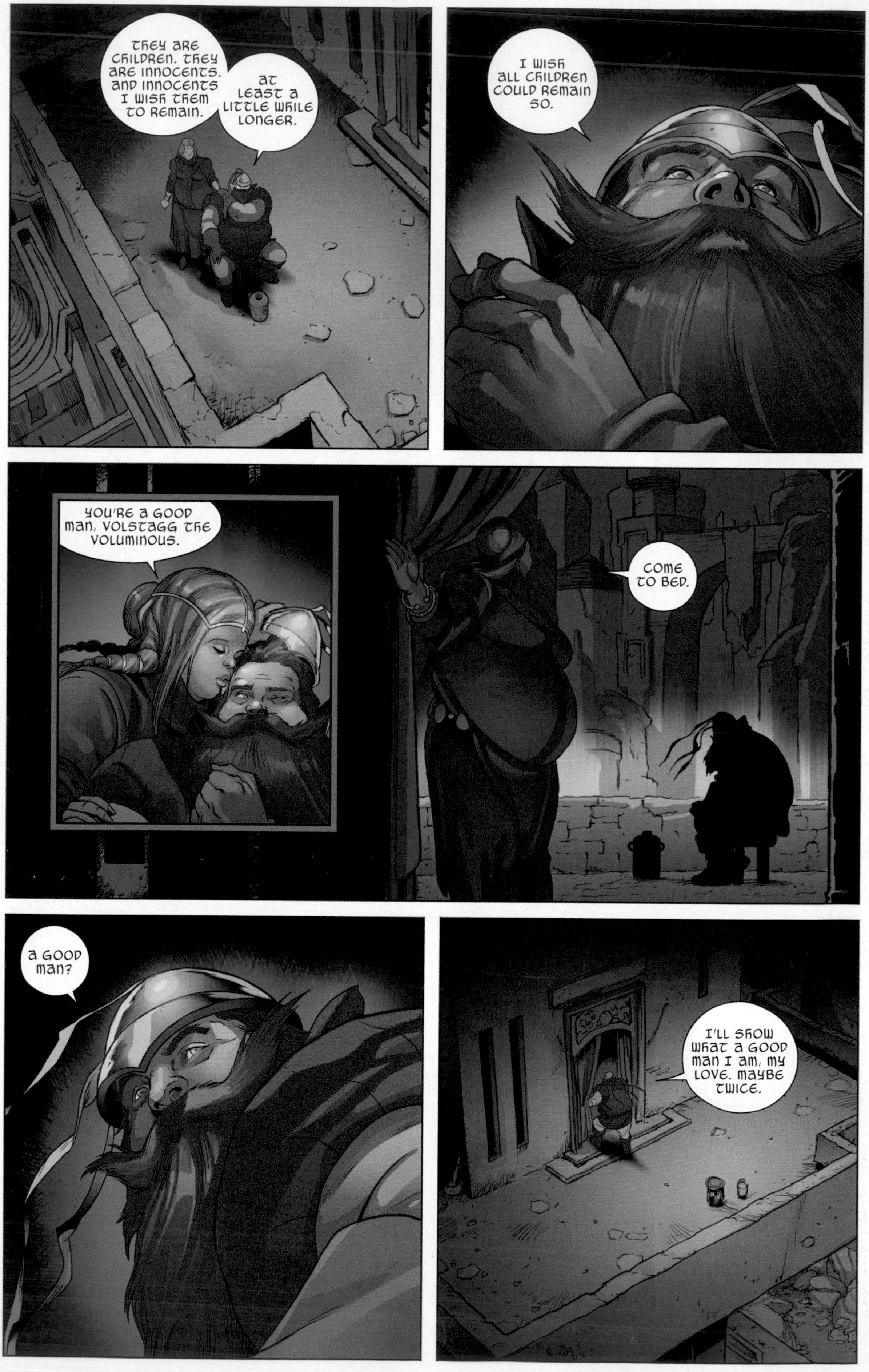
THEY ARE CHILDREN. THEY ARE INNOCENTS. AND INNOCENTS I WISH THEM TO REMAIN.
AT LEAST A LITTLE WHILE LONGER.
I WISH ALL CHILDREN COULD REMAIN SO.
YOU'RE A GOOD MAN, VOLSTAGG THE VOLUMINOUS.
COME TO BED.
A GOOD MAN?
I'LL SHOW WHAT A GOOD MAN I AM, MY LOVE. MAYBE TWICE.

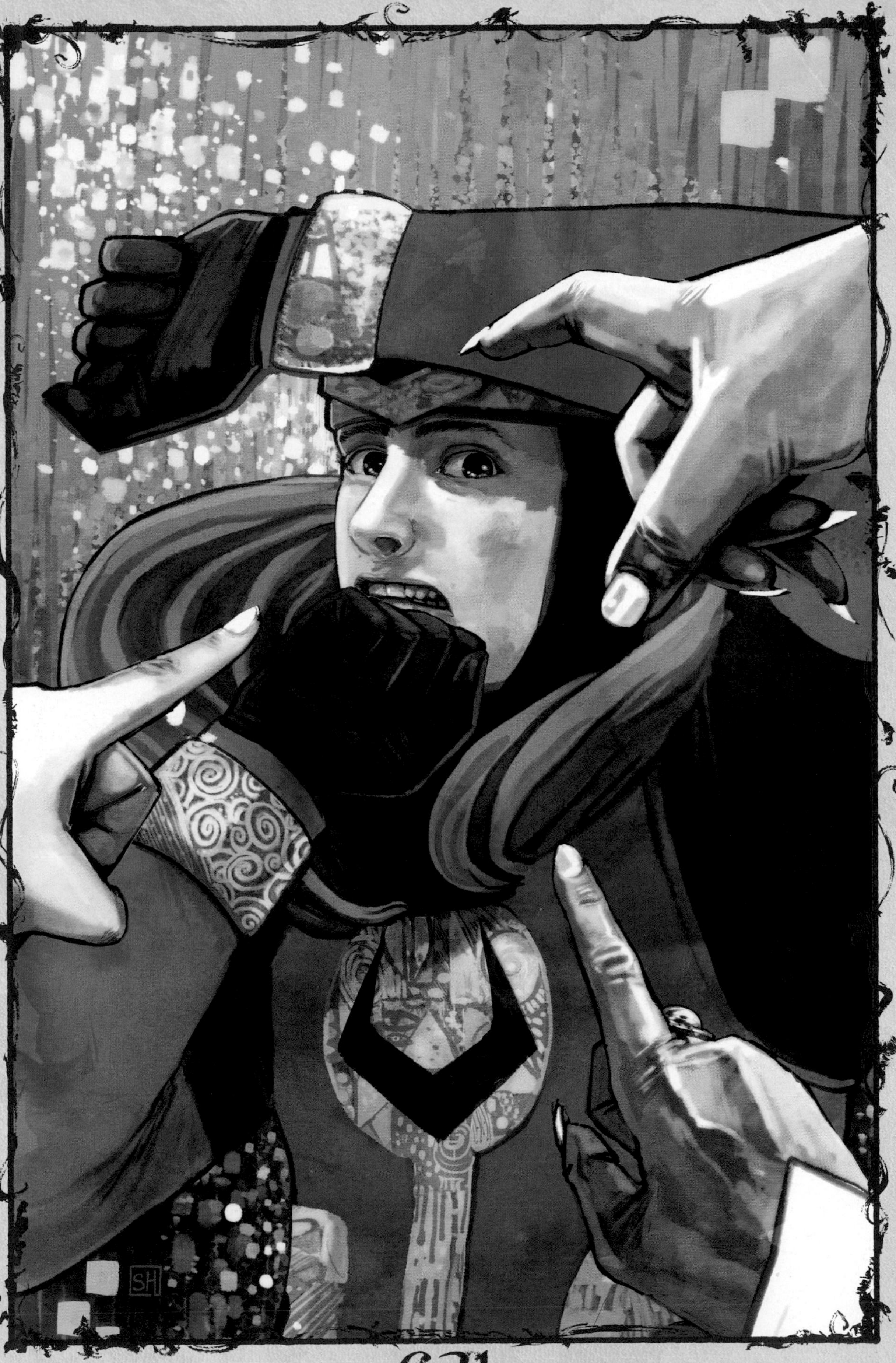

631

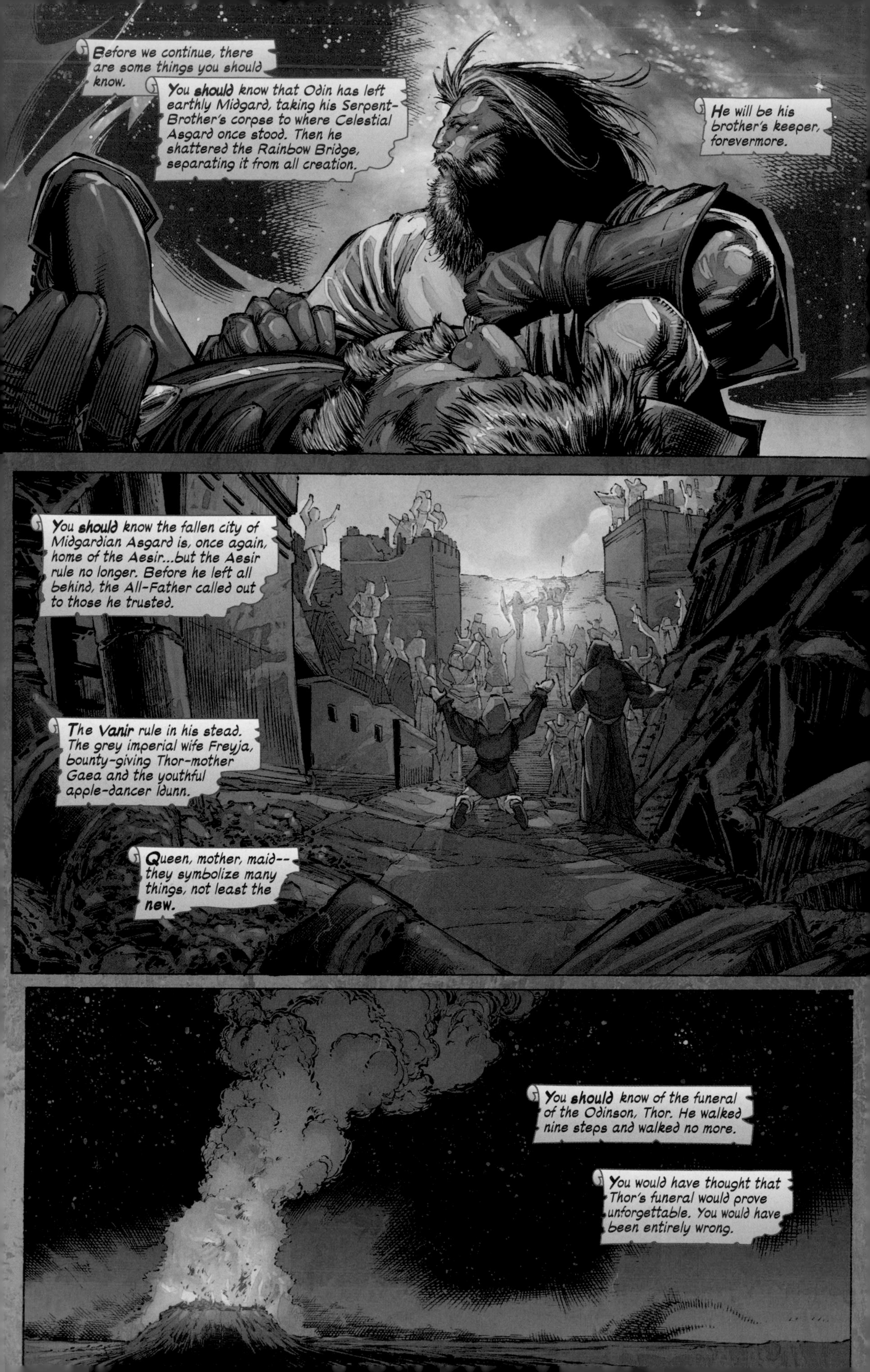
Before we continue, there are some things you should know.
You **should** know that Odin has left earthly Midgard, taking his Serpent-Brother's corpse to where Celestial Asgard once stood. Then he shattered the Rainbow Bridge, separating it from all creation.
He will be his brother's keeper, forevermore.
You **should** know the fallen city of Midgardian Asgard is, once again, home of the Aesir...but the Aesir rule no longer. Before he left all behind, the All-Father called out to those he trusted.
The **Vanir** rule in his stead. The grey imperial wife Freyja, bounty-giving Thor-mother Gaea and the youthful apple-dancer Idunn.
Queen, mother, maid-- they symbolize many things, not least the **new.**
You **should** know of the funeral of the Odinson, Thor. He walked nine steps and walked no more.
You would have thought that Thor's funeral would prove unforgettable. You would have been entirely wrong.

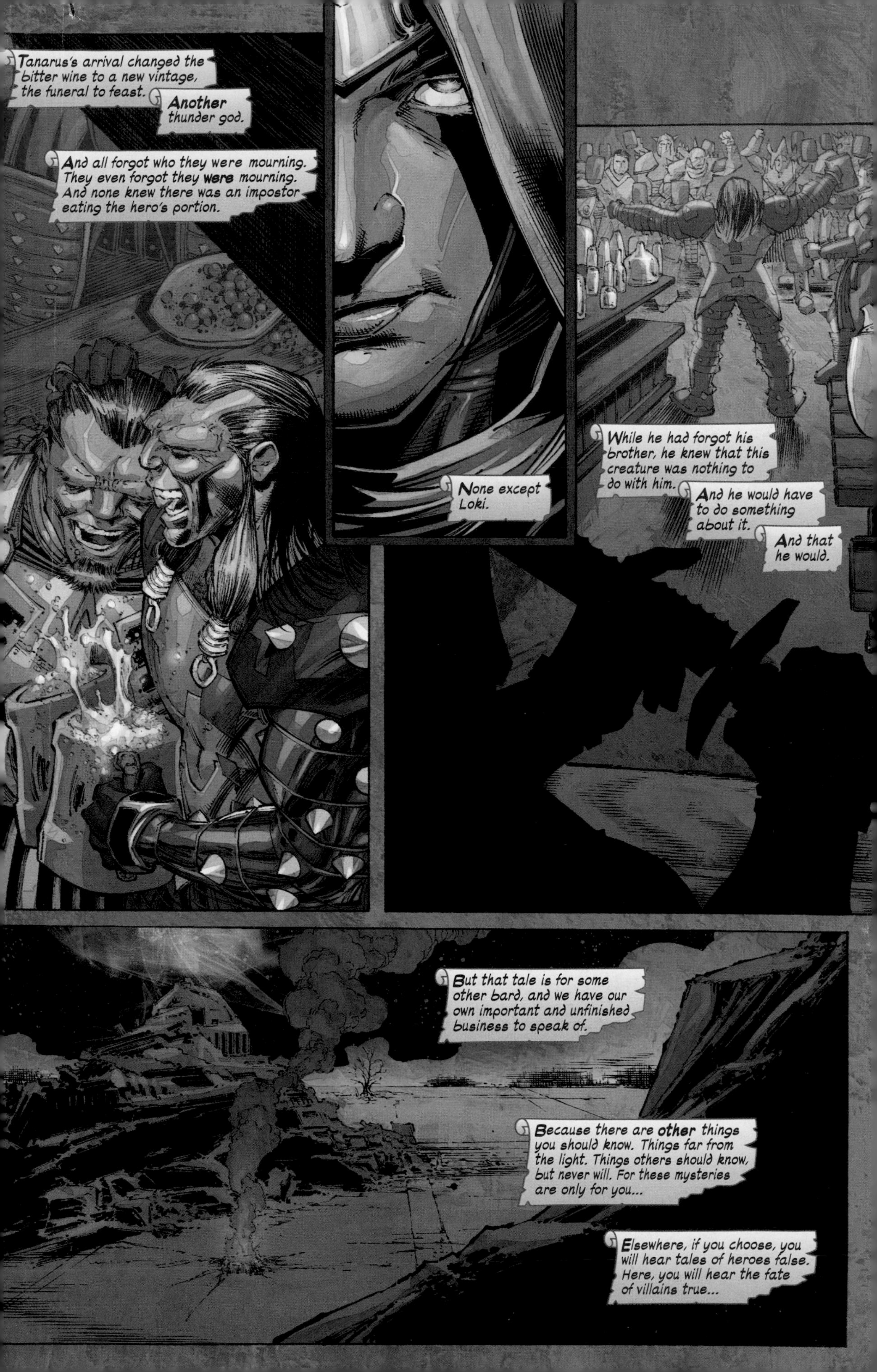
Tanarus's arrival changed the bitter wine to a new vintage, the funeral to feast.
Another thunder god.
And all forgot who they were mourning. They even forgot they were mourning. And none knew there was an impostor eating the hero's portion.
None except Loki.
While he had forgot his brother, he knew that this creature was nothing to do with him.
And he would have to do something about it.
And that he would.
But that tale is for some other bard, and we have our own important and unfinished business to speak of.
Because there are other things you should know. Things far from the light. Things others should know, but never will. For these mysteries are only for you...
Elsewhere, if you choose, you will hear tales of heroes false. Here, you will hear the fate of villains true...

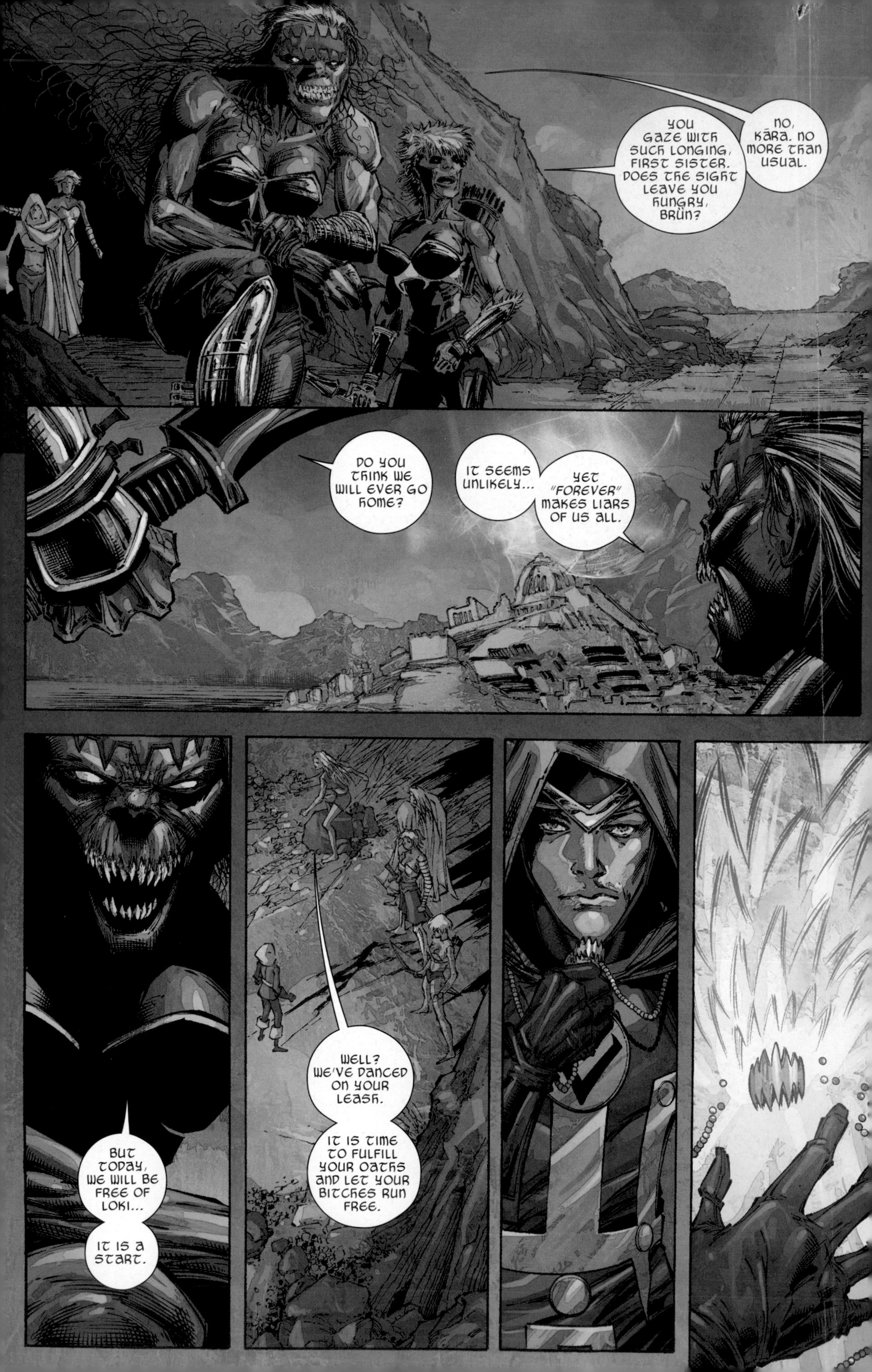
YOU GAZE WITH SUCH LONGING, FIRST SISTER. DOES THE SIGHT LEAVE YOU HUNGRY, BRÜN?
NO, KÄRA. NO MORE THAN USUAL.
DO YOU THINK WE WILL EVER GO HOME?
IT SEEMS UNLIKELY...
YET "FOREVER" MAKES LIARS OF US ALL.
BUT TODAY, WE WILL BE FREE OF LOKI...
IT IS A START.
WELL? WE'VE DANCED ON YOUR LEASH.
IT IS TIME TO FULFILL YOUR OATHS AND LET YOUR BITCHES RUN FREE.

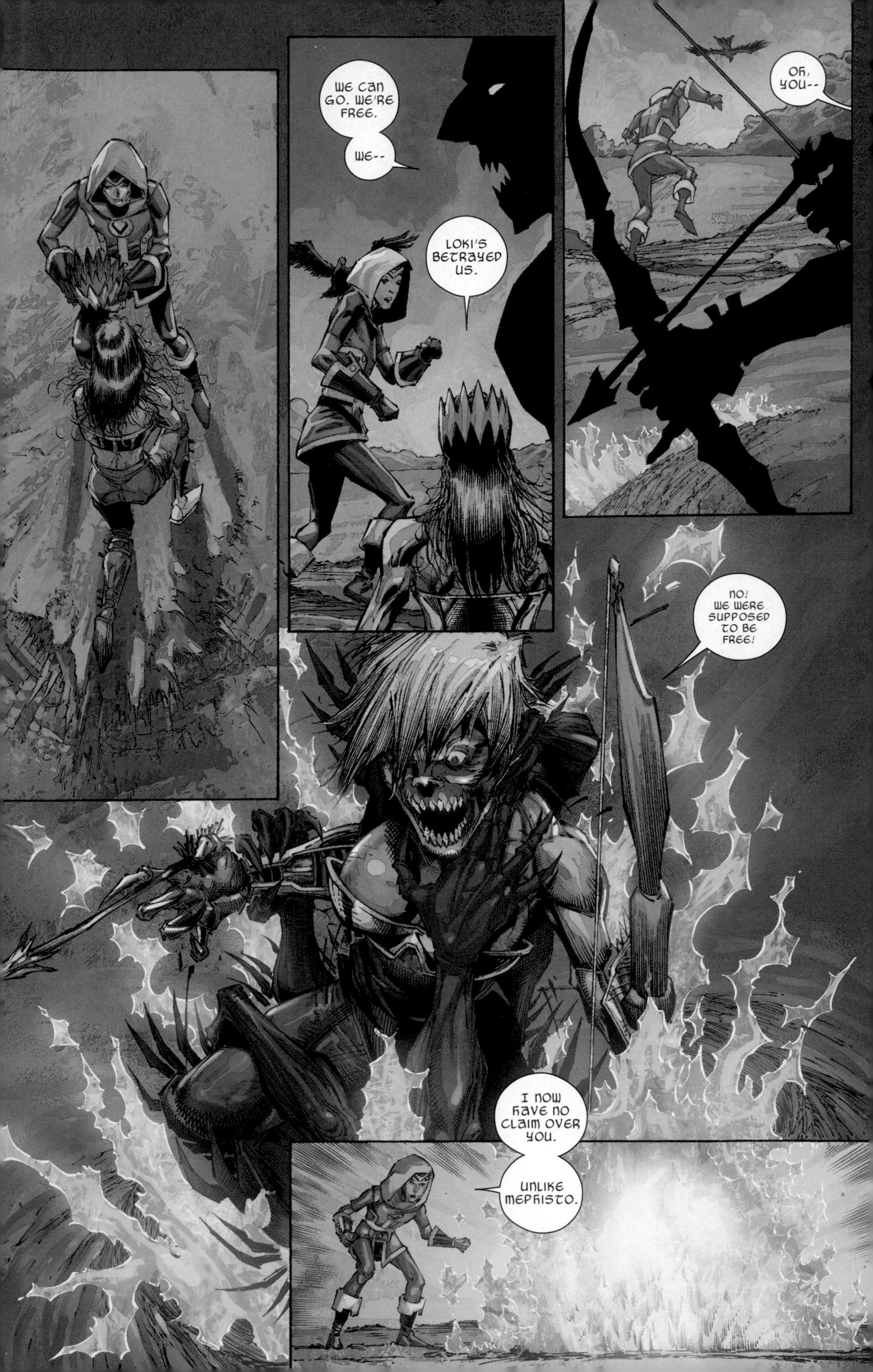
WE CAN GO. WE'RE FREE.
WE--
LOKI'S BETRAYED US.
OH, YOU--
NO! WE WERE SUPPOSED TO BE FREE!
I NOW HAVE NO CLAIM OVER YOU.
UNLIKE MEPHISTO.

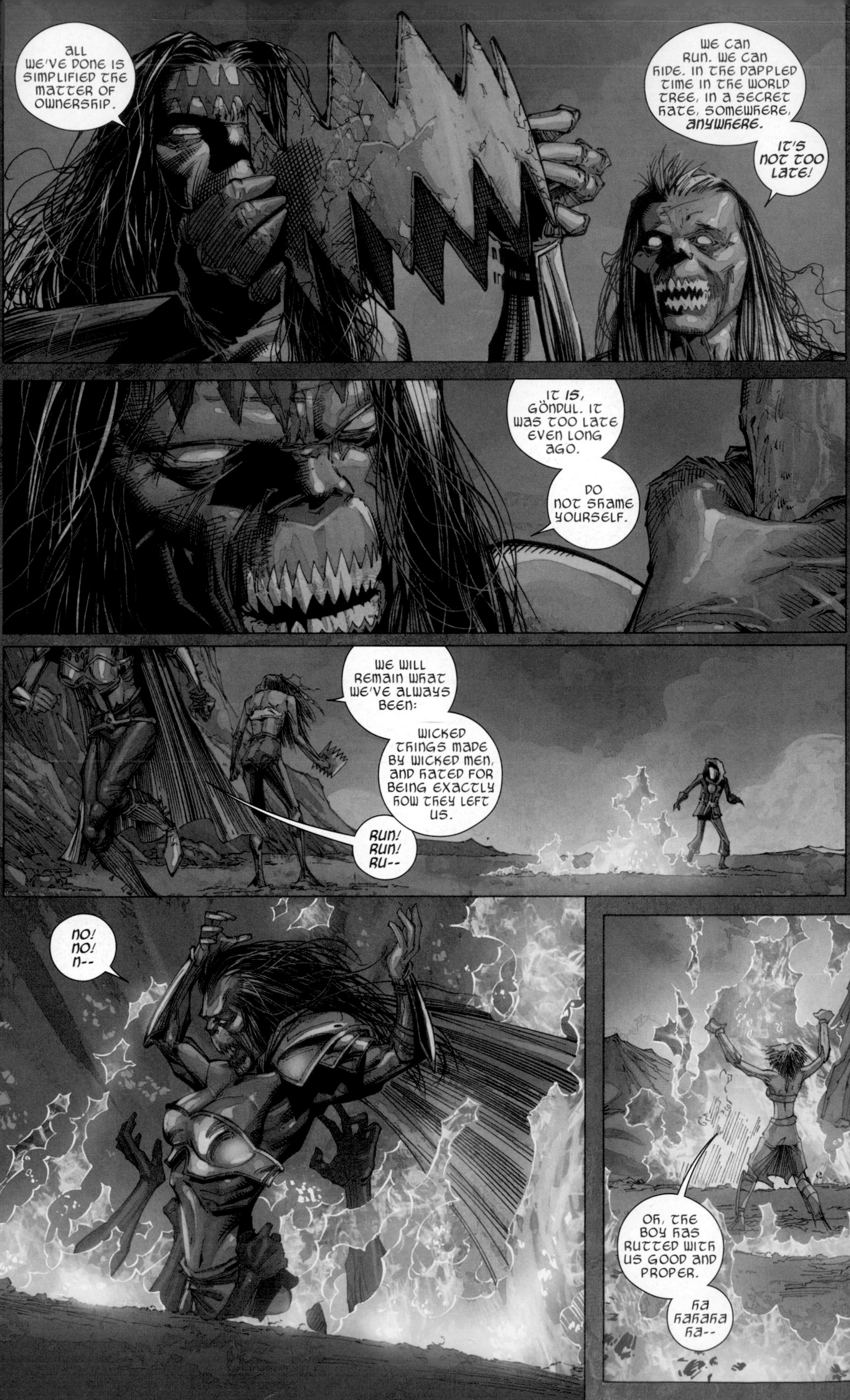
ALL WE'VE DONE IS SIMPLIFIED THE MATTER OF OWNERSHIP.
WE CAN RUN. WE CAN HIDE. IN THE DAPPLED TIME IN THE WORLD TREE, IN A SECRET HATE, SOMEWHERE, ANYWHERE.
IT'S NOT TOO LATE!
IT IS, GÖNDUL. IT WAS TOO LATE EVEN LONG AGO.
DO NOT SHAME YOURSELF.
WE WILL REMAIN WHAT WE'VE ALWAYS BEEN:
WICKED THINGS MADE BY WICKED MEN, AND HATED FOR BEING EXACTLY HOW THEY LEFT US.
RUN! RUN! RU--
NO! NO! N--
OH, THE BOY HAS RUTTED WITH US GOOD AND PROPER.
HA HAHAHA HA--

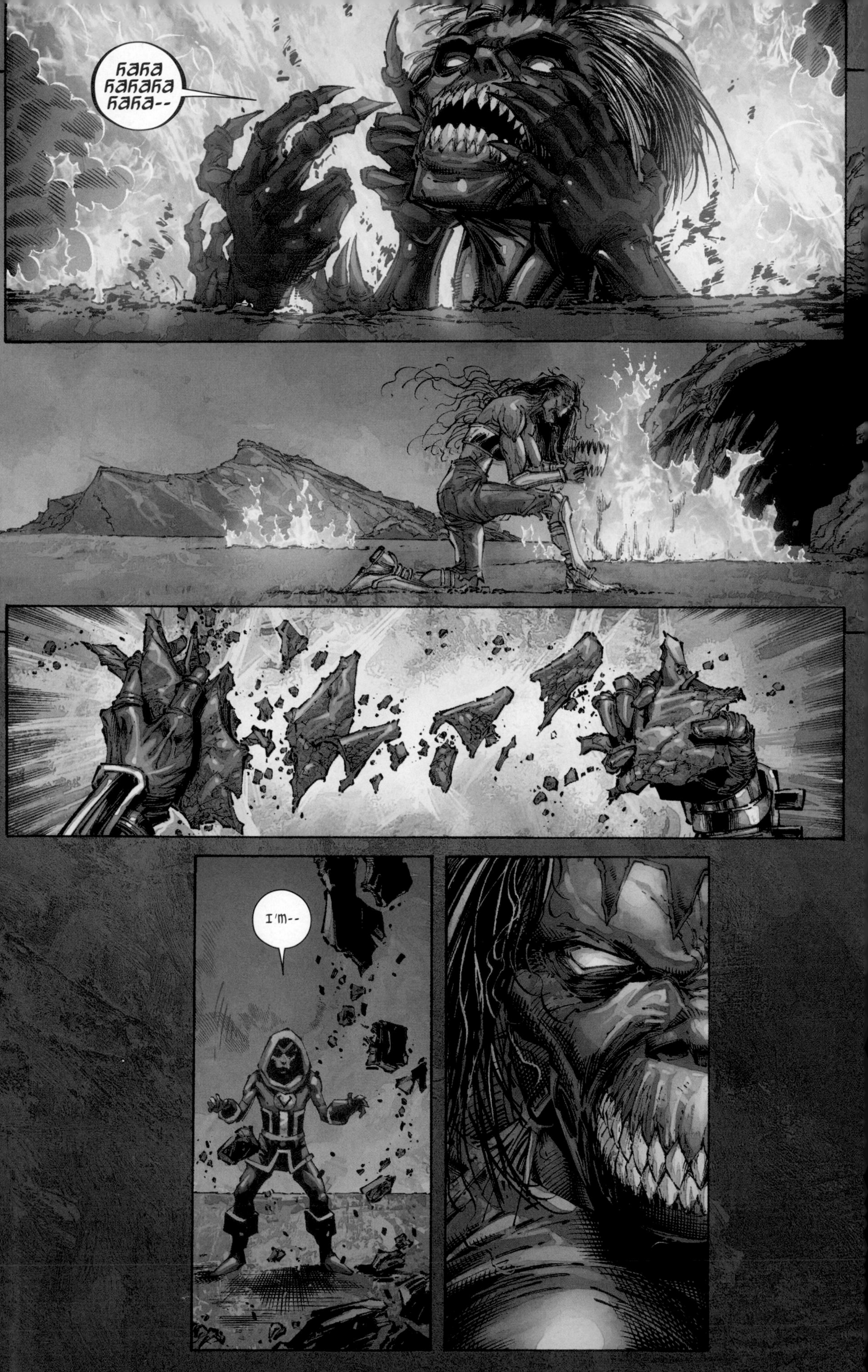
HAHA HAHAHA HAHA--
I'M--

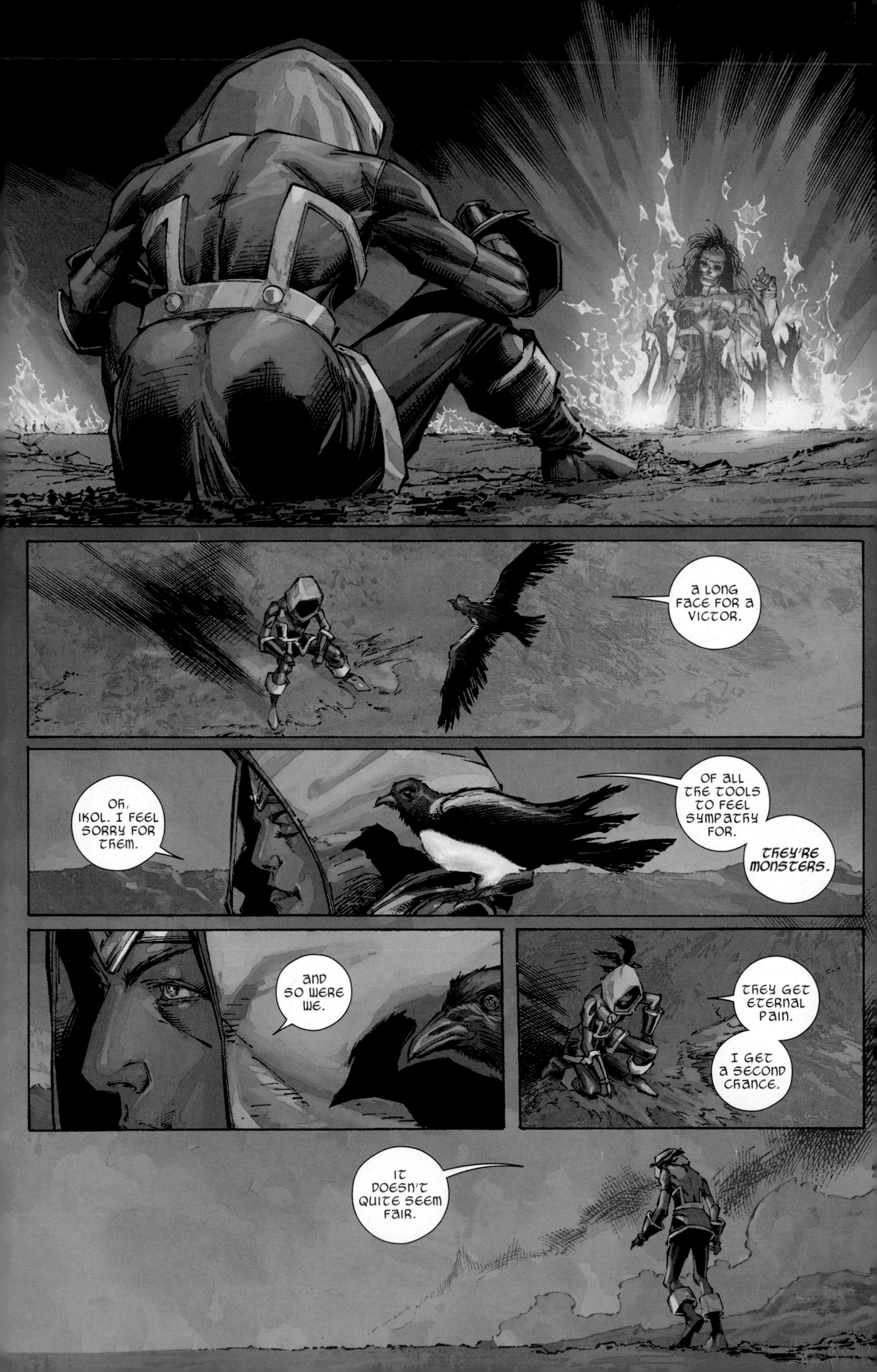
A LONG FACE FOR A VICTOR.
OH, IKOL. I FEEL SORRY FOR THEM.
OF ALL THE TOOLS TO FEEL SYMPATHY FOR.
THEY'RE MONSTERS.
AND SO WERE WE.
THEY GET ETERNAL PAIN.
I GET A SECOND CHANCE.
IT DOESN'T QUITE SEEM FAIR.

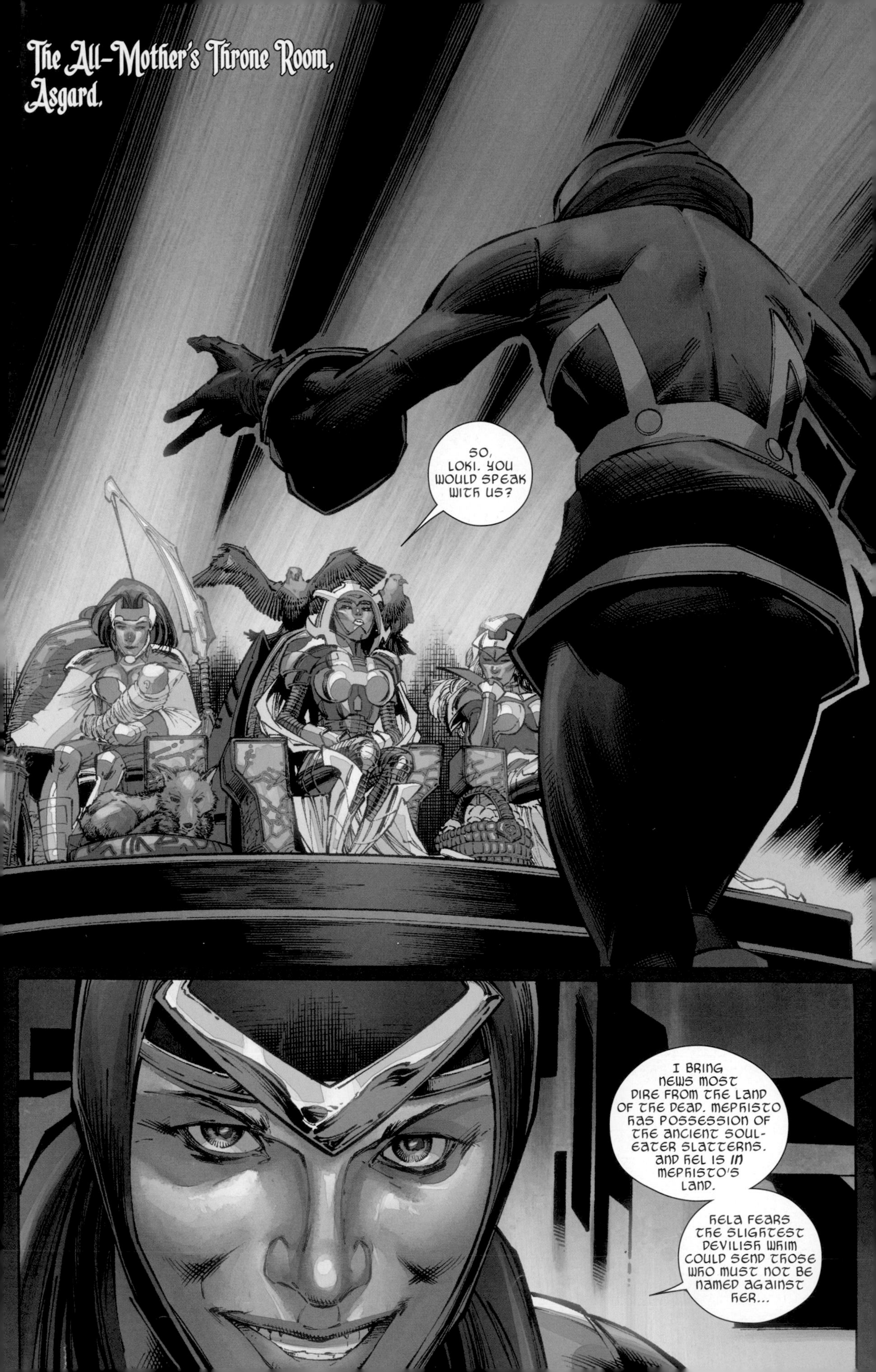
The All-Mother's Throne Room, Asgard.
SO, LOKI. YOU WOULD SPEAK WITH US?
I BRING NEWS MOST DIRE FROM THE LAND OF THE DEAD. MEPHISTO HAS POSSESSION OF THE ANCIENT SOUL-EATER SLATTERNS. AND HEL IS IN MEPHISTO'S LAND.
HELA FEARS THE SLIGHTEST DEVILISH WHIM COULD SEND THOSE WHO MUST NOT BE NAMED AGAINST HER...

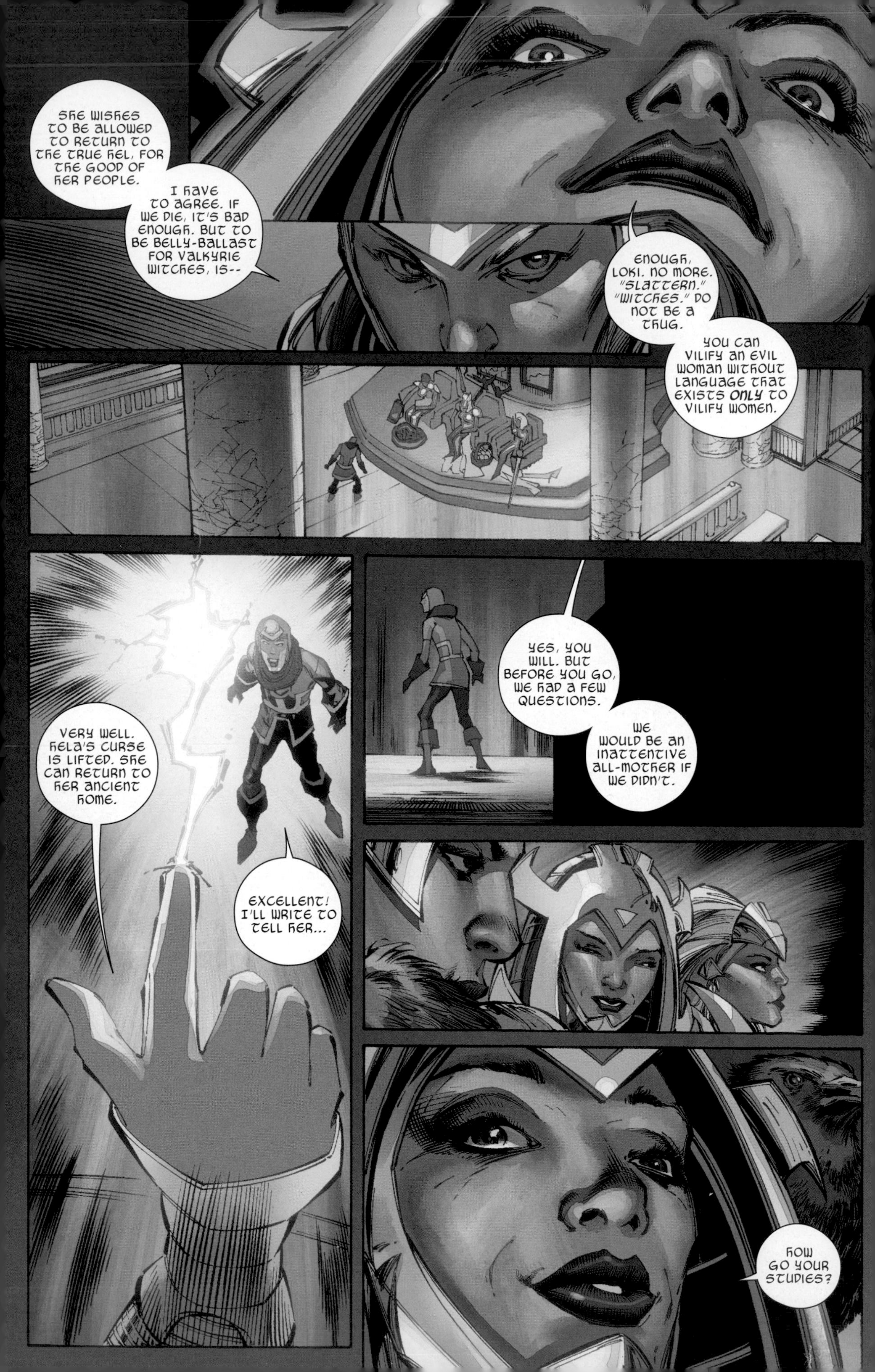
SHE WISHES TO BE ALLOWED TO RETURN TO THE TRUE HEL, FOR THE GOOD OF HER PEOPLE.
I HAVE TO AGREE. IF WE DIE, IT'S BAD ENOUGH. BUT TO BE BELLY-BALLAST FOR VALKYRIE WITCHES, IS--
ENOUGH, LOKI. NO MORE. "SLATTERN." "WITCHES." DO NOT BE A THUG.
YOU CAN VILIFY AN EVIL WOMAN WITHOUT LANGUAGE THAT EXISTS ONLY TO VILIFY WOMEN.
VERY WELL. HELA'S CURSE IS LIFTED. SHE CAN RETURN TO HER ANCIENT HOME.
EXCELLENT! I'LL WRITE TO TELL HER...
YES, YOU WILL. BUT BEFORE YOU GO, WE HAD A FEW QUESTIONS.
WE WOULD BE AN INATTENTIVE ALL-MOTHER IF WE DIDN'T.
HOW GO YOUR STUDIES?

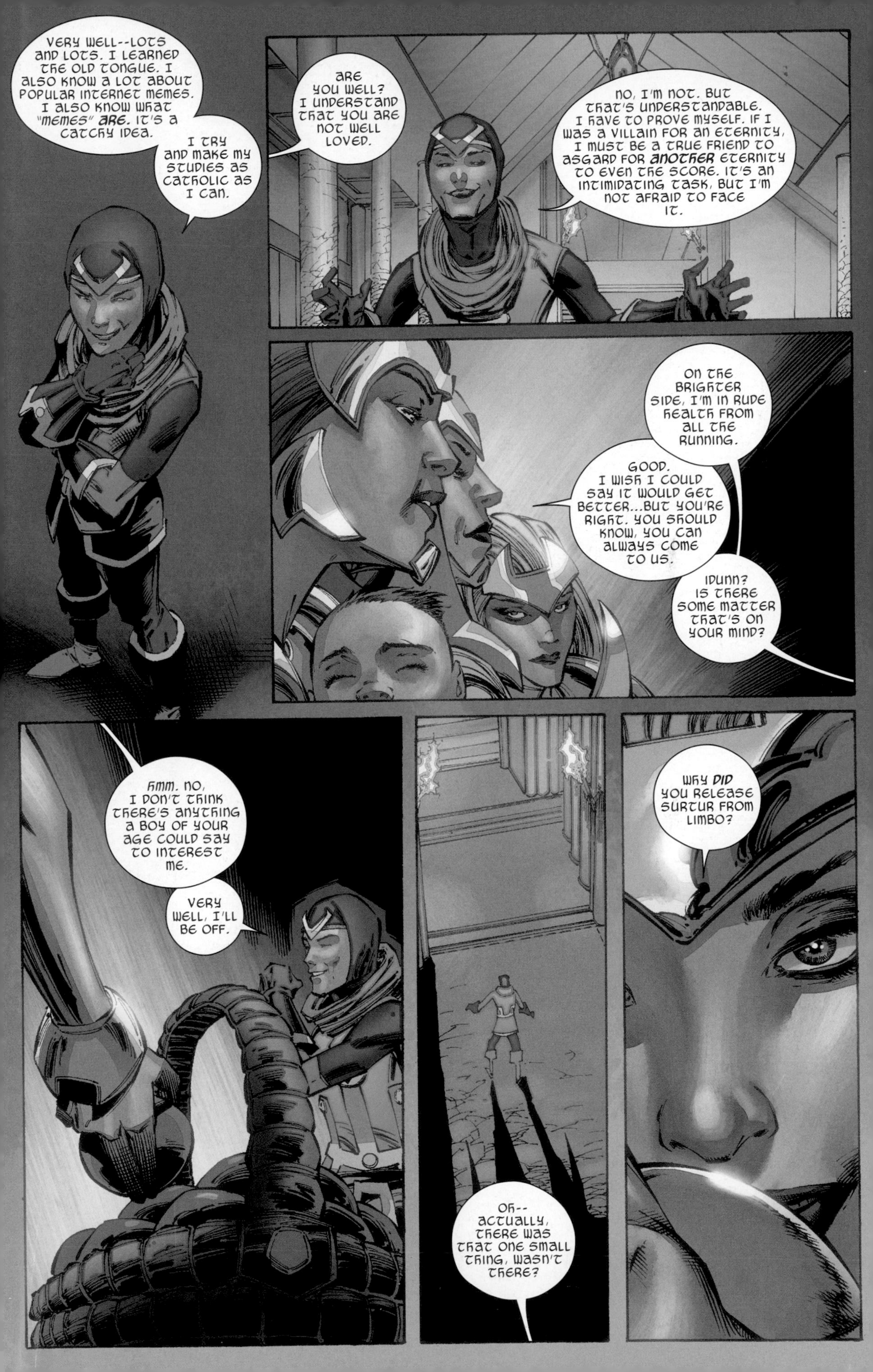
VERY WELL--LOTS AND LOTS. I LEARNED THE OLD TONGUE. I ALSO KNOW A LOT ABOUT POPULAR INTERNET MEMES. I ALSO KNOW WHAT "MEMES" ARE. IT'S A CATCHY IDEA.
I TRY AND MAKE MY STUDIES AS CATHOLIC AS I CAN.
ARE YOU WELL? I UNDERSTAND THAT YOU ARE NOT WELL LOVED.
NO, I'M NOT. BUT THAT'S UNDERSTANDABLE. I HAVE TO PROVE MYSELF. IF I WAS A VILLAIN FOR AN ETERNITY, I MUST BE A TRUE FRIEND TO ASGARD FOR ANOTHER ETERNITY TO EVEN THE SCORE. IT'S AN INTIMIDATING TASK, BUT I'M NOT AFRAID TO FACE IT.
ON THE BRIGHTER SIDE, I'M IN RUDE HEALTH FROM ALL THE RUNNING.
GOOD. I WISH I COULD SAY IT WOULD GET BETTER...BUT YOU'RE RIGHT. YOU SHOULD KNOW, YOU CAN ALWAYS COME TO US.
IDUNN? IS THERE SOME MATTER THAT'S ON YOUR MIND?
HMM. NO, I DON'T THINK THERE'S ANYTHING A BOY OF YOUR AGE COULD SAY TO INTEREST ME.
VERY WELL, I'LL BE OFF.
OH--ACTUALLY, THERE WAS THAT ONE SMALL THING, WASN'T THERE?
WHY DID YOU RELEASE SURTUR FROM LIMBO?

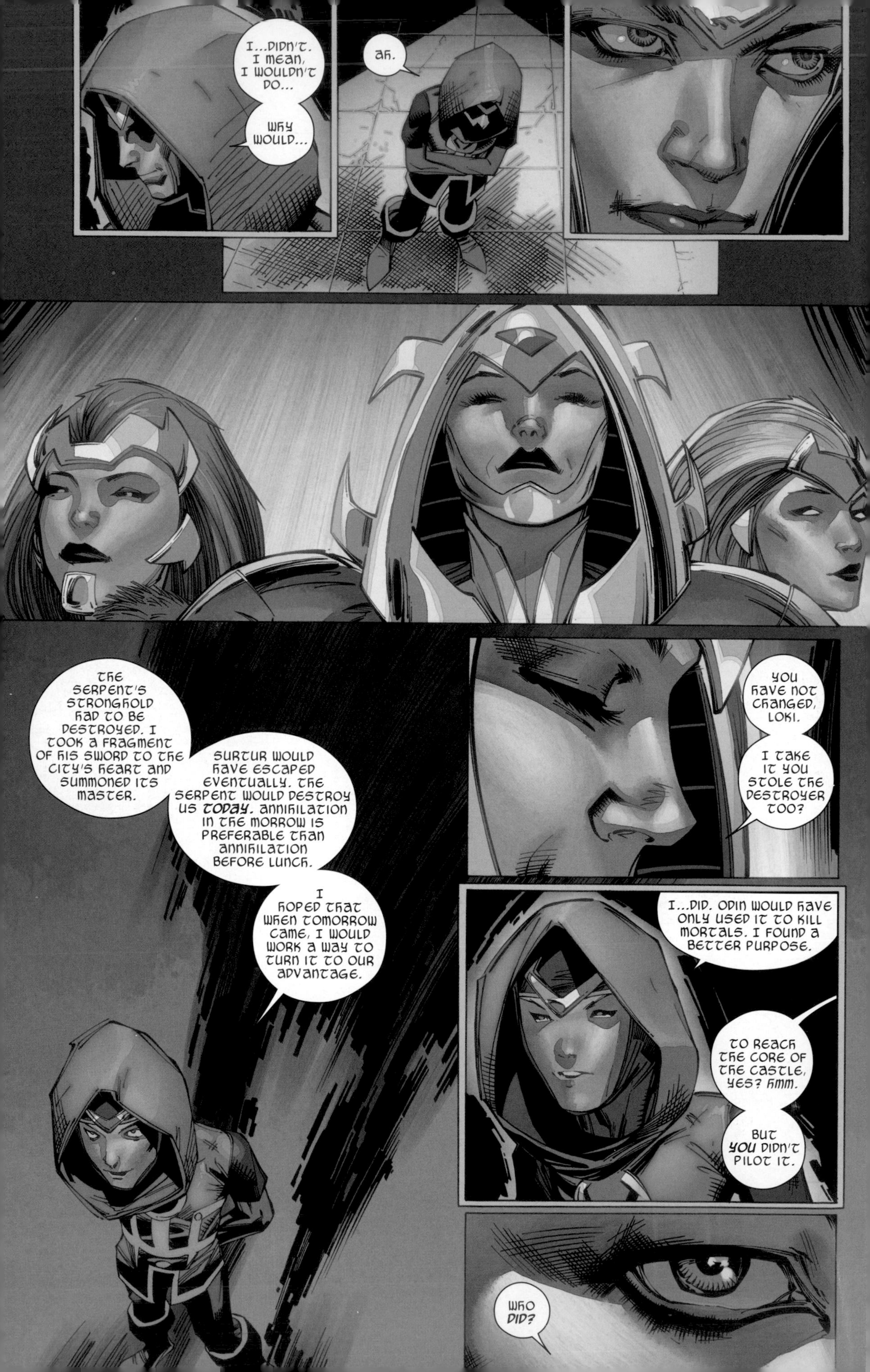
I...DIDN'T. I MEAN, I WOULDN'T DO...
WHY WOULD...
AH.
THE SERPENT'S STRONGHOLD HAD TO BE DESTROYED. I TOOK A FRAGMENT OF HIS SWORD TO THE CITY'S HEART AND SUMMONED ITS MASTER.
SURTUR WOULD HAVE ESCAPED EVENTUALLY. THE SERPENT WOULD DESTROY US TODAY. ANNIHILATION IN THE MORROW IS PREFERABLE THAN ANNIHILATION BEFORE LUNCH.
I HOPED THAT WHEN TOMORROW CAME, I WOULD WORK A WAY TO TURN IT TO OUR ADVANTAGE.
YOU HAVE NOT CHANGED, LOKI.
I TAKE IT YOU STOLE THE DESTROYER TOO?
I...DID. ODIN WOULD HAVE ONLY USED IT TO KILL MORTALS. I FOUND A BETTER PURPOSE.
TO REACH THE CORE OF THE CASTLE, YES? HMM.
BUT YOU DIDN'T PILOT IT.
WHO DID?

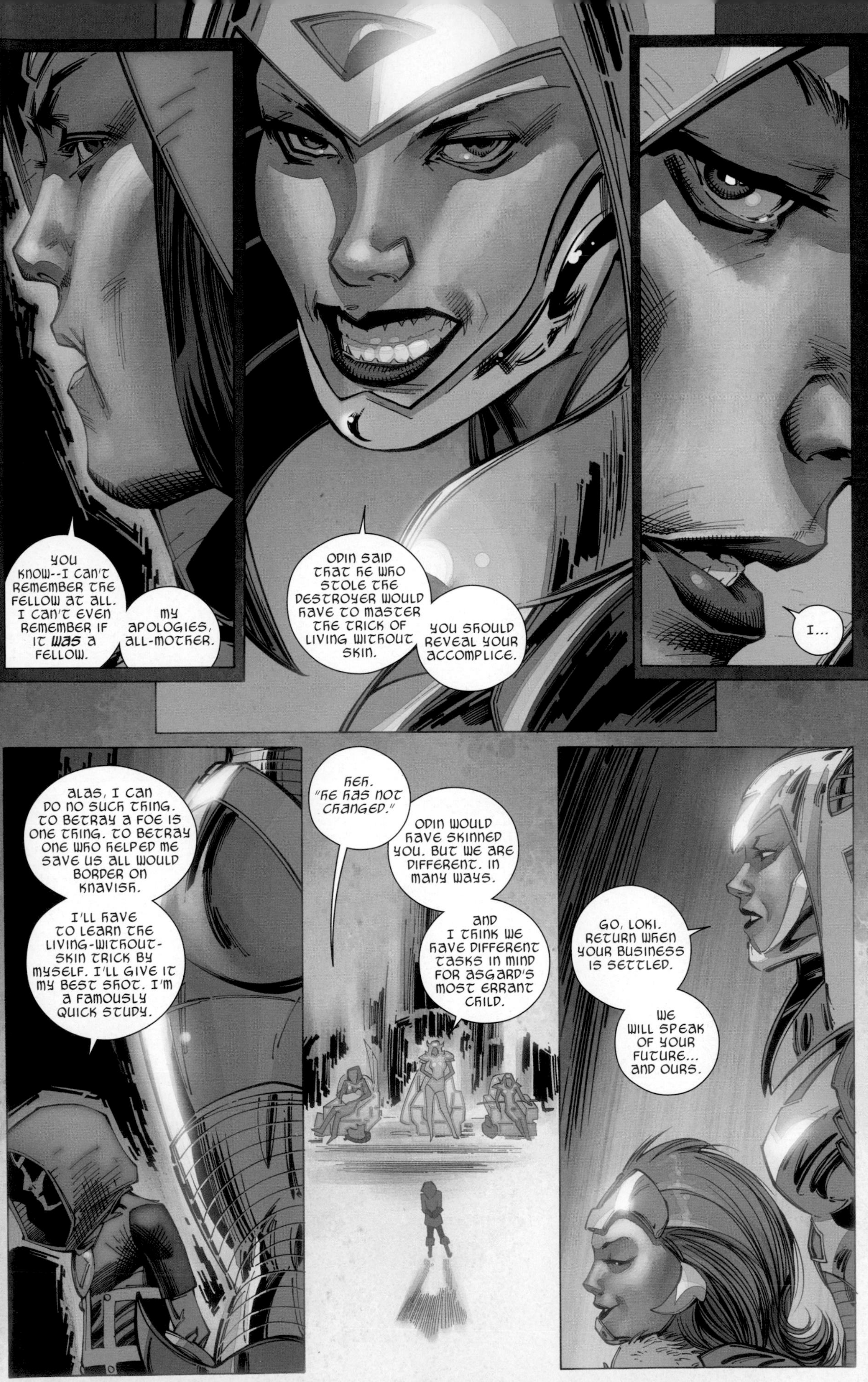
YOU KNOW--I CAN'T REMEMBER THE FELLOW AT ALL. I CAN'T EVEN REMEMBER IF IT *WAS* A FELLOW.
MY APOLOGIES, ALL-MOTHER.
ODIN SAID THAT HE WHO STOLE THE DESTROYER WOULD HAVE TO MASTER THE TRICK OF LIVING WITHOUT SKIN.
YOU SHOULD REVEAL YOUR ACCOMPLICE.
I...
ALAS, I CAN DO NO SUCH THING. TO BETRAY A FOE IS ONE THING. TO BETRAY ONE WHO HELPED ME SAVE US ALL WOULD BORDER ON KNAVISH.
I'LL HAVE TO LEARN THE LIVING-WITHOUT-SKIN TRICK BY MYSELF. I'LL GIVE IT MY BEST SHOT. I'M A FAMOUSLY QUICK STUDY.
HEH. "HE HAS NOT CHANGED."
ODIN WOULD HAVE SKINNED YOU. BUT WE ARE DIFFERENT. IN MANY WAYS.
AND I THINK WE HAVE DIFFERENT TASKS IN MIND FOR ASGARD'S MOST ERRANT CHILD.
GO, LOKI. RETURN WHEN YOUR BUSINESS IS SETTLED.
WE WILL SPEAK OF YOUR FUTURE... AND OURS.

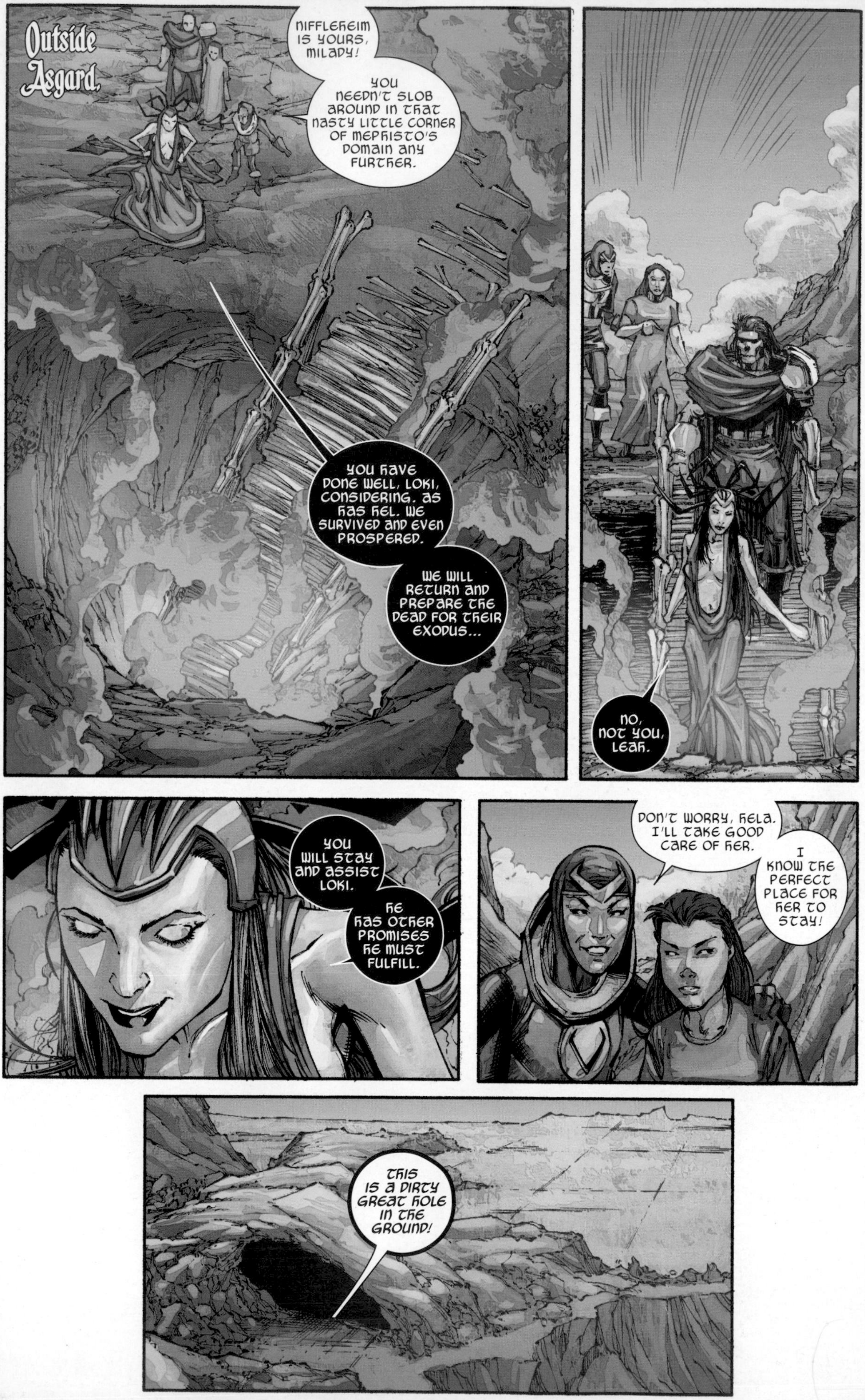
Outside Asgard.
NIFFLEHEIM IS YOURS, MILADY!
YOU NEEDN'T SLOB AROUND IN THAT NASTY LITTLE CORNER OF MEPHISTO'S DOMAIN ANY FURTHER.
YOU HAVE DONE WELL, LOKI, CONSIDERING. AS HAS HEL. WE SURVIVED AND EVEN PROSPERED.
WE WILL RETURN AND PREPARE THE DEAD FOR THEIR EXODUS...
NO, NOT YOU, LEAH.
YOU WILL STAY AND ASSIST LOKI.
HE HAS OTHER PROMISES HE MUST FULFILL.
DON'T WORRY, HELA. I'LL TAKE GOOD CARE OF HER.
I KNOW THE PERFECT PLACE FOR HER TO STAY!
THIS IS A DIRTY GREAT HOLE IN THE GROUND!

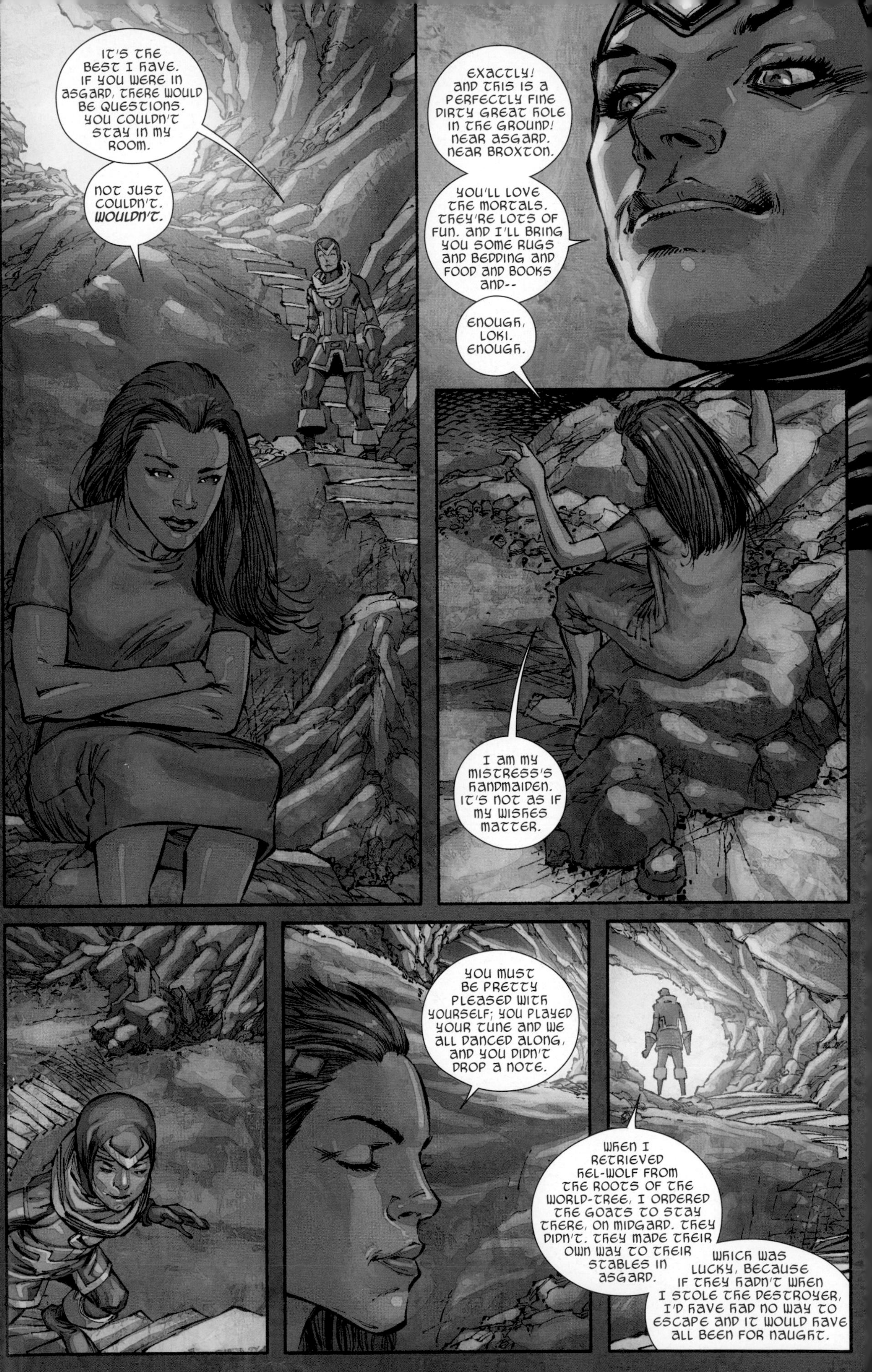
IT'S THE BEST I HAVE. IF YOU WERE IN ASGARD, THERE WOULD BE QUESTIONS. YOU COULDN'T STAY IN MY ROOM.
NOT JUST COULDN'T. *WOULDN'T.*
EXACTLY! AND THIS IS A PERFECTLY FINE DIRTY GREAT HOLE IN THE GROUND! NEAR ASGARD. NEAR BROXTON.
YOU'LL LOVE THE MORTALS. THEY'RE LOTS OF FUN. AND I'LL BRING YOU SOME RUGS AND BEDDING AND FOOD AND BOOKS AND--
ENOUGH, LOKI. ENOUGH.
I AM MY MISTRESS'S HANDMAIDEN. IT'S NOT AS IF MY WISHES MATTER.
YOU MUST BE PRETTY PLEASED WITH YOURSELF; YOU PLAYED YOUR TUNE AND WE ALL DANCED ALONG, AND YOU DIDN'T DROP A NOTE.
WHEN I RETRIEVED HEL-WOLF FROM THE ROOTS OF THE WORLD-TREE, I ORDERED THE GOATS TO STAY THERE, ON MIDGARD. THEY DIDN'T. THEY MADE THEIR OWN WAY TO THEIR STABLES IN ASGARD.
WHICH WAS LUCKY, BECAUSE IF THEY HADN'T WHEN I STOLE THE DESTROYER, I'D HAVE HAD NO WAY TO ESCAPE AND IT WOULD HAVE ALL BEEN FOR NAUGHT.

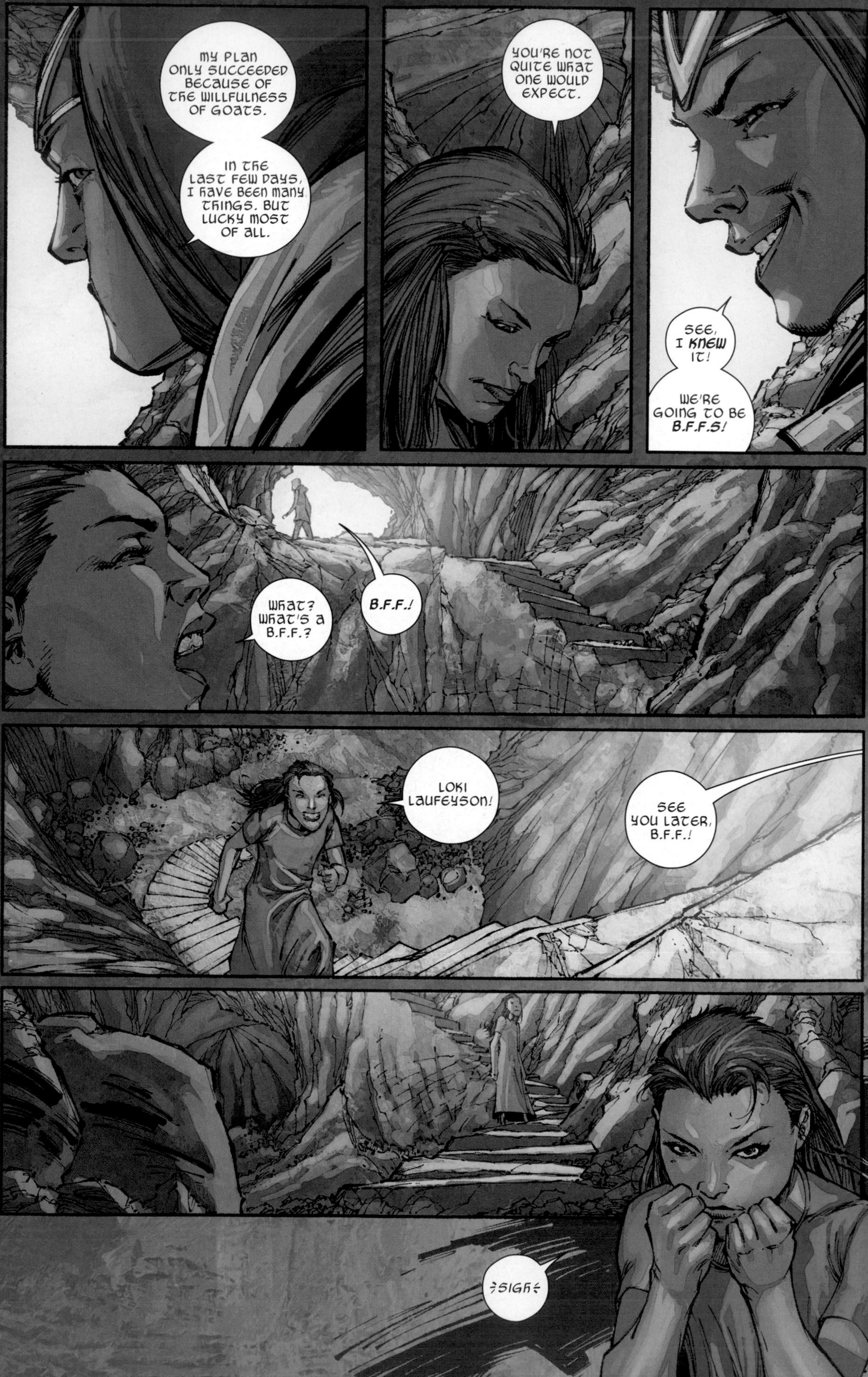
MY PLAN ONLY SUCCEEDED BECAUSE OF THE WILLFULNESS OF GOATS.
IN THE LAST FEW DAYS, I HAVE BEEN MANY THINGS. BUT LUCKY MOST OF ALL.
YOU'RE NOT QUITE WHAT ONE WOULD EXPECT.
SEE, I KNEW IT!
WE'RE GOING TO BE B.F.F.S!
WHAT? WHAT'S A B.F.F.?
B.F.F.!
LOKI LAUFEYSON!
SEE YOU LATER, B.F.F.!
SIGH

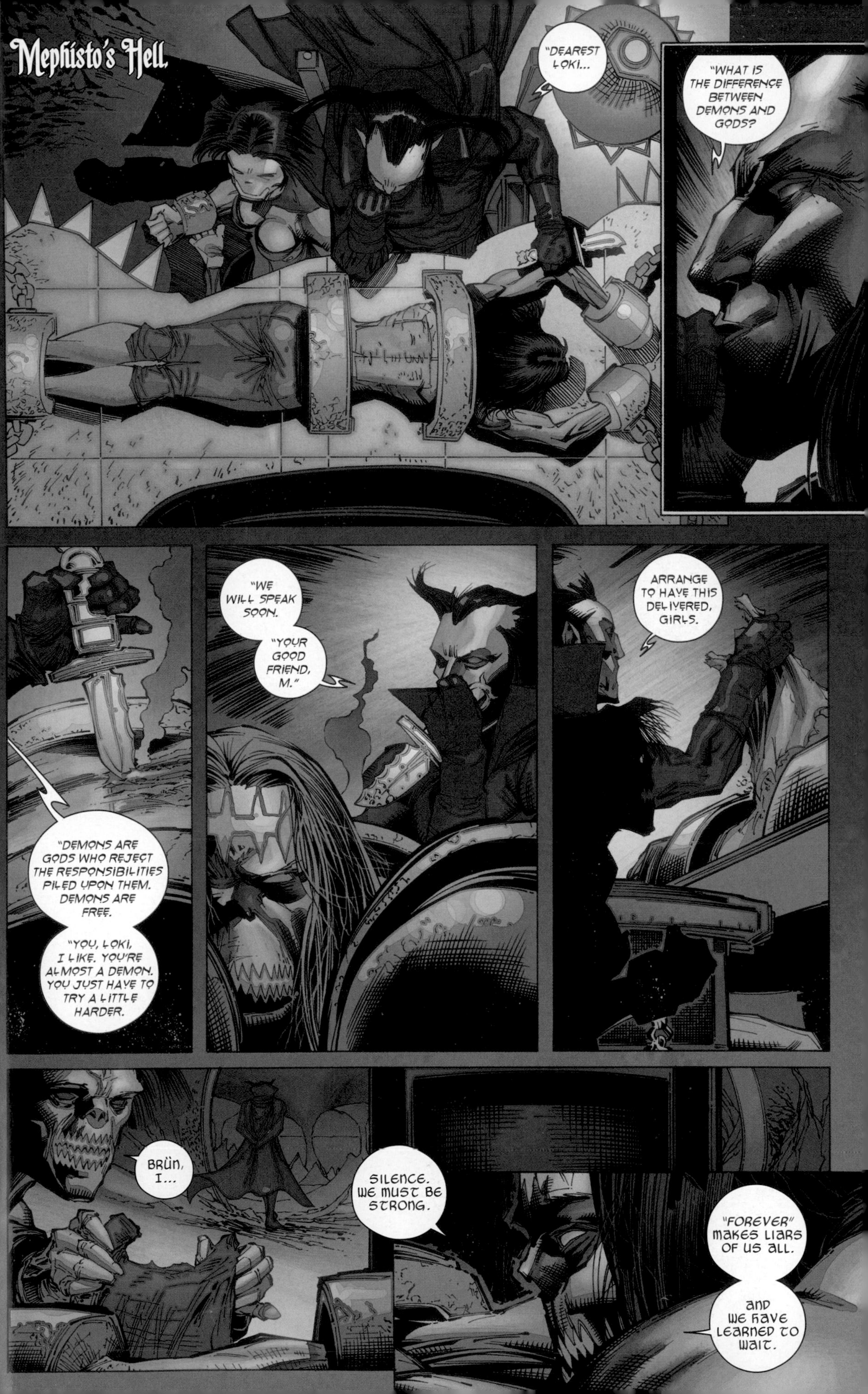
Mephisto's Hell.
"DEAREST LOKI...
"WHAT IS THE DIFFERENCE BETWEEN DEMONS AND GODS?
"DEMONS ARE GODS WHO REJECT THE RESPONSIBILITIES PILED UPON THEM. DEMONS ARE FREE.
"YOU, LOKI, I LIKE. YOU'RE ALMOST A DEMON. YOU JUST HAVE TO TRY A LITTLE HARDER.
"WE WILL SPEAK SOON.
"YOUR GOOD FRIEND, M."
ARRANGE TO HAVE THIS DELIVERED, GIRLS.
BRÜN, I...
SILENCE. WE MUST BE STRONG.
"FOREVER" MAKES LIARS OF US ALL.
AND WE HAVE LEARNED TO WAIT.

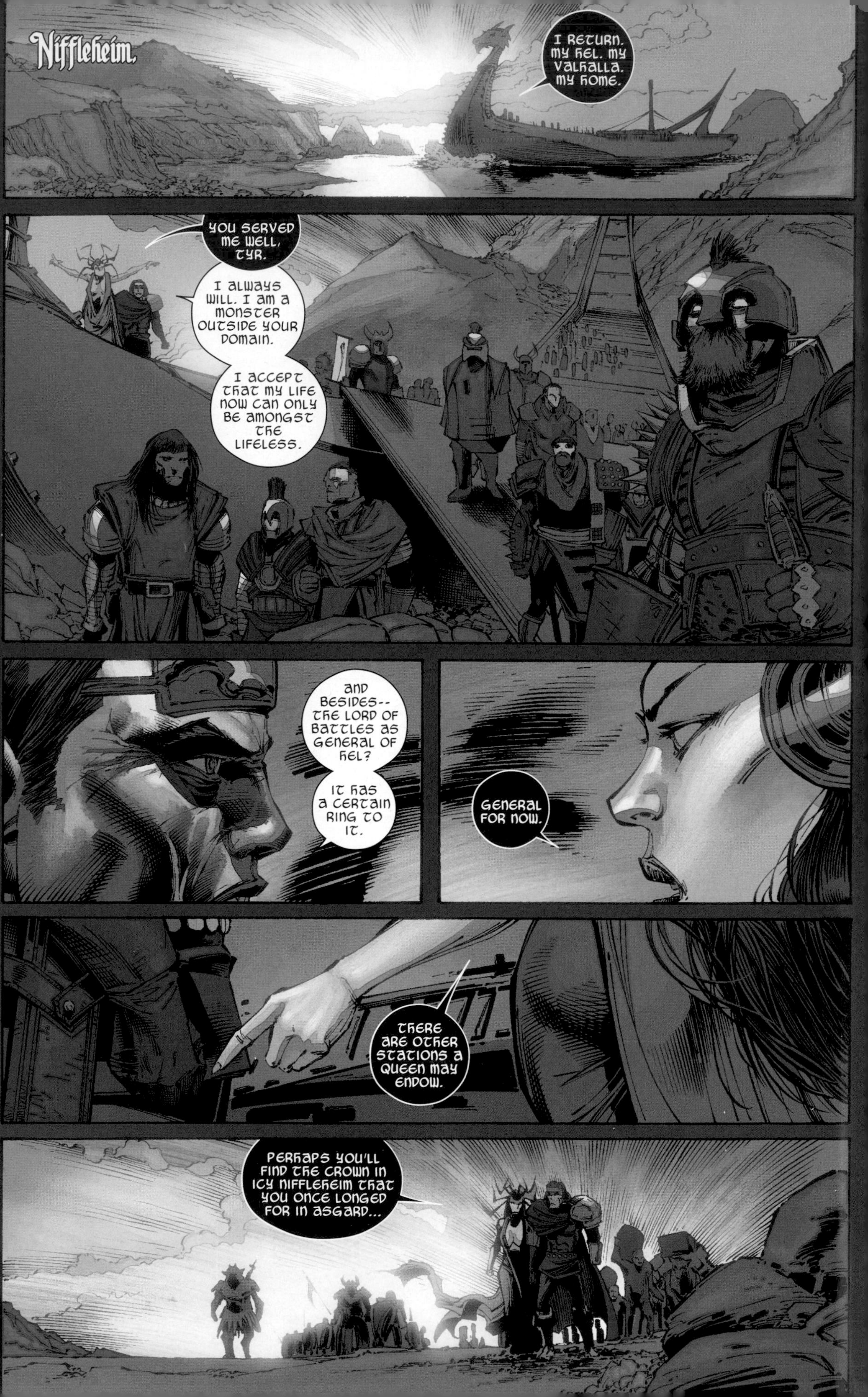
Niffleheim.
I RETURN. MY HEL. MY VALHALLA. MY HOME.
YOU SERVED ME WELL, TYR.
I ALWAYS WILL. I AM A MONSTER OUTSIDE YOUR DOMAIN.
I ACCEPT THAT MY LIFE NOW CAN ONLY BE AMONGST THE LIFELESS.
AND BESIDES-- THE LORD OF BATTLES AS GENERAL OF HEL?
IT HAS A CERTAIN RING TO IT.
GENERAL FOR NOW.
THERE ARE OTHER STATIONS A QUEEN MAY ENDOW.
PERHAPS YOU'LL FIND THE CROWN IN ICY NIFFLEHEIM THAT YOU ONCE LONGED FOR IN ASGARD...

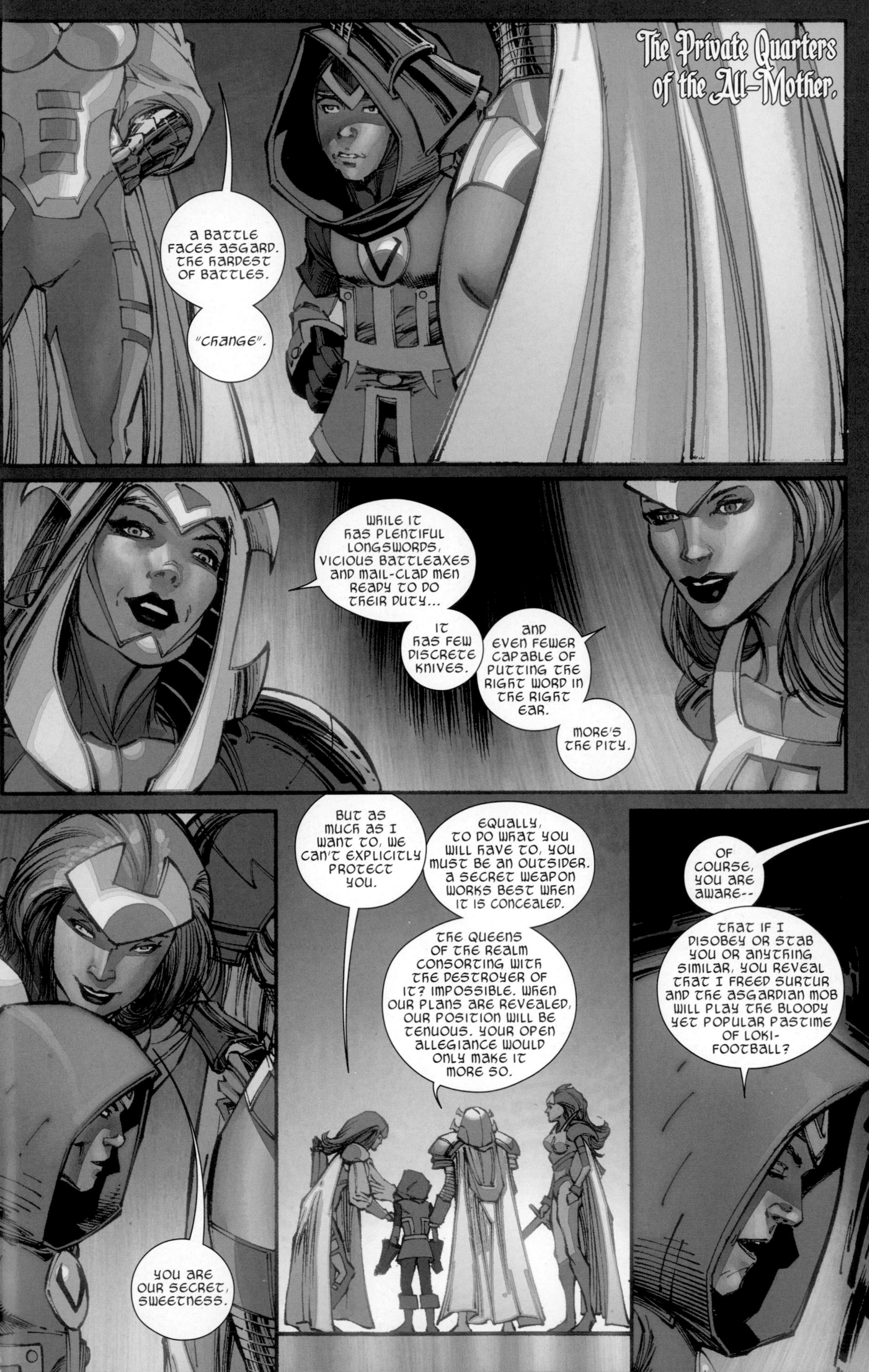
The Private Quarters of the All-Mother.
A BATTLE FACES ASGARD. THE HARDEST OF BATTLES.
"CHANGE".
WHILE IT HAS PLENTIFUL LONGSWORDS, VICIOUS BATTLEAXES AND MAIL-CLAD MEN READY TO DO THEIR DUTY...
IT HAS FEW DISCRETE KNIVES.
AND EVEN FEWER CAPABLE OF PUTTING THE RIGHT WORD IN THE RIGHT EAR.
MORE'S THE PITY.
BUT AS MUCH AS I WANT TO, WE CAN'T EXPLICITLY PROTECT YOU.
YOU ARE OUR SECRET, SWEETNESS.
EQUALLY, TO DO WHAT YOU WILL HAVE TO, YOU MUST BE AN OUTSIDER. A SECRET WEAPON WORKS BEST WHEN IT IS CONCEALED.
THE QUEENS OF THE REALM CONSORTING WITH THE DESTROYER OF IT? IMPOSSIBLE. WHEN OUR PLANS ARE REVEALED, OUR POSITION WILL BE TENUOUS. YOUR OPEN ALLEGIANCE WOULD ONLY MAKE IT MORE SO.
OF COURSE, YOU ARE AWARE--
THAT IF I DISOBEY OR STAB YOU OR ANYTHING SIMILAR, YOU REVEAL THAT I FREED SURTUR AND THE ASGARDIAN MOB WILL PLAY THE BLOODY YET POPULAR PASTIME OF LOKI-FOOTBALL?

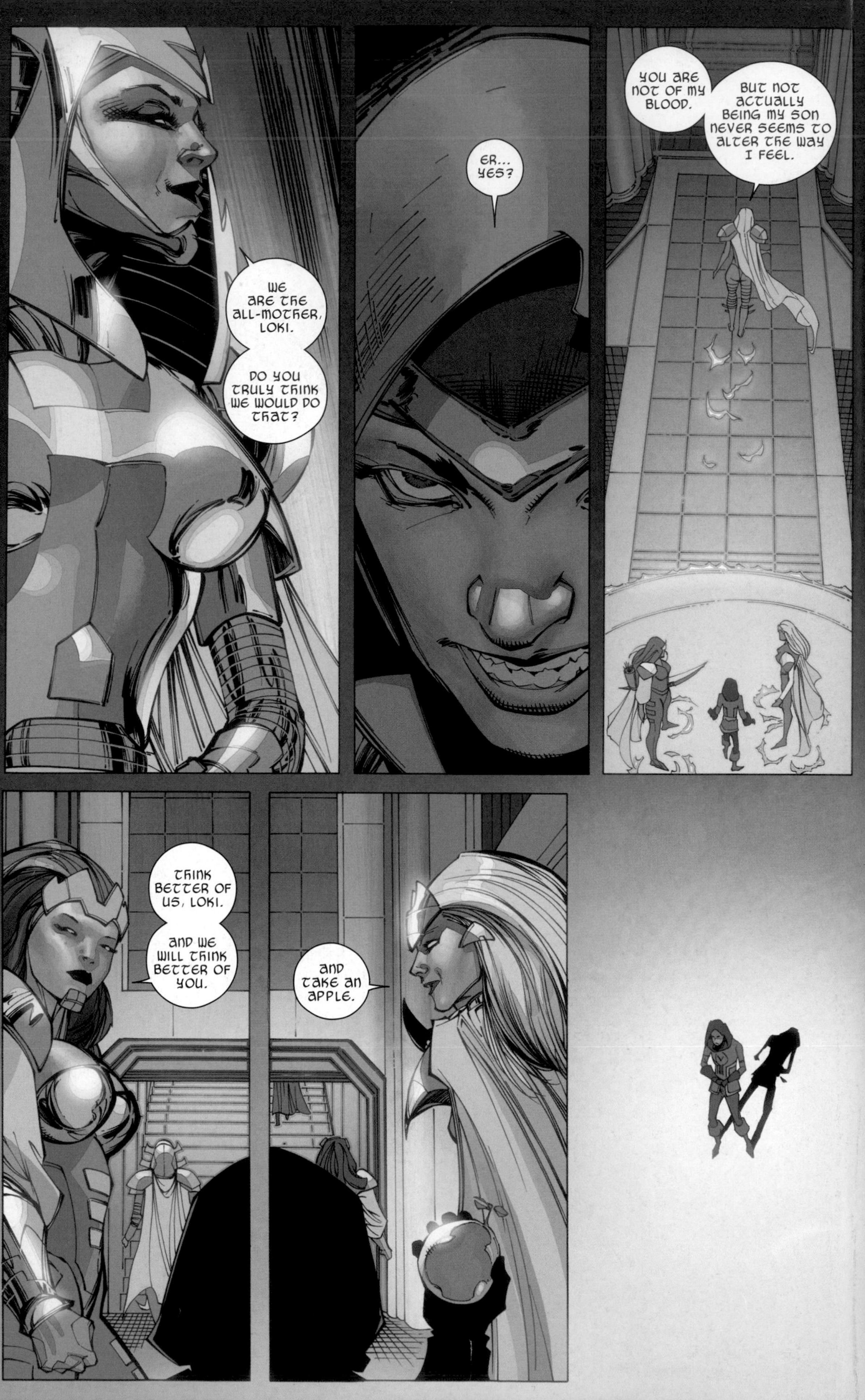

WE ARE THE ALL-MOTHER, LOKI.
DO YOU TRULY THINK WE WOULD DO THAT?
ER... YES?
YOU ARE NOT OF MY BLOOD.
BUT NOT ACTUALLY BEING MY SON NEVER SEEMS TO ALTER THE WAY I FEEL.
THINK BETTER OF US, LOKI.
AND WE WILL THINK BETTER OF YOU.
AND TAKE AN APPLE.

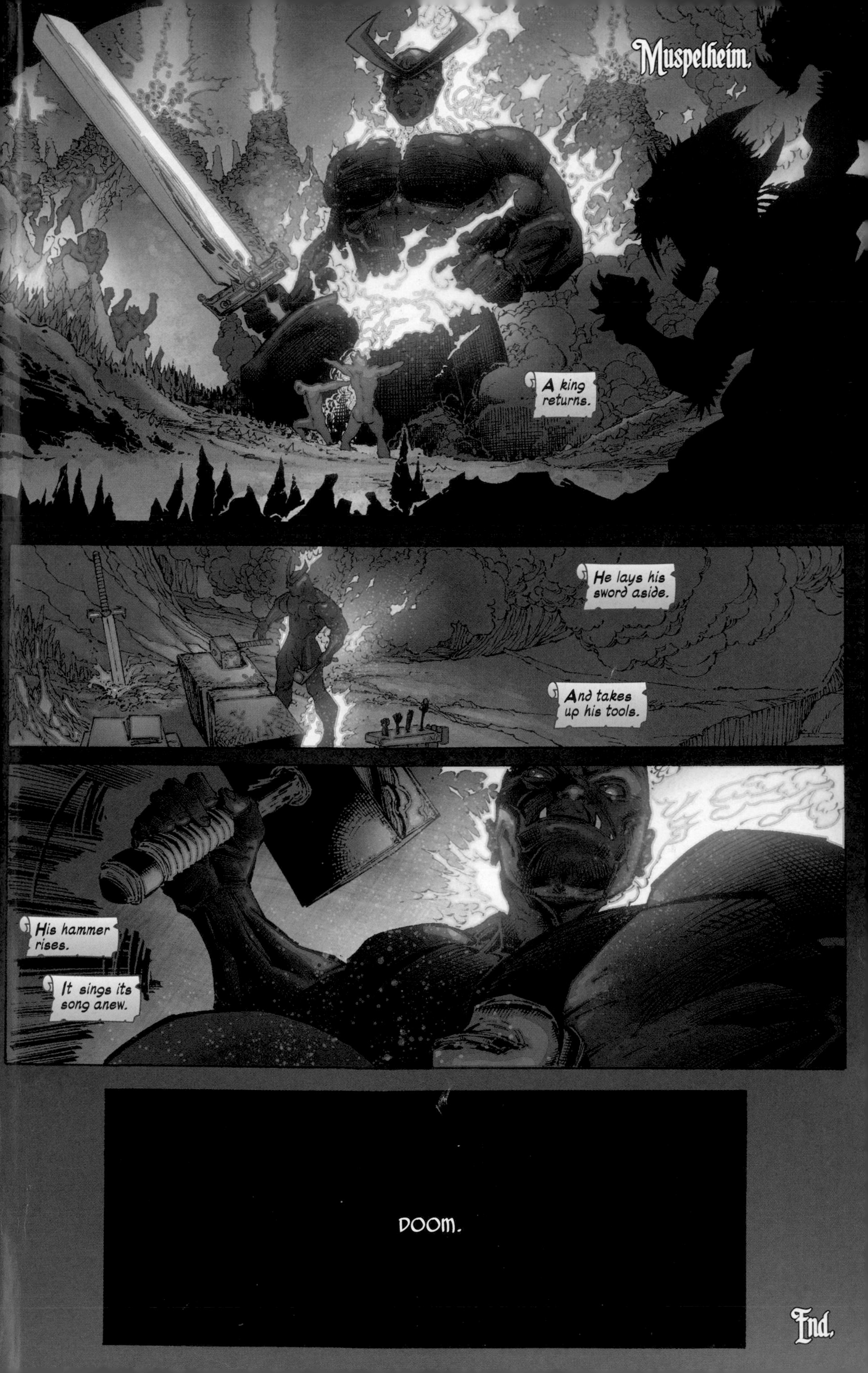
Muspelheim.
A king returns.
He lays his sword aside.
And takes up his tools.
His hammer rises.
It sings its song anew.
DOOM.
End.

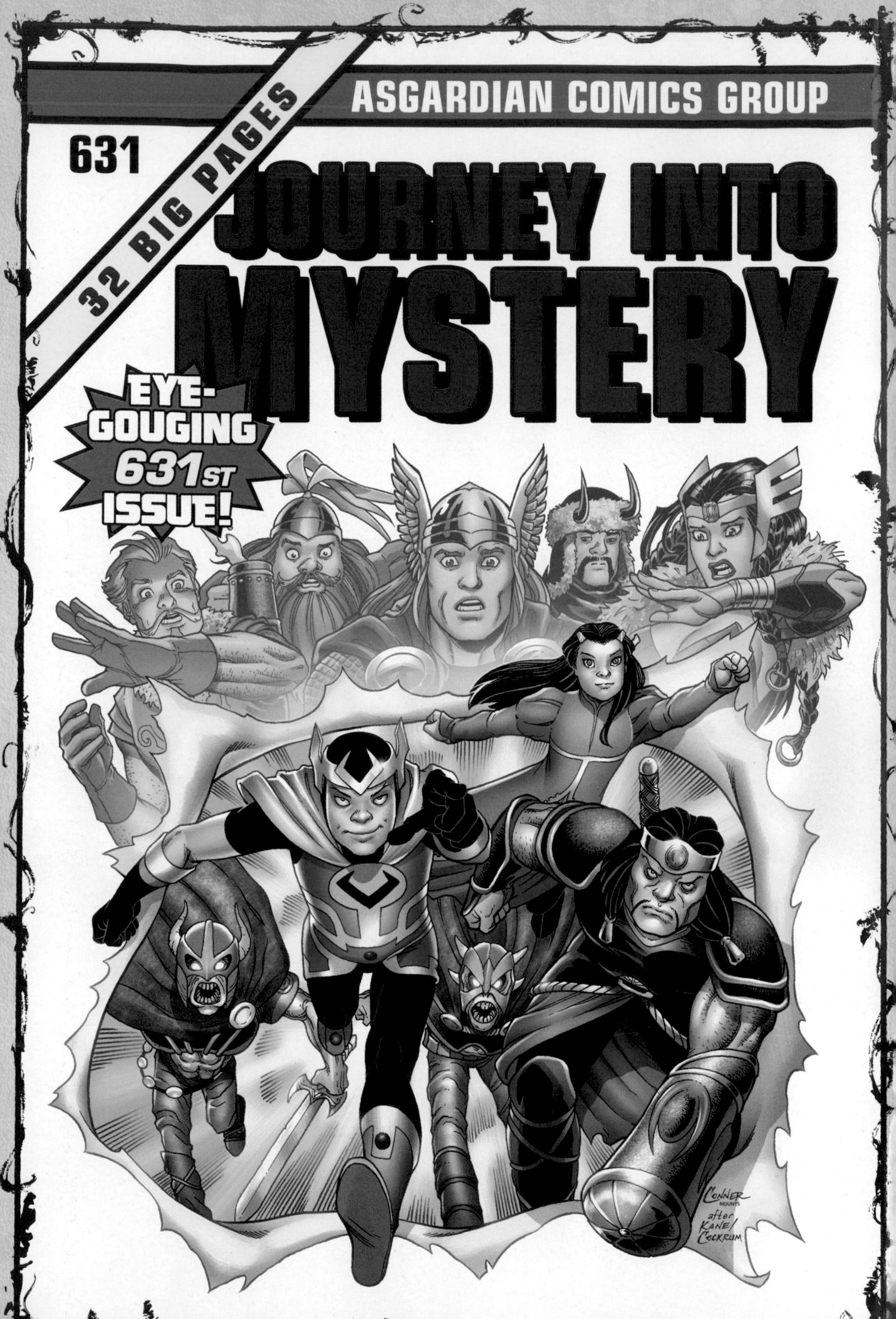
ASGARDIAN COMICS GROUP
631
32 BIG PAGES
JOURNEY INTO MYSTERY
EYE-GOUGING 631ST ISSUE!
CONNER MOUNTS after KANE/COCKRUM

#631 MARVEL 50TH ANNIVERSARY VARIANT BY AMANDA CONNER & PAUL MOUNTS